OPEN EDUCATION

Open Education

International Perspectives in Higher Education

Edited by Patrick Blessinger and TJ Bliss

https://www.openbookpublishers.com

All external links were active on 2/12/2016 unless otherwise stated and have been archived via the Internet Archive Wayback Machine at https://archive.org/web

Updated digital material and resources associated with this volume are available at https://www.openbookpublishers.com/isbn/9781783742783#resources

Every effort has been made to identify and contact copyright holders and any omission or error will be corrected if notification is made to the publisher.

The Hewlett Foundation (http://www.hewlett.org) has generously contributed towards the publication of this volume.

ISBN Paperback: 978-1-78374-278-3
ISBN Hardback: 978-1-78374-279-0
ISBN Digital (PDF): 978-1-78374-280-6
ISBN Digital ebook (epub): 978-1-78374-281-3
ISBN Digital ebook (mobi): 978-1-78374-282-0
DOI: 10.11647/OBP.0103

Cover image: Oditel, Uganda (2011). Photo by Brian Wolfe, CC BY-NC-SA, https://www.flickr.com/photos/mightyboybrian/6324873971

All paper used by Open Book Publishers is SFI (Sustainable Forestry Initiative), and PEFC (Programme for the endorsement of Forest Certification Schemes) Certified.

Printed in the United Kingdom, United States and Australia
by Lightning Source for Open Book Publishers (Cambridge, UK).

Contents

This book is dedicated to educators all over the world and to the members of the International Higher Education Teaching and Learning Association whose passion for teaching, learning, research, and service are helping to transform the academy in many positive ways.

Vision, mission, and values statement

The long-term vision of HETL is to improve educational outcomes in higher education by creating new knowledge and advancing the scholarship and practice of teaching and learning.

To bring that vision to reality, the present mission of HETL is to develop a global community of higher education professionals who come together to share their knowledge and expertise in teaching and learning.

To effectively fulfill that mission, HETL adheres to the values of academic integrity, collegiality, and diversity. As such, HETL supports academic and pedagogical pluralism, diversity of learning, as well as practices that promote sustainable learning and peace.

Membership, conference, publishing, and research information

For information about HETL, please see https://www.hetl.org

Patrick Blessinger
Founder, Director, and Chief Research Scientist
The HETL Association
patrickblessinger@gmail.com

Lorraine Stefani
President
The HETL Association
lorraine.stefani@auckland.ac.nz

Notes on Contributors

Fahriye Altinay has research interests in educational technology and management. Altinay is a lecturer at Near East University, a member of an information technology platform for disabled people, a consultant to the Ministry of Education, and a member of the Turkey Informatics Association. Altinay is a board member of Distance Education Center and has published her work in leading books and journals in the field.

Zehra Altinay is an Associate Professor who teaches doctorate, graduate and undergraduate degree courses in the Ataturk Education Faculty at Near East University. She is the Director of the Societal Research and Development Center, Vice Director of the Institute of Educational Sciences, and a board member of Distance Education Center. Zehra Altınay has published a number of leading articles, including three international book chapters and seven international articles, as well as two national publications. She is an active researcher in four research projects that were funded by the Ministry of Education.

Beatriz de los Arcos is a Research Associate at the Institute of Educational Technology (IET) at The Open University, UK (OUUK). Prior to her work with OER Hub she worked on the production and delivery of online distance language learning courses at the Department of Languages at OUUK. She collaborated on the development, implementation and evaluation of the JISC-funded LORO repository (http://loro.open.ac.uk), which provides open education resourcse for language teaching and learning, and facilitated OT12 MOOC in Open Translation tools and practices, the first ever MOOC produced at The Open University (http://www.ot12.org). With OER Hub she led the project's collaborations and research in the K12 (primary and secondary education) sector, in addition to overseeing data analysis.

Phil Barker is a Research Fellow at Heriot-Watt University. He teaches design for online learning and other courses to information systems students. Phil has contributed to the development of a number of learning resource metadata specifications. He edited and co-authored the Instructional Management Systems (IMS) Meta-data Best Practice Guide for the IEEE 1484.12.1-2002 Standard for Learning Object Metadata. He has been on the technical working group developing the Learning Resource Metadata Initiative (LRMI) since its inception, and is currently a member of the LRMI Task Group of the Dublin Core Metadata Initiative. Along with Lorna Campbell, he provided technical leadership for a three-year UK Open Education Resources Program in Higher Education, which encouraged the use of open and distributed systems to disseminate the resources released as a result of the program.

John D. Belshaw is a historian of Canada and British Columbia with special interests in demographic history, working-class communities, and twentieth century Vancouver. His three latest hard-copy books are *Becoming British Columbia: A Population History*; *Vancouver Noir: 1930–1960* (with co-author Diane Purvey), and an edited collection of articles called *Vancouver Confidential*. In 2015 he completed the open textbook *Canadian History: Pre-Confederation* (https://opentextbc.ca/preconfederation) and followed that up in 2016 with *Canadian History: Post-Confederation* (https://opentextbc.ca/postconfederation). Belshaw has taught internationally and has been a face-to-face and online professor at Thompson Rivers University for nearly twenty years. He has also worked in various administrative capacities and consults with institutions eager to build community-based research capacities.

Patrick Blessinger is the founder, executive director, and chief research scientist of the International Higher Education Teaching and Learning Association (HETL) and an adjunct associate professor in the School of Education at St John's University, New York City. Patrick is the editor-in-chief of two international academic journals and two international book series on higher education, a Governor's Teaching Fellow, and a Fulbright Senior Scholar.

TJ Bliss is a Program Officer in the Education Program at the Hewlett Foundation. In this role, he oversees grant making to expand the reach and efficacy of Open Educational Resources (OER). Before joining the

Foundation, he was the Director of Assessment and Accountability at the State Department of Education in Idaho. TJ was an OER Policy Fellow at the International Association for K-12 Online Learning (iNACOL), where he conducted research on state education policies friendly to open education resources (OER).

Carina Bossu is a Lecturer of Learning and Teaching in Open Educational Practices (OEP) with the Tasmanian Institute of Learning and Teaching at the University of Tasmania, Australia. Her current research is primarily focused on Open Educational Resources (OER) and Open Educational Practices in higher education; more specifically, she is exploring issues related to learning, teaching, and professional development. Bossu has presented and published widely and is currently involved in several research projects investigating different aspects of OER and OEP in higher education.

Lorna M. Campbell works for the Learning, Teaching and Web Division at the University of Edinburgh. She has over fifteen years' experience working in open education technology and interoperability standards and has worked with a wide range of international standards bodies, including Instructional Management Systems (IMS) Global Learning, the Institute of Electrical and Electronics Engineers (IEEE), the International Organization for Standardization (IOS), the British Standards Institution (BSI), the European Committee for Standardization's Information Society Standardization System (CEN/ISSS) Workshop on Learning Technologies, and the Dublin Core Metadata Initiative. She has contributed to the development of metadata specifications including the IEEE Learning Object Metadata (LOM), IMS Learning Resource Meta-Data and the Learning Resource Metadata Initiative (LRMI). Lorna leads the Open Scotland initiative and is co-author of the Scottish Open Education Declaration.

Anna Comas-Quinn is a Senior Lecturer and Associate Head of the Department of Languages at the Faculty of Education and Language Studies at The Open University, UK. She led the development of LORO (http://loro.open.ac.uk), a repository of open educational resources for languages, was a Fellow of the Support Centre for Open Resources in Education (SCORE), and is a long-standing member of the organizing committee of the UK-based OER conference. She has published on technology-enhanced and mobile language learning, teacher professional development, and open educational resources and practices, and co-edited the first book on open practice in language teaching (http://research-publishing.net/publications/2013-beaven-comas-quinn-sawhill).

Rob Farrow is Research Fellow in the Institute of Education Technology (IET) at The Open University, UK. He is a philosopher, interdisciplinary researcher and educational technologist who has worked on many research projects including the European-Commission-funded Mobile Technologies in Lifelong Learning (MOTILL) and European Unified Framework for Accessible Lifelong Learning (EU4ALL) projects. In the Open Learning Network (OLnet) project he was responsible for curating and disseminating evidence about OER. In the OER Research Hub project he worked with a range of key stakeholders to research the non-formal and institutional use of OER.

Lidia Cámara de la Fuente is Applied Linguistics Researcher and Associate Professor of the Philosophical Faculty at Humboldt University of Berlin. She carries out research in two areas: (in)formal learning of second and foreign language(s) through social media in multilingual and multicultural inclusive web communities, and multimodal and multilingual accessibility to information and knowledge for those who are disadvantaged due to disabilities, ethnic and cultural minorities and asylum seekers and refugees. She is a Technology, Entertainment and Design (TED) Associate Member, a Spanish Language Coordinator for the TED Open Translation Project, and a Spanish Language Coordinator for Coursera.

David Gibson is Director of Learning Futures at Curtin University in Perth, Australia and Chair of the education arm of the Curtin Institute for Computation. Gibson's research focuses on games and simulations in education, learning analytics, complex systems analysis and the use of technology to personalize learning via cognitive modeling, design and implementation and he has over ninety publications on these topics. He is the creator of simSchool (http://www.simschool.org), a classroom flight simulator for preparing educators, and eFolio (http://www.my-efolio.com), an online performance-based assessment system, and he provides vision and sponsorship for Curtin University's Challenge, a mobile, game-based learning platform (https://challenge.curtin.edu.au).

Arthur Gill Green is an environmental geographer and a 2016 Faculty Fellow for the BCcampus Open Education Project. He is currently a professor at Okanagan College in British Columbia and a post-doctoral fellow working on OER and Geographic Information Science (GIS) at the Department of Geography at the University of British Columbia. In 2014, he co-authored an open textbook on regional geography. His present research examines best practices for integrating open pedagogy into the teaching of GIS and OER within geography and environmental studies.

Kellie Hall is a motor learning and control specialist based in the Kinesiology Department at Cal Poly State University, San Luis Obispo, California, whose teaching is grounded in learn-by-doing. Hall is interested in providing access to affordable textbooks in the specialty area of Kinesiology.

Mika Hoffman is the Executive Director of Test Development Services at the Center for Educational Measurement for Excelsior College in Albany, New York. She has over twenty years of professional experience in test design, quality control, integration of psychometric analyses, assessments development and production processes for higher education and government. Prior to coming to Excelsior, she managed the high-stakes Defense Language Proficiency Test program at the Defense Language Institute Foreign Language Center. She began her career at Educational Testing Service working on the Graduate Record Examination (GRE) as it transitioned to a computer-adaptive format.

Dirk Ifenthaler's research focuses on the intersection of cognitive psychology, educational technology, learning science, data analytics, and computer science. He developed automated and computer-based methodologies for the assessment, analysis, and feedback of graphical and natural language representations, as well as simulation and game environments for teacher education. His research outcomes include numerous co-authored books, book series, book chapters, journal articles, and international conference papers, as well as successful grant funding in Australia, Germany, and the US (see Dirk's website for a full list of scholarly outcomes at www.ifenthaler.info). Dirk is the Editor-in-Chief of the Springer journal *Technology, Knowledge and Learning*.

Rajiv Jhangiani is a social and personality psychologist who conducts research in political psychology, the scholarship of teaching and learning, and open education. He is an OER Research Fellow with the Open Education Group, a faculty workshop facilitator with the Open Textbook Network, and an Associate Editor of the journal *Psychology Learning and Teaching*. Rajiv has revised two open textbooks—for *Research Methods* (https://opentextbc.ca/researchmethods) and *Social Psychology* (https://opentextbc.ca/socialpsychology)—and advocates for the adoption of open educational and science practices. His forthcoming book is entitled *Open: The Philosophy and Practices that are Revolutionizing Education and Science.*

Andy Lane is Professor of Environmental Systems at The Open University, UK and a Principal Fellow of the Higher Education Academy. He was seconded as the founding Director of the OUUK's multi-award winning OpenLearn platform from 2006–09. He has taken a prominent role in the OUUK's work on Open Educational Resources including serving as a board member of the Open Education Consortium from 2008–10, being involved in a number of European OER initiatives as well as UK projects. He was a Senior Fellow in the Support Centre for Open Resources in Education at the OUUK from 2009–12 and involved in organizing a number of OER conferences. He has authored or co-authored many teaching texts, research papers and other publications dealing with systems thinking and environmental management; the use of diagramming to aid systems thinking and learning; and systems of open education, especially the use of open educational resources.

Patrina Law is Head of Free Learning at the Open University, UK where she has spent the last fifteen years of her career. She has moved through various roles in higher education, with an emphasis on eLearning, outreach, and researching and commissioning impactful free learning. Her research interests at present surround understanding informal learners, the impact and implications for digital badging for higher education and how this translates to good open educational practice for the University, for which she has won several awards.

Audeliz Matias is an Assistant Professor of Science, Math and Technology for the Center for Distance Learning at the State University of New York (SUNY) Empire State College. Prior to joining as a faculty member, she served as the coordinator of curriculum and instructional design for the science, maths and technology area for three years at the Center for Distance Learning. Audeliz is involved in innovation and emerging technology efforts for teaching and learning and has seven years' experience developing fully online courses. Her scholarly interests focus on geoscience education and effective practices in online learning, including the use of social and media environments, open educational resources, mobile learning, multimedia maps, experiential learning, and the use of scientific datasets to promote active learning.

Patrick McAndrew is Professor of Open Education and Director of the Institute of Educational Technology (IET) in The Open University, UK. IET is a strategic academic unit carrying out research, supporting the University and offering postgraduate qualifications in online and distance education. In his own research Patrick has taken a leading part in the development of approaches to open and free learning. Recent projects in this area include OpenLearn, OLnet, Bridge to Success and the OER Research Hub. He has had an active role in over forty funded-projects across technology enhanced learning.

Howard Miller is Professor of Education at Mercy College, Dobbs Ferry, New York, where he serves as chair of the Department of Secondary Education. Previously, he was a member of the Teacher Education Faculty at Lincoln University, Missouri. Howard began his career as a classroom teacher, and for twenty years taught reading and English in public schools in the United States. He has presented numerous professional workshops and has published close to four dozen articles and book reviews in professional journals. He has been actively engaged with the use of Open Educational Resources for the past five years, has presented at the Open Education Conference, co-authored an article on the use of OER at Mercy College (http://er.educause. edu/articles/2013/11/adopting-oer-a-case-study-of-crossinstitutional-collaboration-and-innovation) and recently served as guest editor of an OER-themed issue of the open online journal *Global Education Review* (http://ger.mercy.edu/index.php/ger).

Ruth Olmsted is a Faculty Program Director in the School of Liberal Arts at Excelsior College, Albany, New York, where she has specific oversight of the BA/BS in Liberal Arts degree programs. These degree programs are the College's most flexible offerings, affording students many opportunities to use credit-by-exam and other forms of prior learning assessment, as well as transfer credit, to meet distribution, depth, and level requirements. Previously, Ruth spent twenty years in what is now the Center for Educational Measurement, overseeing the editorial and test development functions and both electronic and paper-based portfolio assessment. She also has many years of teaching experience, both face-to-face and online.

Davor Orlic co-founded videolectures.net with 20,000 educational videos, created the *Opening up Slovenia* national education case study, established the UNESCO Chair on Open Technologies for OER and Open Learning and conceptualised the Internet of Education paradigm. He is now managing the Knowledge 4 All Foundation with sixty global members in machine learning. He is active in artificial intelligence research, open education, policies and business innovation in education and has international professional experience in project management — connecting research, technology and business — in the Ed Tech landscape. Davor will be curator of the second UNESCO OER World Congress in 2017.

Dana Ospina is the Open Education Library Fellow at Kennedy Library, Cal Poly State University, San Luis Obispo. In this capacity, she creates and supports initiatives and programming on such issues as affordability, access, and open culture. Ospina is responsible for developing the Kennedy Library's pilot open educational resources program.

Ebba Ossiannilsson was awarded the European Distance and E-Learning Network (EDEN) Fellow title in 2014, and became Open Education Europa Fellow in 2015. Since 2000 she has worked at Lund University, Sweden, as an eLearning, open online learning expert with a special focus on quality. Ossiannilsson is the research leader for the

International Council for Open and Distance Education (ICDE) research study on a global overview of quality models, and the evaluator of the Supporting Quality in e-learning European NeTworks (SEQUENT) project on quality. Ossiannilsson collaborated with the European Commission Education and Training working group on Digital and Online Learning, and with the Commonwealth of Learning. She was guest editor of the *Education Sciences Journal* Special Issue on MOOCs (2016), and contributes frequently as a keynote speaker at international conferences. She has a passion for contributing to open education and collaborated with the United Nations (UN) System Task Team on the UN Development Agenda "Realizing the Future We Want for All" (http://www.un.org/en/development/desa/policy/untaskteam_undf/report.shtml). She has produced over 130 publications.

Helen Partridge is the Pro Vice Chancellor (Scholarly Information and Learning Services) at the University of Southern Queensland, and an Adjunct Professor at the Queensland University of Technology (QUT). From 2007 to 2013 she coordinated QUT's library and information studies (LIS) education program. Partridge has published widely in the area of teaching and learning and has received a number of teaching awards including a Teaching Fellowship in 2008 from the Australian Learning and Teaching Council (ALTC) that explored the impact of social media on the LIS profession and its education. From 2009 to 2011 she worked with eleven Australian educational institutions on an ALTC project that established a framework for the education of the information professions in Australia. Helen has twice been elected to the Board of Directors of the Australian Library and Information Association (ALIA), and was appointed a Fellow of the Association in 2012. Helen's research focuses on the interplay between information technology and learning.

Kati Peltonen currently works as a Research, Development and Innovation (RDI) Director of Wellbeing and Regenerative Growth Focus in Lahti University of Applied Sciences in Finland. She is a member of the quality development team in Lahti University of Applied Sciences and has also worked for several years as a Lecturer in the Faculty of Technology in Lahti University of Applied Sciences. Her research interests focus on entrepreneurship, entrepreneurship education, and teaching. She has published in both national and international peer reviewed journals and publications on topics including entrepreneurial pedagogy, team learning and team teaching and teachers' competence development. She also has twenty years of experience in various positions in international business as well as being one of the owners of Entre House and the co-founder and CEO of EnTree Academy, both operating in the field of further education and professional development.

Rebecca Pitt is a Research Associate at the Institute of Educational Technology (IET) at The Open University, UK. Beck worked as project and research support on the Gates-funded Bridge to Success project, which collaborated with community colleges in the Maryland area to remix the existing OU whole course OER for use as bridging content for students beginning their college studies. Beck was responsible for a range of collaborative activity during the OER Research Hub Phase I including research with open textbook providers OpenStax CNX, Siyavula and the BC Campus Open Textbook project. She also led the development and delivery of the OER Research Hub's P2PU course Open Research, which was awarded a RCUK/Open University Engaging Research award in February 2015.

Lizabeth Schlemer is a professor in engineering at Cal Poly State University, San Luis Obispo, California, where she has taught for twenty-three years. Her main area of research is engineering education, specifically project based learning and the use of Online Educational Resources (OER) to enable self-directed learning. She has most recently been researching learning environments for diversity and institutional change.

Pete Schwartz is an associate professor at Cal Poly State University, San Luis Obispo, California. His research explores sustainable living, how people adjust to transitions and how we learn basic physics. He endeavors to learn collaboratively with his students. He is also exploring an alternative way to teach physics classes, and in particular for introductory mechanics where he has invoked what he calls "Parallel Pedagogy" in a flipped classroom methodology based on video lectures. The learning model is described in this short video (https://www.educanon.com/public/32670/93718/different-mechanics-class).

Adrian Stagg is an eLearning Designer in Learning and Teaching Services at the University of Southern Queensland. Adrian's current areas of interest are the use and reuse of open educational resources in higher education and the institutional enablers and barriers to widespread adoption and support of open practice. He is pursuing doctoral research through the University of Tasmania that will seek to understand the practitioner experience of openness in Australian higher education.

Ken Udas currently serves as the Deputy Vice Chancellor of Academic Services and CIO of the University of Southern Queensland, Australia. He has served as the CEO of UMass Online and spent three years as the Executive Director of Penn State World Campus. Ken has also held positions as the Director of the SUNY Learning Network and as the Director of the eLearning Group at the Open Polytechnic of New Zealand. Ken is the co-founder of the Educause Constituency Group on Openness and the Jasig 2-3-98 project that are focused on the emergence and adoption of open technologies, practices, policies, and initiatives, and how they affect the delivery and support of education. He is currently chairing the Educators Working Committee for the Free, Libre, and Open Works project hosted by the Open Source Initiative. He sporadically publishes his less developed thoughts on higher education in *Latent Pattern Transmission.*

Ilkka Väänänen has over twenty years' experience with Finnish higher education institutions. In the last ten years he has worked as a research director at the multidisciplinary Lahti University of Applied Sciences (Lahti UAS) in Lahti, Finland, focusing on strategic management and leadership of research, development and innovation activities (RDI). He currently works as a senior researcher at the Well-being and Regenerative Growth Focus Area in Lahti UAS, and is the editor-in-chief of the *Finnish University of Applied Sciences* journal. He has published recently on user driven innovations, authentic learning environments and open applied research. He is involved in many regional RDI projects, where his specific interest is in RDI integrated learning that promotes regional developing.

Linda Vanasupa explores how to create learning environments that support all learners in their holistic development, herself included. She is a professor of materials engineering at Cal Poly State University, San Luis Obispo, California. She is the author of twenty-nine journal articles, three book chapters, and fifty-six OERs, among other publications.

Catherine Waitinas is an Associate Professor of English at Cal Poly State University, San Luis Obispo, California, who primarily teaches American Literature courses at undergraduate and graduate levels. Her research interests include Walt Whitman, literary mesmerism (including mesmeric sexual consent or the lack thereof), and literary pedagogy.

Martin Weller is Professor of Educational Technology at the Open University, UK. He chaired the OU's first eLearning course in 1999 with 15,000 students, and has been the Virtual Learning Environment (VLE) Director at the OU. He was part of the team that initiated the OpenLearn project and is currently Director of the OER Research Hub project. He is author of two books: *The Digital Scholar* and *The Battle for Open*. He blogs at edtechie.net.

Nathan Whitley-Grassi is the Assistant Director of Educational Technologies at SUNY Empire State College (ESC). Whitley-Grassi teaches courses on various Science, Technology, Engineering and Maths (STEM) and Education topics at the ESC School of Graduate Studies and courses in Education and Ecology and Evolution topics at the undergraduate level at ESC. His interests involve increasing access to STEM experiences through innovative technology integration.

Amy Wiley teaches courses in Argument and Comparative Literature in the English Department at Cal Poly State University, San Luis Obispo, California, where she has been an adjunct faculty member since 2004.

David Wiley is Chief Academic Officer of Lumen Learning, an organization dedicated to increasing student success, reinvigorating pedagogy, and improving the affordability of education through the adoption of open educational resources by schools, community and state colleges, and universities. He is also currently the Education Fellow at Creative Commons and adjunct faculty in the graduate program in Instructional Psychology and Technology at Brigham Young University, Provo, Utah, where he leads the Open Education Group (and was previously a tenured Associate Professor).

Deborah Wilhelm studies adult learning methods and formation. A former Lecturer in technical writing at Cal Poly State University, San Luis Obispo, California, she now teaches homiletics and theology at the Aquinas Institute of Theology and Loyola University, New Orleans, Louisiana.

Linda S. Williams is Professor of Business Management and Administration at Tidewater Community College (TCC) in Chesapeake, Virginia. In 2013, she led the faculty team that launched TCC's Z-Degree, the first Associate of Science degree in the US based entirely on openly licensed content, and continues to lead the program's expansion. She is also project coordinator and participant in the Kaleidoscope Project, project leader for TCC's participation in the Virginia Community College System's Zx23 Project and as course author for the Gates Foundation Next Generation Courseware Introduction to Business course. As a Chancellor's Innovation Grant recipient, she authored a comprehensive faculty development course to educate faculty on the proper adoption, adaptation and deployment of open educational resources. This course, "Pathways: Adopting OER into the Classroom", is now being delivered to faculty across the US. In addition to her work with OER, Linda maintains a strong presence in the classroom and in 2015, was the recipient of TCC's Faculty Senate Outstanding Faculty Award for Teaching Excellence.

Kevin Woo is an Assistant Professor for the SUNY Empire State College's New York City location. Kevin currently teaches a number of studies in behavior, ecology, and conservation, but also engages in interdisciplinary studies across other areas of study. Currently, his research focuses on the evolution of animal communication and cognition, and he has studied the behavior of marine mammals, lizards, birds, and invertebrates. He is also the Assistant Director for the Center for the Study of Pinniped Ecology and Cognition (C-SPEC), based out of St. Francis College, Brooklyn, New York.

Foreword

The last several decades have seen dramatic changes to education. Our fundamental accounts of learning have broadened from purely behavioral explanations to include cognitive, social, constructivist, and connectivist perspectives. The tools we use to support learning have broadened from books, paper, and pencils to include computers of all shapes and sizes, networks, and a wide range of static and interactive digital resources. The institutions we use to support learning have broadened to include those that are public and private, large and small, accredited and not, online and on campus. The values of the institutions that support learning have broadened as well, including a new recognition of the critical role diversity plays in a facilitating a vibrant, evolving ecosystem of ideas and benefits to society.

Where do we position openness in a narrative of the evolution of education? Openness has little to contribute to our fundamental accounts of learning. The foundational role of open licenses in open education might suggest that openness be considered a tool we use to support learning. The inclusion of "open" in the names of institutions might suggest that openness describes a type of institution. However, these simplistic, impoverished views underestimate openness, confusing its everyday implements with its deeper nature.

When properly understood, openness is a value – like diversity. In fact, I believe diversity is one of the best metaphors for understanding the place of openness in education. Decades ago, the value of diversity in the educational enterprise was deeply underappreciated and education was the worse for it. Over a period of years, we have slowly improved education's recognition of the crucial contributions of diversity through a coordinated effort comprised of campus conversations, workshops, trainings, initiatives, and a range of other memetic vehicles. Where administrators, faculty, staff, and students have truly internalized the value of diversity, they act in ways that allow everyone around them to enjoy the benefits of diversity.

As I ponder the core beliefs embodied in openness (considering openness as a value), I return again and again to sharing and gratitude. I share because others have shared with me, and sharing with others seems the most appropriate way to express gratitude for what I have received. Like Newton, I recognize that if I have seen further it is by standing on the shoulders of giants. Should I then, from my heightened station, fight to prevent people from standing on my shoulders? Or do I have an obligation to those before and after me to leverage every means available to me, including modern technologies and open licenses, to enable as many people to stand there as possible? And is it not true that the more people we can help make their way atop our shoulders, and the faster we can enable others to climb atop theirs, the sooner we can solve global wicked problems like poverty, hunger, and war that threaten all humanity?

When administrators, faculty, staff, and students embrace the value we call openness they create, share, and use open educational resources. They publish their research in open access journals. They employ open pedagogies and other open educational practices. They reward and recognize those in their institutions who engage in these behaviors and others that embody the ideals of sharing and gratitude. They work to remove barriers, remove obstacles, and remove friction from pathways to learning for all. Out of their deep gratitude for what others have shared with them, intellectually and in other ways, they do everything in their power to share with others.

The importance of openness in education is only now beginning to be appreciated, and I hope this volume can increase the pace of its spread. This volume contains stories of people and institutions around the world acting in accordance with the value of openness, and relates the amazing results that come from those actions. I hope it will inspire you. I hope that as you read these stories you will feel an inward stirring of gratitude for what you have received from those giants who went before us, and that out of the rich soil of that gratitude will grow a commitment to share – a commitment to openness.

David Wiley

Preface

Patrick Blessinger and TJ Bliss

The Book

Higher education systems around the world are experiencing great change brought about by the global demand for tertiary education, which is at an all-time high. Open education (e.g., open educational resources, open courseware, open textbooks, massive online open courses) provide a means by which society can help meet this growing demand. Within this context, this volume examines the research literature on this topic and it explores, via cases studies, how higher education systems are changing structurally as a result of the open education movement. Open education is part of the wider movement to democratize tertiary education, and to treat lifelong learning as a human right (Altbach, Gumport and Berdahl, 2011; Blessinger and Anchan, 2015; Burke, 2012; Iiyoshi and Kumar, 2008; Kovbasyuk and Blessinger, 2013; Palfreyman and Tapper, 2009; Trow and Burrage, 2010).

Purpose

The main purpose of this volume is to examine the emerging trends and common themes taking place in open education around the world and to provide education professionals, policymakers and interested readers with a global overview of the open education movement. Each chapter investigates a different aspect of open education within a different cultural and institutional context. Using case study data, this

  http://dx.doi.org/10.11647/OBP.0103.01

volume addresses the following questions: What are the global macro pressures impacting open education? What are the more granular micro pressures underlying the emerging trends in open education? What are the major changes occurring in tertiary education as a result of these pressures? How can we best interpret and explain these trends and themes to develop a plausible theory of open education?

Understanding open education within the broader context of the changing landscape of higher education is important because it allows practitioners to reflect on specific changes taking place. While some educational models today focus on disruptive technological innovations as a catalyst for change, a central theme in this volume is to analyse changes in tertiary education through the lens of democratization and human rights.

In the past higher education was mainly the domain of a few. In recent decades, however, it has gradually become more accessible to larger segments of society — a phenomenon that is currently concerning a growing number of countries. These developments not only reflect the growing democratization of society and the increasing emphasis on human rights around the world but also the rising demand for a diversified and flexible system of higher learning to meet the increasingly complex needs of global societies.

For the purposes of this book, a broad definition of open education is used. More specifically, this book uses the definition of open educational resources (OER) used by The William and Flora Hewlett Foundation: "teaching, learning, and research resources that reside in the public domain or have been released under an intellectual property license that permits their free use and re-purposing by others".[1]

Aims

The main thesis of this book is that open education provides a viable means by which anyone can pursue lifelong learning though access to free, openly licensed, high quality educational resources. Open education, and OER in particular, is in the early stages of its development. The typical diffusion cycle for new products, services, and innovations

---

1   See http://www.hewlett.org/programs/education/open-educational-resources

consists of stages for introduction, adoption, growth, and maturity. In the early stages of the cycle, basic models, concepts and standards are defined. In the adoption stage, more and more people and organizations begin to use and find new applications for these products, services, and innovations. For instance, as the idea of OER began to spread in the late twentieth century and early twenty-first century, MIT began to post its courses on the internet. This radical idea, known as the MIT OpenCourseWare project, now has over 2000 courses available to the public for free. Other universities have followed MIT's example.

As with the broader movement to democratize education at all levels, the common underlying force driving these changes — irrespective of national geography or technological innovation — is the on-going development of democratically oriented societies (e.g., public policy reforms, rising global demand for higher education and lifelong learning opportunities). Within the last few decades we have seen an explosion of new ways, such as OER, massive open online courses and online universities, as a way to broaden access to higher education courses.

In this volume, the chapter authors provide their unique perspectives and their own interpretations of open education providing a multi-disciplinary, interdisciplinary, and global perspective on the major changes and challenges facing open education today. Although every country is different in terms of cultural and historical development the chapter authors focus on the most salient features of the open education movement as a whole, such as access, agency, participation, quality education and mass learning.

By looking at whether democratic ideals are adequately reflected in open education this book also touches upon wider issues concerning higher education today, such as diversity, inclusion, affordability, justice and human rights.

Chapter Overviews

Chapter 1, "Introduction to Open Education: Towards a Human Rights Theory" by the volumes' editors and Chapter 2, "Emancipation through Open Education: Rhetoric or Reality?" by Andy Lane are cases in point of the wider issues emerging from an analysis of the ideals and aspirations of open education. Whilst Chapter 1 introduces the concept of open education in the context of learning understood as a basic human right, Chapter 2 further explores its impact on the democratization of higher education. Lane examines the potential freedoms that open education can bring to both learners and teachers in the future whilst acknowledging that open education's impact on society *vis-à-vis* the existing modes of closed education (formal, non-formal and informal) is still low. In order for education to be truly open to all the prevailing social, cultural and economic norms that still privilege an education acquired through the existing physical, political and legal infrastructures need a complete re-think.

In Chapter 3, Phil Barker and Lorna M. Campbell address the issue of "Technology Strategies for Open Educational Resource Dissemination" by looking at a range of digital content hosted by institutions in websites, specific topic repositories, sites for sharing specific types of content (e.g., video, images, and ebooks), general topic repositories, and sites that aggregate content from a range of collections. The authors examine the technologies used, and the way content is promoted, and supported for users, financed and presented. A correct and exhaustive description of digital resources is particularly important to ensure content retrieval and reuse; for this reason, librarians should be involved in the process because the description of resources should not be seen as a purely technical activity.

Chapter 4, "Identifying Categories of Open Education Resource Users", by Martin Weller, Beatriz de los Arcos, Rob Farrow, Rebecca Pitt and Patrick McAndrew, describes the measure of success of the OER movement in disseminating high-quality learning material and in influencing policy. Yet the OER movement stands at the cusp of mainstream adoption, which in order to be fully achieved requires reaching out and actively involving additional audiences. The key to this process is the future ability of OER advocates to cater for the main types of OER users — active users, facilitators and consumers — and their ability to devise new strategies to ensure that the diverse needs of existing OER users are met.

In Chapter 5, "Situated Learning in Open Communities: the TED Open Translation Project", by Lidia Cámara de la Fuente and Anna Comas-Quinn, discusses the TED Open Translation Project (TED OTP), an online community of volunteers involved in the crowd-sourced translation of audiovisual open content. TED OTP provides students with concrete linguistic tasks whilst contributing to a wider dissemination of ideas across languages and cultures. The authors explore student experiences at the intersection of learning in formal and informal contexts experienced at TED OTP and assess the value added by this type of translation practice and the type of learning skills gained by participants.

Chapter 6, "Educational Policy to Support the Open Educational Practice: Charting the Australian Higher Education Landscape", by Adrian Stagg and Carina Bossu, explores how open education policy has gained greater attention by governments, primarily as a way to reduce total educational costs for taxpayers. These policy reforms run parallel to the social inclusion movement which aims at broadening participation in higher education especially for students of low socio-economic backgrounds. However, the authors identify two major issues in these policy reforms: the flawed metrics often used by policy-makers, and a widespread lack of understanding of the dynamics of both social inclusion and open education. The authors explore how open education can benefit from social inclusion arguing that an integrated approach to educational policy will be more beneficial to the broader educational ecosystem.

In Chapter 7, "The Identified Informal Learner: Recognising Assessed Learning in the Open", Patrina Law discusses the development of badged open courses (BOCs) launched by the Open University (OU) in the UK in 2015. Law analyses the results of the OpenLearn, a study which looked at the impact in terms of outreach of the badged open courses and the employability of tis students. Law's analysis concluded that the awarding of branded badges for courses attended, together with students' assessment and feedback mechanisms, motivate and reward informal learners. Moreover, badges also provided a click-through mechanism for participants to enrol in a formal course at the Open University, thus opening the way for further educational opportunities.

Chapter 8, "Transformation of Teaching and Learning in Higher Education towards Open Learning Arenas: A Question of Quality", by Ebba Ossiannilsson, Zehra Altinay, and Fahrive Altinay, examines the changing contours of the academic debate on learning and teaching as the increased digitization of education continues to impact society.

Widening access in higher education is at the top of the global agenda as governments see lifelong education as a means to improved employment, entrepreneurship, and innovation in the labour market. The authors focus on the role of open educational practice and open educational culture.

In Chapter 9, "Three Approaches to Open Textbook Development", Rajiv S. Jhangiani, Arthur G. Green and John D. Belshaw outline the three main approaches currently underlying the development of open textbooks: creation and adaptation projects, individual and collaborative efforts, traditional timeline and compressed timeline models. The authors discuss the similarities and differences of these approaches and the way particular educational disciplines and philosophies influence the development of open textbooks.

In Chapter 10, "What Does It Mean to Open Education? Perspectives on Using Open Educational Resources at a US Public University", by Linda Vanasupa, Amy Wiley, Lizabeth Schlemer, Dana Ospina, Peter Schwartz, Deborah Wilhelm, Catherine Waitinas, and Kellie Hall, the authors discuss OER as a disruptive innovation. Whilst at a basic level OER may be viewed as a simply replacing a traditional text with an OER resource, the process of adopting and adapting OER unearths a host of fundamental questions about the value of education, the meaning of authority and credibility, the risks associated with change, whilst at an individual level challenging our own identities as participants in higher education.

Chapter 11, "Expanding Access to Science Field-Based Research Techniques for Students at a Distance through Open Educational Resources", by Audeliz Matias, Kevin Woo, and Nathan Whitley-Grassi, argues that the adoption of OERs by the STEM community has yet to become an integral part of classroom education in these disciplines. They argue that many STEM faculty have been reluctant to adopt OER because locating and integrating these resources into courses is often fraught with problems and time-consuming. To help ameliorate these issues the authors devised a process to helps generating OERs for STEM related topics focusing on three specific areas — microscopy, interpretation of geologic history, and biodiversity.

In Chapter 12, "A Practitioner's Guide to Open Educational Resources: A Case Study", Howard Miller discusses the practical issues facing OER provision, such as the need to minimize the cost of expensive textbooks and provide greater opportunities for access to higher education. The author examines the issues arising when a textbook-dependent lecture series becomes an OER course, especially when the OER is adopted by an institution that does not have an OER-supportive infrastructure — for instance where there are no experienced OER users to serve as models and mentors, where the librarians are not well-versed in identifying and accessing OER, or where there are no course designers able to provide assistance. Based on the experience of one college professor's journey to OER, amidst these challenges this contribution provides a model of an OER-based course for instructors interested in adopting OER.

Chapter 13, "Open Assessment Resources for Deeper Learning", by David Gibson, Dirk Ifenthaler, and Davor Orlic, outlines the design of a global open assessment resources (OAR) item bank. This bank includes automated feedback and scoring tools for OER that supports a wide range of assessment applications, e.g., quizzes, tests, virtual performance assessments, and game-based learning. The aims of OAR centre on authentic assessment, reusability, modularity and automated assembly and presentation of assessment items. The authors discuss assessment structure, assessment processes, quality issues, and the alignment of OER to a global technology infrastructure and the six core services for delivery — content, interaction, assessment, credentialing, support and technology.

In Chapter 14, "Promoting Open Science and Research in Higher Education: A Finnish Perspective" Ilkka Väänänen and Kati Peltonen discusse the drive towards a wider availability of open research information embodied by the Open Science and Research Initiative for 2014–17. Through this programme Finland aims to become the leading country for open science and research by enabling a more effective utilization of research results for the benefit of society. The authors examine Lahti University of Applied Sciences as a case study of the challenges and opportunities arising from the implementation of the open science and research framework.

In Chapter 15, "Credentials for Open Learning: Scalability and Validity", Mika Hoffman and Ruth Olmsted discuss the challenge of aligning OER with standardized exams and of achieving consensus among educational institutions on the value and type of academic accrediting. The authors describe the process for creating exams and then define a method for building the bridge between OER and the exam. Finally, the authors advocate separating credentialing from the learning process as a means to greater scalability of OER.

In Chapter 16, "Open Education Practice at the University of Southern Queensland" by Ken Udas, Helen Partridge and Adrian Stagg, the authors discuss the social justice ethos informing the University of Southern Queensland in its effort to re-position and re-vision itself as a university grounded in the principles of open education. The authors describe how USQ is striving to create a culture of openness and justice and how implementing open education practices are helping with this effort. The authors explore the key issues confronting USQ such as barriers, challenges, and opportunities in implementing open education practices.

Conclusion

This volume provides a snapshot of the emerging phenomenon of open education around the world and of the increasing impact of OERs on all levels of education, particularly on higher education. It also investigates open education's current trajectory and deep transformations at work providing an analysis of principles, themes, trends and mechanisms underlying these changes, and projecting possible scenarios of what higher education will look like in the coming decades.

This book also explores the ideals informing the OE movement, in particular the democratic and human rights ideals concerning the values of diversity, inclusion, equality, equity, and justice; how these values contribute to the expansion of open education resources; and the shock waves they are sending through global higher education as a result of the shifting tectonic plates in the educational landscape. The editors hope that this collection of case studies will be useful not just to those interested in OE, but more generally to those concerned with the future higher education. Thus, this volume is meant not only for faculty, students, and course designers but it is also meant to provide insights into the emerging trends in global higher education for politicians, higher education policymakers and for anyone interested in the emerging directions in higher education and lifelong learning.

References

Altbach, P. G., Gumport, P. J., and Berdahl, R. O. (Eds.) (2011), *American Higher Education in the Twenty-Frist Century: Social, Political, and Economic Challenges*, Baltimore: The Johns Hopkins University Press.

Blessinger, P. and Anchan, J. P. (Eds.) (2015), *Democratizing Higher Education: International Comparative Perspectives*, New York: Routledge.

Burke, P. J. (2012), *The Right to Higher Education: Beyond Widening Participation*, Abingdon: Routledge.

Iiyoshi, T., and Kumar, M. S. V. (Eds.) (2008), *Opening Up Education: The Collective Advancement of Education through Open Technology, Open Content, and Open Knowledge*, Cambridge, MA: MIT Press.

Kirby, D. (2009), Widening Access: Making the Transition from Mass to Universal Post-Secondary Education in Canada. *Journal of Applied Research on Learning*. Vol. 2, Special Issue, Article 3, http://www.ccl-cca.ca/pdfs/JARL/Jarl-Vol2Art3-Kirby_EN.pdf

Kovbasyuk, O., Blessinger, P. (Eds.) (2013), *Meaning-centered Education: International Perspectives and Explorations in Higher Education*, New York: Routledge.

Palfreyman, D., and Tapper, T. (Eds.) (2009), *Structuring Mass Higher Education: The Role of Elite Institutions*, New York: Routledge.

Trow, M., and Burrage, M. (2010), *Twentieth-Century Higher Education: Elite to Mass to Universal*, Baltimore: Johns Hopkins University Press.

1. Introduction to Open Education: Towards a Human Rights Theory

Patrick Blessinger and TJ Bliss

Education is recognized as a fundamental human right. Yet, many people throughout the world do not have access to important educational opportunities. Open education, which began in earnest in the late 1960s with the establishment of open universities and gained momentum in the first part of this century through open educational resources and open technologies, is part of a wider effort to democratize education. Designed for access, agency, ownership, participation, and experience, open education has the potential to become a great global equalizer, providing opportunity for people throughout the world to exercise this basic human right.

http://dx.doi.org/10.11647/OBP.0103.01

Introduction

What does it mean to be open, as opposed to closed? As with any word, several meanings can be attached to it. Perhaps it is best to first discuss the more general meaning of the term and then explore the more specific meanings as we develop an analysis of open education. The word open, broadly speaking, means to be flexible, free, and welcoming, and relative to closed, it means non-prejudiced, non-restricted, and unfettered. Of course, there are different degrees and types of openness as well as different goals and outcomes that are sought in open education. Common themes that tend to cut across all these aspects of open education are the ability to cultivate personal agency, self-determination, and self-regulated lifelong (every life stage) and life-wide (across all life activities) learning. In so doing, democracy is strengthened and human rights are supported — this is the focus of open education in this volume.

The condition of being open has many qualities and characteristics but these characteristics, relative to one's ability to access, participate in, and leverage the full benefits of open education, have the following dimensions: spatial, temporal, and process. Therefore, these core dimensions serve as a good starting point to explain the nature of open education.

Regarding the spatial dimension, open education (e.g., open educational resources, open courseware, massive online open courses) allows people to access and participate in education regardless of their physical/geographic location, provided of course that they have the means (e.g., computer, smart phone, internet access) to connect to the resources. Thus, improvements in open education technologies allow more people to overcome physical and geographical barriers and constraints. As mobile and other information technologies become more affordable, the opportunity to access these resources increases.

Regarding the temporal dimension, open education allows people to access and participate in education regardless of the time of day, month, or year, and independent of others' time considerations. In other words, open education need not be a synchronous form of communication as in the traditional higher education model, but rather communication and participation become in this context an asynchronous form of learning and communication. As with the spatial dimension, improvements in course design and information and communication technologies allow more people to overcome time barriers and constraints.

Regarding the process dimension, it is important that open educational platforms and systems be created using sound design principles, valid and reliable teaching methods, and learning theories. Within this dimensional framework, open education consists of the following core components:

- Subject-matter experts (i.e., professors, scholars, teachers, educators) create the content.

- Students are free to select those courses and other educational resources that they believe will be most beneficial to them (i.e., it is a voluntary system to satisfy the learning needs of the students). Within the structural constraints of the educational platform and the usage policies and rules, students are free to determine if, when, and how they will access and participate in open education and they are free to self-determine what learning needs (outcomes) they want to meet.

- Organizations (i.e., universities, non-governmental organizations) create the structure and rules by which the content is packaged and structured as well as the basic rules governing how content is produced and consumed, including feedback systems that are used to continuously make improvements and meet the needs of both the experts and students.

As noted by Kahle (2008), the core underlying principles involved in open education include the following:

- Design for access
- Design for agency
- Design for ownership
- Design for participation
- Design for experience

Open education is designed for access because it removes the traditional barriers that people often face in obtaining knowledge, credits, and degrees — including but not limited to cost. Access is fundamental to open education and is the basic principle that has informed and driven the open education movement from its inception.

Open education goes beyond access: it is designed for the agency of students and teachers and affords them increased control of content and technology. As Kahle (2008, p. 35) explains: Openness "is measured by the degree to which it empowers users to take action, making technology [and content] their own, rather than imposing its own foreign and inflexible requirements and constraints". Open education pre-supposes the participation of the learner and the educator, and it seeks to amplify their agency.

Open education is also designed for ownership when technology and content are licensed in such a way that users can both modify and retain the resource in perpetuity. David Wiley originally defined open content using a "4 R" framework, which includes the rights to reuse, revise, redistribute, and remix creative works. But in response to academic publishers pushing access codes and short-term leases on educational content, Wiley made explicit something he had long seen as an underlying implicit principle of open content: the right to retain, which includes the rights to make, own, and control copies of the content (Wiley, 2014).

Open education is designed for participation when it is well-designed for access, agency, and ownership. In other words, these aspects lead to participation by learners and educators. As open education promotes these fundamental principles, students and teachers are more likely to collaborate and participatory in inclusive activities. Indeed, one of the goals of open education is to move learners closer to the center of a community of practice, specifically through providing opportunities and infrastructure for participation and collaboration.

Finally, open education is designed for experience, or at least it can be, when educators and systems focus on making content and technology appealing and user-friendly. Kahle (2008, p. 42) argues that "design for experience recognizes that all participants, particularly busy educators and students, quickly form opinions as to what resources are interesting, helpful, and worth their investment of time. Design for experience is a form of human-centered design". Insofar as creators of content and technologies recognize this important principle, open education can appeal to a broader audience than students and educators, thus amplifying access, agency, ownership and participation to anyone with a desire to learn.

The open education movement can also be viewed as part of a wider drive to democratize tertiary education, which, in turn, can be viewed as part of the movement to establish tertiary education and lifelong learning as a human right. Since this chapter starts with the normative premise that open education should be used as a means to promote and facilitate lifelong learning, the next section will discuss the history of open education and then segue into the rationale for tertiary education and lifelong learning as a human right, which will lay the groundwork for a human rights theory of lifelong learning.

The human rights view of lifelong learning focuses not on the socio-economic and personal benefits that education produces (albeit very important) but rather on the claim that universal education makes on others. A human right is a very broad construct from which other issues and rights flow (e.g., civil rights, social inclusion, humane treatment of people). A human right is defined as a justified claim on others (McGowan, 2013). In addition, one of the goals of the UN Millennium Development Goals initiative is to move towards a more inclusive and quality education system that recognizes tertiary education alongside primary and secondary education.[1] Human rights are justified because they protect humanity from the abuse of others and they defend those aspects of society (e.g., life, liberty, and security) that are considered fundamental to human life, and as such, they are the most urgent claim on others. In the final analysis, by viewing learning and education through the lens of human rights, universal education throughout the course of life becomes an important condition for justice in a democratic society.

Blessinger discusses this theme further this way:

> Given the huge importance of lifelong learning to the overall well-being of society and the economy, access to and participation in meaningful lifelong educational opportunities is one of the chief human rights issues of our generation. As such, the emerging global higher education system hints at the prospect of a more inclusive global knowledge society. (2015b).

---

1   https://scholarlykitchen.sspnet.org/2016/09/08/guest-post-inasps-john-harle-on-why-publishers-need-to-pay-attention-to-the-sustainable-development-goals

In 2007, UNESCO and UNICEF further delineated the right to education into three areas: the right of *access* to education, the right to *quality* education, and the right to *respect* within the learning environment. Defined this way, these rights therefore have implications for governments, educational institutions, and non-governmental organizations with regard to their responsibility towards how they provision educational resources and how they lead learning environments.

Concerning *access*, open education puts the responsibility and duty of care primarily on the service provider and others to ensure a ubiquitous, affordable way for people to access a wide range of educational resources. Concerning *quality*, it puts the responsibility primarily on the service provider (i.e., the educational institution) and the content creators (i.e., the faculty or other subject matter expert) to define the framework and process of who, what, when, where, why, and how the content will be created and the criteria by which to evaluate and assess the quality of the content and the effectiveness of teaching and learning. Concerning *respect*, it puts the responsibility primarily on the service provider to define the policies and rules to cultivate an environment of mutual respect and on the teachers and students, as the two primary agents in the teaching-learning process, to treat others with respect and dignity. Thus, open education will be most effective if it addresses all these components.

Brief History of Open Education

At its core, the open education movement has been about access. In the late 1960s, efforts began to remove barriers to entry for students desiring to pursue tertiary education. For example, the Open University of the United Kingdom (OU-UK, http://www.open.ac.uk) was established in 1969 with the mission to help facilitate educational opportunities and greater social justice by providing high-quality university education to anyone who has a desire to learn and realize their potential. Since the founding of the OU-UK, many other open universities have been established in countries throughout the world, ranging from Bangladesh to Canada to South Africa.

In the late 1990s, as the internet was becoming more ubiquitous, many prestigious institutions of higher education in the United States began looking for ways to further disseminate the educational content promulgated within their classrooms. At the same time, forward thinking education technologists were recognizing the power of the internet to democratize education at all levels and exponentially increase access to educational content for people across the globe. In 1998, David Wiley coined the term "open content", which he described as a creative work that others are allowed to copy, share, and modify. Wiley created a basic open license that creators could place on their works to signify these permissions.

As the idea of open content for education began to spread, Charles Vest, then President of the Massachusetts Institute of Technology (MIT), sought funding from private foundations to video-tape and post content from MIT courses on the internet. This radical idea became the MIT project (http://ocw.mit.edu/index.htm), which continues to publicly and freely share the content from over two thousand MIT courses. Other universities followed MIT's example, dramatically expanding the open courseware movement over the next several years.

Recognizing the power and potential of open content to increase access to education, private philanthropic foundations, particularly the William and Flora Hewlett Foundation in California, began supporting the development and spread of open courseware and other types of open educational content. In 2002, at a UNESCO meeting of developing nations, known as the Forum on the Impact of Open Courseware for Higher Education in Developing Countries, the term "Open Educational Resources" (OER) was officially adopted to describe open content used for educational purposes. The forum agreed on the following definition of OER: the open provision of educational resources, enabled by information and communication technologies, for consultation, use and adaptation by a community of users for non-commercial purposes (UNESCO, 2002, p. 24).

In the same year, Lawrence Lessig, Hal Abelson, and Eric Eldred received funding to establish a new non-profit called Creative Commons, which produced flexible copyright licenses that people could use to openly license their creative works. These licenses have become the gold standard for establishing the legal aspect of OER. The

Hewlett Foundation defines OER as "teaching, learning, and research resources that reside in the public domain or have been released under an intellectual property license that permits their free use and re-purposing by others", and requires that all works created with project grant funding be licensed with a Creative Commons Attribution license.[2] Many other foundations and government agencies throughout the world have adopted similar open policies, leading to a significant increase in the supply of OER.

For the first five or so years after the UNESCO meeting in Paris, most of the OER available for professors to adopt existed in piecemeal form and was mostly suitable as a supplement to primary course content. Starting in 2009, advocates and supporters of OER began to recognize that for OER to enter mainstream adoption, open content would need to be produced in a format that professors would be better able to adopt as primary course material: the textbook. With support from foundations and governments, work began to produce and disseminate what have become known as "open textbooks". For example, over the past four years, OpenStax College at Rice University (https://openstax.org) has produced twenty open textbooks for the highest enrolled college courses in the United States; and the state of California and the province of British Columbia have each compiled a library of open textbooks for the highest enrolled courses in their respective systems. These open textbooks have been adopted by thousands of professors, positively impacting hundreds of thousands of students. In addition, the Open Textbook Network and the Open Textbook Library at the University of Minnesota (https://open.umn.edu) provide access to a growing list of open textbooks.

Most recently, an effort has begun to bring adoption of OER in higher education to scale. In 2013, Tidewater Community College established the first degree program entirely based on OER. In June 2016, the college reform network, Achieving the Dream (http://achievingthedream. org), provided pass-through funding to nearly 40 community colleges in the United States to establish OER degrees within the next 2 years. These degree programs will impact many students and do much to bring OER into mainstream adoption in higher education. On the

---

2 See http://www.hewlett.org/programs/education/open-educational-resources

international front, the OERu partnership (https://oeru.org) is working with over thirty partner institutions around the world to establish a fully articulated, credit-bearing first year of study based exclusively on OER that students around the world can enroll in for free.

Open education is more than just open content, of course, but the OER movement is a remarkable example of the power of openness to increase educational access for all. The real potential of open education is to actually improve learning for all. In the next several years, Open Educational Practice is expected to increase. It will include teaching techniques that draw on open educational resources, open technologies, and open systems to increase the flexibility and authenticity of learner experiences (Conole and Ehlers, 2010), ultimately resulting in better learning for students and better teaching for educators globally.

Open Education to Democratize Education

Open education is not a substitute for traditional higher education provisioning, nor is it intended to be. The desire-to-learn model of open education supplements the ability-to-pay model of higher education. For many people who use open education services, they provide a supplementary type of education that adds to the mix of educational offerings available. Thus, open education need not represent an "either/or" proposition and it need not compete with (nor necessarily intends to) traditional higher education but rather it provides an additional means by which people can access knowledge and engage in lifelong learning. In fact, some of the largest providers of open educational resources are the traditional brick-and-mortar higher education institutions because they understand that open education is not a pure substitute for traditional place-based higher education and because it makes it easier for them to prepare materials for MOOCs, for example (based on existing courses), and because it is easier for them to utilize existing instructional staff and institutional expertise.

The goals of students using open education and the goals of those who undertake traditional higher education are often very different. Most students in traditional place-based higher education want to obtain a degree whereas most in open education want to pursue learning but not necessarily obtain a degree. In addition, many people do not have the time to devote themselves exclusively, or even part-time, to place-based education. Fixed time and place requirements are major obstacles to enrolment for many students. To ameliorate this obstacle, in some countries university fees are kept very low and virtually non-existent for low-income students and for students who live at home the total cost of attendance is extremely low. A key distinction between traditional and open education is that traditional higher education institutions provide services (e.g., accredited degrees, extensive instructional and support staff, research output) that some open education services may not, nor necessarily intend to. Thus, both systems have emerged to address different types of learners who have different goals and needs.

Most nations have gradually shifted away from an elitist system of higher education and towards a universal access model of higher education. In the universal access model a multiplicity of institutional types (e.g., technical colleges, community colleges, liberal arts colleges, research universities) and a multiplicity of access types (e.g., online universities, open universities, open courseware, open educational resources), as well as hybrid institutions together with further and continuing education programs are combined in unique ways to serve the varied needs of society. This shift has created a more diversified system of institutional types, access methods, and program and course offerings for every stage of life or career and is reflective of the continuing democratization of knowledge and the growing demand for higher education worldwide (Blessinger and Anchan, 2015; Blessinger, 2015a, b; OECD, 2012; Trow, 1974; Yu and Delaney, 2014).

The main distinguishing features of open education is that it consists of free, unfettered, anytime, anywhere access to educational resources that are meaningful and useful to those who wish to utilize those resources. Effective open education platforms and processes center on meeting the needs and aspirations of people throughout every life stage (lifelong learning) and across all life activities (life-wide learning). Since every person is part of the broader social structures in which they live, the most effective open education platforms are those that create opportunities for shared meaning-making, collaborative activities, and creative participation. Thus, open education should not only be a personal meaning-making experience but also a social one. As such, the open education model moves away from the knowledge scarcity model and toward a knowledge abundance model (McGrath, 2008; Batson, Paharia, and Kumar, 2008).

As such, additional models are needed to work alongside (not replace) traditional educational structures. With the knowledge abundance model, knowledge is made available to anyone who wishes to consume it, regardless of their ability to pay or their ability to participate in place-based education. The emerging abundance model is reflective of the broader democratization of knowledge that is unfolding around the world. The abundance model represents an emerging paradigm shift from knowledge that is owned and controlled by knowledge elites to knowledge that is accessible to anyone.

As mentioned earlier, the emergence of massive open online courses, open universities, and open educational resources represent concrete exemplars of this paradigm shift. As noted by Blessinger (2016a), this is not an entirely new phenomenon because there have been revolutionary moments in human history (e.g., invention of the printing press in the 15th century, the spread of public libraries in the nineteenth century, the development of the internet in the twentieth century) that have served as catalysts to de-monopolize higher learning and to open access to knowledge to wider segments of society. Blessinger (2016a) puts it this way: "The wide-ranging utility of the printing press laid the foundation for future political, social, economic and scientific revolutions such as the Renaissance and the Reformation, which paved the way for mass learning and the modern hyper-connected global knowledge society". This trend continues to this day. Thus, one can see how these events are connected, although, at the time they emerged, their future impact was often unforeseen and often shunned and even fiercely opposed by those who wanted to maintain the status quo.

Thus, as discussed by Blessinger and Anchan (2015), the underlying forces driving the development of open education are the basic human needs to learn and grow throughout every stage of life. The change model also supports a *democratic theory of higher education* postulating that the goal of university-level education is to cultivate personal agency through the development of knowledge, skills, and capacity; opportunities to learn throughout life should therefore be provided to all.

These political, social, economic, scientific, and technological revolutions and factors are connected and they impact each other in concrete ways. The role and purpose of tertiary education continues to expand. The importance of lifelong and life-wide learning continues to grow and it is now regarded as necessary to social and personal development and therefore as a human right. As such, the role of tertiary education has expanded to include the production of social and cultural capital, not just human and economic capital.

Lynch (2008) argues that we should not automatically equate access to information (e.g., internet based information) to access to education (i.e., education is a system of formal learning). This is especially true if we take a broader definition of education to include sociocultural processes which implies that education should also be about social and emotional learning, not just cognitive learning. Treating education as a social process emphasizes the point that learning is socially situated (Lave and Wenger, 1991) and that learning is also a personal meaning-making process (Kovbasyuk and Blessinger, 2013). Yet, notwithstanding the importance of these processes, effective educational systems also require the elimination of unnecessary and arbitrary barriers that may inhibit its access and participation.

Whether one uses a narrow definition of education or a broad definition, open education can be adequately described as a form of universal education available to all through freely accessible and ubiquitous knowledge bases. Although open education need not, strictly speaking, be electronic in form, electronic technology does nonetheless provide a low cost and relatively easy means for people anywhere at any time to learn in a social and personalized way, thus making the ideal of "education for all" an emerging reality.

Open Education as Social Inclusion

Given higher education's history of exclusion and elitism, the emergence of *education for all* and *education as a right* is imperative (Blessinger, 2016e; Burke, 2012; McCowan, 2013; UNESCO/UNICEF, 2007; Spring, 2000; Vandenberg, 1990). Learning is a social process and formal systems of learning are necessary for social reproduction and the continual development of society. As with all living creatures, all people are born depending on others for their survival and development. They depend on others (e.g., family, school, community) to learn the required knowledge and skills to live within society. Education is therefore social in nature and a type of learning community. Although the ultimate purpose of education is to produce learning, education also inherently serves political, economic, social, and humanistic purposes. With globalization, humans live in an increasingly interconnected and interdependent world. The more complex the world becomes and the faster that change happens, the greater the need for lifelong and life-wide education. Different models and systems of open education help meet this need (Altbach, Gumport and Berdahl, 2011; Barnett, 2012; Burke, 2012; Dewey, 1916; Kezar, 2014; Knapper and Cropley, 2000; Kovbasyuk and Blessinger, 2012).

In the US, for example, higher education and lifelong learning have been marked by four broad movements (or waves) over the last 150 years. The first wave was the result of the Morrill Act of 1862 which created a system of land-grant universities through the US; the second wave was the creation of the community and technical college system that began at the beginning of the twentieth century and the G.I. Bill of 1944, both of which extended access to higher education to millions of US citizens; the third wave was the use of information and communication technologies (e.g., television, internet) and distance education opportunities which helped create the anytime, anywhere educational movement; and the fourth wave which has been brought about by the acceleration of globalization and the internationalization of higher education resulting in the growing recognition that lifelong learning and education is a human right which further expands the democratic social contract to education to all segments of society (Blessinger, 2015c, d, e). We suggest that the OE movement, and open methods as part of this, be considered a fifth wave in the history of education.

Open Education to Support Education as a Human Right

One of the main reasons why higher education has become so diversified (in terms of institutional types and educational delivery models) and widely available to anyone who wishes to avail her/himself of it is because a university or college degree has become the gateway to professional careers and specific job opportunities, whether they be white, pink or blue collar. For instance, nearly all professions such as medicine, law, education, and engineering are only available to those with advanced university degrees. Many careers that once only required a high school diploma now require a college degree. In most countries certification and apprenticeships are now required in most vocational fields such as medical and legal assisting, welding, electronics, cosmetology, real estate, and culinary arts. Jobs have become more complex and more demanding throughout the labour market.

Thus, it is no surprise that tertiary institutions of all types have grown in importance. Societies around the world are placing greater faith and reliance in educational systems to address a growing array of social and economic problems. Universal education is now widely viewed as one of the basic requirements for a modern society and it serves as a chief catalyst for socio-economic and personal development. Education at all levels (i.e., primary, secondary, tertiary) is now widely considered a human right because it yields so many positive benefits at a social, economic, and personal level (Hanushek and Woessmann, 2007), because it has become so vital to the development of social reproduction (Bourdieu and Passeron, 1977) and because continual learning is so necessary to human agency and development. Because of these factors, it would be an injustice to deny or constrain people from learning throughout the entirety of their lives (Kovbasyuk and Blessinger, 2013; Spring, 2000; Vandenberg, 1990).

MOOCs, open educational resources, open universities, and the like therefore provide a low cost or zero cost means for anyone to access high quality educational materials. The costs associated with producing open educational services typically come from a variety of sources such institutional budgets, government support, and non-governmental support (e.g., foundations). In addition, studies have shown that costs for textbooks, for example, can be dramatically reduced using OER (Hilton, Robinson, Wiley, and Ackerman, 2014). Open education resources and platforms may be structured either as formal learning (i.e., part of a structured curriculum) or as non-formal learning (i.e., not structured as part of a curricula program leading to a certificate or degree but rather as one-off courses).

In the years following WWII, the human and civil rights movement took on a new sense of urgency. This sense of urgency was a result, in large measure, of the crimes against humanity perpetrated by some people during WWII. When the full extent of these crimes was revealed it became clear that the civilized world community needed to intervene on a global scale. So, the United Nations, acting in their capacity as representatives of the world community, adopted *The Universal Declaration of Human Rights* — UDHR (United Nations, 1948) which articulated those basic human rights that applied to all nations and cultures.[3] The UDHR states that everyone has a right to education at all levels.

To conclude, this chapter has discussed how democratic societies have gradually moved away from elitist and exclusivist systems of higher education that were based on power and privilege claims in favor of open and inclusive systems of higher education based on justice and human rights claims. This phenomenon represents a major paradigm shift in higher education. Since democratic societies are fundamentally based on principles of rights and justice, it should not come as a surprise that this transformation is occurring, albeit incrementally. Thus, the emergence of open education is a reflection of the broader democratic society in which it functions.

The UNESCO *Universal Declaration on Democracy* (1997) states that, "A sustained state of democracy thus requires a democratic climate and culture constantly nurtured and reinforced by education and other vehicles of culture and information".[4] Thus, lifelong education, not just basic education, is needed to nurture and strengthen democracy. It does this by creating flexible and open educational structures that allow all people to engage in lifelong and life-wide learning. Given the increasing impact of globalization and the increasing importance of continual lifelong education for all, it is clear that treating education as a human right is imperative.

---

3   Recently a prestigious group of scholars, politicians and activists, under the leadership of former British Prime Minister Gordon Brown and the auspices of New York University's Global Institute for Advanced Study, convened the Global Citizenship Commission to re-examine the spirit of The Universal Declaration of Human Rights. Their findings are published in Gordon Brown (Ed.), *The Universal Declaration of Human Rights in the 21st Century* (Cambridge: Open Book Publishers, 2016), http://doi.org/10.11647/OBP.0091, http://www.openbookpublishers.com/product/467. See, in particular, Section 6.3.d, "Human Rights Education" (pp. 97–99) and the online Appendix "Advancing Transformative Human Rights Education", https://www.openbookpublishers.com/shopimages/The-UDHR-21st-C-AppendixD.pdf

4   http://www.ipu.org/cnl-e/161-dem.htm.

In a democratic society, the right of voting has been viewed as the "great equalizer" because it allows citizens to have a voice in how their society is governed. Open education can also be viewed as a potential "great equalizer" since it allows people to continually improve their knowledge and skills throughout the course of their lives. And just like voting, it helps to extend the democratic social contract to all and is reflective of how the democratic social contract continues to be restructured in meaningful ways. Thus, open education also has the potential to strengthen democracy and respect for human rights by creating a more educated and informed citizenry.

References

Altbach, P. G., Gumport, P. J. and Berdahl, R. O. (2011), *American Higher Education in the Twenty-first Century: Social, Political, and Economic Challenges*, Baltimore: The Johns Hopkins University Press.

Barnett, R. (2012), *The Future University: Ideas and Possibilities*. London: Routledge.

Batson, T., Paharia, N. and Kumar, M. S. V. (2008), A Harvest Too Large?: A Framework for Educational Abundance, in T. Iiyoshi and M. S. V. Kumar (Eds.), *Opening up Education: The Collective Advancement of Education through Open Technology, Open Content, and Open Knowledge*, pp. 89–103. Cambridge, MA: MIT Press.

Blessinger, P. (2016a), A Catalyst for Change, *University World News*, London, http://www.universityworldnews.com/article.php?story=201602091 44724889

Blessinger, P. and Anchan, J. P. (Eds.) (2015), *Democratizing Higher Education: International Comparative Perspectives*, New York: Routledge.

Blessinger, P. (2015a), Towards an Inclusive Global Knowledge Society, *University World News*, London, http://www.universityworldnews.com/article.php?story=20150929193529682

Blessinger, P. (2015b), Why Global Higher Education Must Be Democratized, *University World News*, London, http://www.universityworldnews.com/article.php?story=2015090815175230

Blessinger, P. (2015c), The Future of Higher Education: Towards a Democratic Theory of Higher Education, in P. Blessinger and J. P. Anchan (Eds.), *Democratizing Higher Education: International Comparative Perspectives*, New York: Routledge.

Blessinger, P. (2015d), Why Universal and Life-Long Higher Education is the Next Step in Advancing the Social Contract, *Scholars Strategy Network*, http://www.scholarsstrategynetwork.org/content/why-universal-and-life-long-higher-education-next-step-advancing-social-contract

Blessinger, P. (2015e), Lifelong Learning as a Human Right, *University World News*, http://www.universityworldnews.com/article.php?story=2015030315 0758108

Bourdieu, P. and Passeron, J. (1977), *Reproduction in Education, Society, and Culture*, London: Sage, http://dx.doi.org/10.2307/589547

Brown, G. (Ed.), *The Universal Declaration of Human Rights in the 21st Century* (Cambridge: Open Book Publishers, 2016), http://doi.org/10.11647/OBP.0091, http://www.openbookpublishers.com/product/467

Burke, P. J. (2012), *The Right to Higher Education: Beyond Widening Participation*. Abingdon: Routledge, http://dx.doi.org/10.4324/9780203125571

Conole, G. C., and Ehlers, U. D. (2010), *Open Educational Practices: Unleashing the Power of OER*, Paper presented to UNESCO Workshop on OER in Namibia 2010, Windhoek, http://efquel.org/wp-content/uploads/2012/03/OEP_Unleashing-the-power-of-OER.pdf

Dewey, J. (1916), *Democracy and Education: An Introduction to the Philosophy of Education*, New York: Macmillan, https://s3.amazonaws.com/arena-attachments/190319/2a5836b93124f200790476e08ecc4232.pdf

Hanushek, E. and Woessmann, L. (2007), *The Role of Education Quality for Economic Growth*, Washington: World Bank, http://dx.doi.org/10.1596/1813-9450-4122

Hilton, J. L., Robinson, T. J., Wiley, D., and Ackerman, J. D. (2014), Cost-Savings Achieved in Two Semesters through the Adoption of Open Educational Resources. *The International Review of Research in Open and Distributed Learning*, 15(2), http://www.irrodl.org/index.php/irrodl/article/view/1700/2833

Iiyoshi, T. and Kumar, M. S. V. (Eds.) (2008), *Opening up Education: The Collective Advancement of Education through Open Technology, Open Content, and Open Knowledge*, Cambridge, MA: MIT Press.

Kahle, D. (2008), Designing Open Education Technology, in T. Iiyoshi and M. S. V. Kumar (Eds.), *Opening up Education*, pp. 27–45. Cambridge, MA: MIT Press.

Kezar, A. (2014). *How Colleges Change: Understanding, Leading, and Enacting Change*. New York: Routledge.

Knapper, C. K. and Cropley, A. J. (2000), *Lifelong Learning in Higher Education*, Sterling: Stylus Publishing.

Kovbasyuk, O. and Blessinger, P. (2013), *Meaning-centered Education: International Perspectives and Explorations in Higher Education*, New York: Routledge, http://dx.doi.org/10.4324/9780203115084

Lave, J. and Wenger, E. (1991), *Situated Learning: Legitimate Peripheral Participation*, Cambridge, UK: Cambridge University Press, http://dx.doi.org/10.1017/cbo9780511815355

Lynch, C. (2008), Digital Libraries, Learning Communities and Open Education, in T. Iiyoshi and M. S. V. Kumar (Eds.), *Opening up Education*, pp. 105–118, Cambridge, MA: MIT Press.

McCowan, Tristan (2013), *Education as a Human Right: Principles for a Universal Entitlement to Learning*, New York: Bloomsbury Publishing, http://dx.doi.org/10.5040/9781472552938

McGrath, O. (2008), Open Educational Technology: Tempered Aspirations, in T. Iiyoshi and M. S. V. Kumar (Eds.), *Opening up Education*, pp. 13–26, Cambridge, MA: MIT Press.

OECD (2012), *Education at a Glance: OECD Indicators 2012*, OECD Country Note, http://www.oecd.org/education/CN - United States.pdf

Spring, J. (2000), *The Universal Right to Education: Justification, Definition, and Guidelines*, New Jersey: Lawrence Erlbaum, http://dx.doi.org/10.4324/9781410601889

Trow, M. (1974), Problems in the Transition from Elite to Mass Higher Education, in OECD (Ed), *Policies for Higher Education*, pp. 51–101, Paris: OECD.

UNESCO (1997), *Universal Declaration on Democracy*, Paris: United Nations, http://www.unesco.org/cpp/uk/declarations/democracy.pdf

UNESCO (2002). *Forum on the Impact of Open Courseware for Higher Education in Developing Countries: Final Report*, http://unesdoc.unesco.org/images/0012/001285/128515e.pdf

UNESCO/UNICEF (2007), *A Human Rights Based Approach to Education for All*, New York: United Nations, http://www.unicef.org/publications/files/A_Human_Rights_Based_Approach_to_Education_for_All.pdf

United Nations (1948), *The Universal Declaration of Human Rights*, New York: United Nations.

Vandenberg, D. (1990), *Education as a Human Right: A Theory of Curriculum and Pedagogy*, New York: Teachers College Press, http://dx.doi.org/10.5860/choice.28-2854

Wiley, D. (2014), *The Access Compromise and the 5th R*, http://opencontent.org/blog/archives/3221

Yu, P. and Delaney, J. A. (2014), The Spread of Higher Education Around the Globe: A Cross-country Analysis of Gross Tertiary Education Enrollment, 1999–2005, *Educational Policy*, 28(5), http://dx.doi.org/10.1177/0895904814531648

2. Emancipation through Open Education: Rhetoric or Reality?

Andy Lane

Many claims have been made as to the potential freedoms offered through open education and how these freedoms may change or democratize higher education. However, are those freedoms truly helping those most in need of emancipation, and what freedoms do they provide for learners or teachers? This chapter tries to answer that question by firstly examining the various discourses surrounding education and emancipation and also open education. It notes that the framing of education and open education can be subject to differing perspectives and outlooks, including distinctions between formal, non-formal and informal education and the relationships between teachers and learners. The chapter then provides a critical overview of the emancipatory effects of open education on learners and teachers (and organizations) as instantiated in open universities, massive open online courses (MOOCs) and open educational resources (OER). It examines the key features and freedoms offered by these examples in relation to formal, non-formal and informal education and in relation to the existing modes of closed education and argues that despite the promise of open education it has had relatively little impact on these existing modes and that the reality will be less profound than the rhetoric suggests.

http://dx.doi.org/10.11647/OBP.0103.02

Introduction

Many claims have been made as to the potential of open education to change or democratize higher education but are they truly helping those most in need of emancipation, whether learners or teachers, who may still have little voice or agency within the educational settings they experience? This chapter tries to answer that question by (1) examining the various discourses surrounding education and emancipation and also open education; (2) providing a critical overview of the emancipatory effects of open education on learners and teachers (and organizations) as instantiated in open universities, massive open online courses (MOOCs) and open educational resources (OER); and (3) outlining the complex roles of open education as an emancipatory force.

Emancipation and Education

Emancipation has a variety of related definitions but the one most pertinent to this chapter is: *the fact or process of being set free from legal, social, or political restrictions.*[1]

Discussion about, and action around, emancipation has often been used in relation to the rights of specific, sizeable groups within society such as the emancipation of slaves (freedom from bondage) or the emancipation of women as part of the suffrage movement (freedom to vote in elections). It implies a power relationship whereby one group within society is, consciously or sometimes unconsciously, oppressing another group in society that is looking for or expecting equality of treatment.

Education, as a significant human activity system (Checkland, 1999), is itself seen by many as both a means to achieve emancipation for all groups within society (emancipation of people *through* education) and as a process within which there can be restrictions placed on certain groups within society by other participants that need to be overcome in that process (emancipation of learners and teachers *within* education).[2]

---

1   From Oxford Dictionaries online, http://www.oxforddictionaries.com
2   This is a term used to describe purposeful systems where, because of the human factor, the purposes and the activities involved are varied and changing, as distinct from having just one attributed purpose or set of activities as with a mechanical or engineered system.

In addition, there are others who would argue for emancipation *of* education (as a human activity system) from its existing structures and practices so that all are equally empowered to act within and benefit from education as a human activity system. Lastly, it is possible to consider that some people are able to free themselves from most of the structures and strictures of education as a human activity system through becoming fully autonomous learners or autodidacts (emancipation *from* organized education).

The first role of education as enabling emancipation in general is instantiated in declarations from the United Nations where education is deemed a fundamental human right and essential for the exercise of all other human rights.[3] Such rights have themselves been incorporated into United Nations sponsored activities such as the Millennium Development Goals and the more recent Sustainable Development Goals.[4] In part this role reifies the products of education as a human activity system in terms of the knowledge and knowledgeable citizens it produces (Kahn, 2014) and looks for transformations within the existing systems of power structures and relationships within society rather than radical transformation of those power structures and relationships (Freire, 1970; De Lissovoy, 2011; Suoranta, 2015).

The second role of education as a process within which certain groups in society are marginalized, disempowered or discriminated against even though it is one they do, or can, in principle participate in, also has these two elements: (i) that of transforming or empowering such groups within existing structures and relationships amongst the main actors within education (learners, teachers and educational institutions) and (ii) that of transforming such structures and relationships between those actors to ensure equity (Freire, 1970; De Lissovoy, 2011); which moves into the third role of education; namely the emancipation of education itself.

An example of the first element is of widening participation in higher education by under-represented groups (enabling transformation *within* one part of the human activity system); an example of the second element is of students and teachers treating each other as equals in the co-production of knowledge and ways of knowing within a

---

3   See https://www.nesri.org/programs/what-is-the-human-right-to-education
4   See https://sustainabledevelopment.un.org/?menu=1300

self-organized network (encouraging transformation *of* the human activity system itself). In the third category are some highly capable leaners who do not require any further social learning with either teachers or other learners to meet their learning needs and so are self-contained within their own personal human activity system.

From even this brief account it can be seen that restrictions on access to, and engagement with, education have many layers of complexity including what type and level of education is involved, whose perspective is being taken and which rights might be involved. Thus many countries by law require all children up to a certain age to have schooling but equally some parents or social groups may not like the style of teaching or the curriculum being offered within schools, and seek to undertake home schooling. Similarly, universities may use one language for teaching, learning and assessment in a country with multiple languages which then privileges the culture and ways of knowing and knowledge production of one social or ethnic group (Gunawardena and LaPointe, 2008). Another example of exclusion is where the naming and surrounding discourse of an educational philosophy or movement may itself be deemed restrictive as noted by Wals and Jickling (2002):

> [...] education for sustainability runs counter to prevailing conceptions of education: it breathes a kind of intellectual exclusivity and determinism that conflicts with ideas of emancipation, local knowledge, democracy and self-determination. The prepositional use of "for" prescribes that education must be in favour of some specific and undisputed product, in this case sustainability. At the same time, an emphasis on sustainability, or sustainable development, might hinder the inclusion of other emerging environmental thought such as deep ecology and ecofeminism. (p. 222)

Throughout any discussion of the emancipatory effects of education will be the contrasts and compromises between the intentions and the actions of different groups of actors, in particular learners and teachers, but also educational institutions, and thus how emancipatory and systemic those intentions and/or actions might be. Further, as education is a human activity system it is also necessary to examine the role of the educational infrastructure in enabling participation, that is the physical structures that enable that human activity to take place. Two examples of infrastructure are the buildings and campuses of educational organizations with their geographical and temporal constraints and the internet/World Wide Web providing extensive storage for educational resources and communication tools to facilitate discourse between learners/students and teachers, free of time and place. Equally, there is a need to examine what emancipation means within formal education (education leading to state recognized qualifications), non-formal education (certificated or non-certificated courses provided by organizations for their employees or for the public), and informal education (which is self-organized by the individual learner or learners) (OECD, 2016).

The Promise of Open Education

The phrase "open education" implies that there must also be closed education or education where there are restrictions or a lack of freedoms to exercise this fundamental human right. Legal restrictions are intentional restrictions in that they are purposefully designed to do so. Social and political restrictions can be a mixture of the intended and unintended flowing from the dominant societal structures and relationships and in particular matters of economics (Lane, 2013). For example, the participation rate in higher education in most countries has increased substantially in the past fifty years (OECD, 2015) as more higher education institutions were opened and more places within those institutions made available but this has led to significant debates and different policy responses as to who pays for this expansion of infrastructure and capacity and whether that includes students paying directly through tuition fees or indirectly, with most other citizens, through the taxes they pay; or effectively a mix of both through income contingent loans. The tension between public and private funding for education also relates to the public and private benefits of education which in themselves are influenced by the nature of ideas, information and knowledge. As noted by Benkler (2006):

> [...] certain characteristics of information and culture lead us to understand them as "public goods", rather than as "pure private goods" or "standard economic goods". When economists speak of information, they usually say that it is "nonrival". We consider a good to be nonrival when its consumption by one person does not make it any less available for consumption by another. (pp. 35–36)

However, while ideas, knowledge and information may be free in one sense and are both inputs and outputs of education as a human activity system, the particular form they are contained in e.g. a book, a patent, are protected by laws so that they can be commercially exploited. This protection then enforces a form of scarcity in that work or resource which gives them both a sale value and a use value (Lane, 2013). This in turn reinforces education as a commercial transaction involving private goods such that wealth inequalities also influence access to and engagement with elements of education as a human activity system (Nunan, 2008). Similar arguments of scarcity apply to the physical infrastructure of classrooms and lecture halls. However, others argue that digital technologies are only increasing a trend within capitalism of "prosumption", involving both production and consumption (Ritzer and Jurgenson, 2010), and that this can equally apply to education as a human activity system.

This interplay of (infra)-structural and economic factors makes fundamental change difficult even when there are social and political drivers for such change. Thus there has also been much policy and practice in recent years to widen participation in higher education such that the absolute numbers from disadvantaged groups have benefitted. But equally all social groups have seen higher participation rates such that often the relative proportion of disadvantaged students benefitting compared to all students has remained much the same (Chowdry *et al.*, 2010). At the same time some authors question whether the discourse around such policy and practice is misdirected and tends to conserve rather than challenge existing norms (Pitman, 2015).

Open education is predicated on freedoms that variously address some of the (time and place-based) restrictions noted above for closed education. The forms and way in which freedoms have been expressed and enabled have varied over the decades. To begin with, the open and distance education movement that emerged from the 1970s onwards (Lane, 2015) with its focus on open entry to degree courses (i.e. freedom from selection in that no prior qualifications were required) has been supplemented, some say supplanted (Nkuyubwatsi, 2016; Loeckx, 2016), by the OER movement since the 2000s (i.e. freedom legally to reuse, revise, remix and redistribute educational works through use of open licenses as noted by Wiley and Green (2012) and Orr *et al.* (2015));

while these "free" resources have, since 2010, been drowned out in media reporting by "free to participate in" massive open online courses or MOOCs (Daniel, 2012; Kelly, 2014).

Throughout this time there has been a changing balance between the freedom of works (e.g. open access to an educational resource) and the freedom of people as an act of emancipation (e.g. the ability of students without qualifications to enroll on degree courses and the ability of teachers to revise and adapt openly licensed educational resources) (Winn, 2012). This, in itself, has led recently to discussion about open educational practices (Cannell, Macintyre and Hewitt, 2015) as an innovative social practice involving partnerships and social networks co-creating educational resources and opportunities. However, just because something is openly (and freely) available and accessible, it does not mean that a learner or teacher can readily benefit from the freedom to use these OER if they do not have the means to do so because they lack freedoms from other constraints (e.g. ownership of digital devices; language skills) or do not have the knowledge to enact open educational practices (Farnes, 1988; Lane 2012; Winn, 2015).

To further unpack the different ways in which emancipation for learners and teachers within (adult) education is or might be realized through openness, I will look at the three modes of openness in the three forms of education already touched upon — open universities and formal education, MOOCs and non-formal education, and OER and informal education.

Open Universities

"Open universities" are a discrete type of university dedicated to using non-campus based systems of distance teaching (Lane, 2012; 2015). Not all such universities have open in their name and not all operate an open entry policy to their undergraduate courses, a defining feature of the first "open university" — The Open University in the United Kingdom, founded in 1969. Even today it is the only UK higher education institution to not have some means of selecting its undergraduate students by prior formal qualifications. The Open University, like almost all other open universities (Peters, 2008), was established through law by government to offer an alternative route or "second" chance for those without formal qualifications. It can therefore be argued that such open entry overcomes certain legal, political and also social restrictions on what is expected of a university student to enable emancipation both through and within education for adult learners as students.

Open entry therefore provides freedom to enroll for those who can afford to pay the tuition fees and who feel emotionally and culturally able to participate (Gunawardena and LaPointe, 2008). The model of teaching used by open universities also means that they can teach very large numbers taking the same course presentation and so overcome some of the physical restrictions of place-based universities (Lane, 2015). In 2013–14 39% of the 180,000 or so undergraduate students studying with The Open University had insufficient or no school leaving qualifications to gain entry to other universities, 21% lived in the most deprived areas of the UK and 10% had declared disabilities, but equally 23% already had a higher education qualification (Open University, 2015). Openness cannot be selective and while it may help the disadvantaged it also helps the already advantaged. It is reported that those with degree level qualifications on entry at The Open University are more than twice as likely (55% as against 20%) to complete courses compared to those with no previous educational qualifications (Simpson, 2009), non-completion rates that are higher than at place-based universities (although all these comparisons raise issues of the definition of non-completion/dropping out and conversely what is seen as a measure of success by learners as opposed to teachers, educational institutions and governments as noted by Grau-Valldosera and Minguillón, 2014). Further, open entry can be tempered by many other factors including access to appropriate technologies. With courses now requiring internet access for remote experiments or collaborative group work this can and does exclude some people who have been able to study print based courses, such as prisoners. Equally, digital assistive technologies can make studying more possible for some disabled students. Inevitably the reality, as Newell (2008) notes is that distance education may be seen as both enabling (e.g. overcoming inability to attend; flexibility of study hours) and disabling (e.g. lack of social engagement; capital and running costs; use of distance education to avoid making campuses accessible).

While The Open University was set up an alternative model for providing and accessing higher education it can be argued that it has not led to an emancipation of education by changing some of the fundamental structures and relationships of higher education beyond those of time (to some extent) and place. Distance teachers, albeit as course teams, devise the curriculum and develop the teaching materials. Yet while students are encouraged to debate and discuss what they are learning there is no greater co-production of knowledge than in a place-based university setting. Indeed the distributed nature of the students and limitations of communication technologies can make student involvement in co-production more challenging.

For its first thirty years, The Open University's curriculum was a very broad one and students could take a wide variety of courses to gain an unnamed Bachelor's degree. However, each course still largely followed strict schedules with regular assignments. Under pressure from students, named degrees were introduced with more restricted pathways. Increasingly this has meant that whereas previously the course teams had more freedom to define the scope of what they taught, increasingly they have to ensure that their course fits the needs of the named qualification(s) they contribute to and the needs of the different cohorts of students taking those qualifications.

Similarly, the requirements of the wider higher education system in the UK has shaped what The Open University does. It no longer receives its teaching grant directly from government as it did for twenty-five years. Like all other UK universities, it receives some teaching grant through separate funding bodies and some through tuition fees, with substantive increases to much higher fee regimes. This has led to reductions in part time student numbers overall though not significantly more for widening participation groups. The Open University has also had to fit in with UK-wide periodic external Quality Assurance reviews, and be part of the annual UK-wide National Student Survey despite the many differences in the types of student and ways of teaching that it employs. These many systemic, structural changes that The Open University has had to adapt to, have then variously affected the freedoms of both learners and teachers, as have the various forms of supportive funding for widening participation.[5]

---

5   http://www.hefce.ac.uk/lt/nss

Systemic social and technological changes such as digital technologies and their use in education have also become political issues as the inequalities in access to such technologies, or equally the telecommunications infrastructure that supports those technologies, also impact on the new modes of education they support (Gulati, 2008). This is particularly important for open education as deployed by open universities as it impinges greatly on the capacity and capability of teachers to deliver technology-enhanced learning (Wright *et al.*, 2009); as well as learners having the requisite digital and information literacy skills (Lane, 2012); and it also impinges on the underlying education for all social justice missions of open universities (Tait, 2013; Lane, 2015).

Ironically, whereas until very recently The Open University was the only fully distance teaching university in the UK, one amongst 130 or so HEIs, the advent of the internet has enabled many more of these universities (and those in other countries) to offer online distance teaching courses to students. Much of this has been at postgraduate level, where there is more part time study, open entry is not a feature, and has not been necessarily about significant increases in student numbers or widening participation. But both this trend, and these issues, have been influenced by the advent of MOOCs.[6]

Massive Open Online Courses

The major premise of MOOCs is that they are open entry and, although as courses they are still timetabled over set times, the learner is free to study anywhere using the infrastructure of the internet. However, while no prior qualifications are needed, good internet connectivity is essential to be able to participate. In many cases a certificate or statement of participation can be gained but, although there are some pilot projects looking at ways of formally recognizing such study, usually no formal higher education credit is directly awarded. This is why I label them as non-formal courses that are developed and run by existing universities or other learned bodies with a pre-determined curriculum and scheduling. However, this is not where the idea of MOOCs started. The original

---

6   In 2014 the newly established Arden University (http://www.rdi.co.uk/about-us) was given degree awarding powers in the UK.

pioneers of MOOCs, in 2008, embraced a more emancipatory philosophy through a constructivist and connectivist approach to the pedagogy they employed (Daniel, 2012). These so-called "cMOOCs", loosely defined as discursive communities creating knowledge together, are distinct from the more instructivist and behaviorist style "xMOOCs" (Daniel, 2012).[7] The xMOOCs, focusing on knowledge duplication, exploded into the global consciousness soon after and that led to the establishment of platforms Coursera,[8] Udacity,[9] edX[10] and FutureLearn[11] through which many organizations can deliver such open online courses.

While there are some similarities between MOOCs and online courses from open universities (Lane, Caird and Weller, 2014) there is a big difference in how the organizations that support them were established. Open universities are largely products of government and fit into prevailing political structures and discourses. MOOC platforms have been private developments with no or very little legal or political input or restrictions to date. Any social restrictions are similar to those influencing students at open universities, with uptake preferentially favoring those people who already have previous qualifications (anywhere between 70 and 90% of people taking MOOCs have higher education qualifications (Kelly, 2014; Rohs and Ganz, 2015) but without the built-in support mechanisms for the less advantaged seen within Open University courses.

Most MOOC platforms offer a wide range of courses across most curriculum areas that can be taken in any order, as was largely the case in the early days of The Open University, although the MOOCs are also relatively short (3 to 10 weeks/ 10–50 study hours) compared to the much larger formal courses currently available from The Open University (300 or 600 hours). MOOCs also exhibit much higher dropout rates than formal distance courses with 70–90% not completing the course (Jordan, 2014), but there has been much debate as to whether this is a valuable measure or not of success when the courses are free (i.e. no fee) to study,

---

7   Several authors have proposed typologies for MOOCs; this is one of the earliest.
8   https://www.coursera.org
9   https://www.udacity.com
10   https://www.edx.org
11   https://www.futurelearn.com

and which mirrors in part the debate within formal online education raised by Grau-Valldosera and Minguillón (2014).

This debate has two parts to it. One, that comparing retention in MOOCs to retention in other type of online courses is unfair as the investment made by participants is completely different (paying high fees for a course and/or committing to studying for a qualification over several years compared with clicking on the "Register" button and then studying for several weeks — or not as the case may be). Two, that retention may be a poor way of judging the success of a MOOC as research shows that MOOC participants engage with MOOCs in many different ways to suit their purposes (Ferguson and Clow, 2015).

The enormous freedom of choice and opportunity to study (or not), for the reasons one wants, can be seen as liberating for learners, providing both emancipation through education and partly emancipation within education. However, this only partly provides emancipation within education as generally there is very limited co-development of courses and/or co-production of knowledge through MOOCs except for those that deliberately take a cMOOC approach, which tends to happen outside the major platforms. Furthermore, MOOCs provide limited emancipation for teachers as well. They do offer scope for teachers from the same educational institution to collaborate on devising and running the course (as noted above for course teams in open universities). They allow them to experiment and do things that might not be allowed or encouraged within the structures of formal courses but they are also restricted by the rules imposed by the MOOC platforms such as the length of courses, when they are presented, and what (open) licence may be applied to the course.

MOOCs have also been subject to a lot of speculation as being disruptive innovations within education (Kelly, 2014; Loeckx, 2016). While it is argued that this disruption would significantly change education as a human activity system by unbundling different parts of the system (an issue which has also been considered in the past for open and distance education as noted by Peters, 2008 and Nunan, 2008) this is largely done through the lens of a "broken" education system (Weller, 2015) and/or liberal market economics with different organizations competing heavily for students (although ironically some have suggested this would lead to a rather monopolistic system of a handful of universities globally as discussed by Loeckx, 2016). This might be seen as the hoped for emancipation of education, except for the fact that few talk about empowering the roles and positions of learners (students) and teachers within this system apart from a clarion call of education for all which many now dismiss (Rohs and Ganz, 2015).

Much of the early hype around MOOCs has abated, partly because of the difficulty in finding sustainable revenue models in the absence of teaching grants and tuition fees and partly because of the dominance of existing legal, political and social structures and relationships that support the current higher education system. For instance, in 2012, the percentages of GDP from public and private sources respectively spent on higher education were 1.4 and 1.4 for the US; 1.2 and 0.6 for the UK and 1.2 and 0.0 for Germany — with the OECD average being 1.2 and 0.4 (OECD, 2015) — all representing trillions of dollars of investment in existing provision. As well as these substantial sums of money, governments variously regulate higher education, such as approving who can award degrees in their country, which forms of teaching may be recognized, what fees might be charged, how many students can be taught and setting up quality assurance agencies to oversee the sector. The investment, value and interest in MOOCs is minuscule compared to these existing investments, as it has been for open universities compared to place-based universities, and it is likely that MOOCs will similarly provide a niche position in the overall system with varying contributions to emancipation.

Open Educational Resources

OER can range from a single learning object to all the education material from a taught course (but without the structured input of teachers as they then tip it over into being a formal or non-formal open online course). They therefore support informal learning by learners and provide inspiration and assets for teachers to use as the basis for new resources and courses. It is generally agreed that an OER should be available for free and openly licensed (Orr, Rimini and Van Damme, 2015) in order to derive the emancipatory effects of what have been called the 4 Rs (Hilton *et al.*, 2010). These 4 Rs are:

1. Reuse — to use the work verbatim.

2. Revise — to alter or transform the work.

3. Remix — to combine the work (verbatim or altered) with other works.

4. Redistribute — to share the verbatim work, the reworked work or the remixed work with others.

More recently a fifth R has been added:

5. Retain — to be able to retain a copy of the work(s) (Wiley, 2014).

These 5 Rs embody freedoms or permissions, through the legal force of the open license, which learners and teachers can then, in principle, exercise through open educational practices (Murphy, 2014). They therefore remove significant legal barriers to the use of educational resources. However, it is not enough to have freedoms in principle if a person (learner or teacher) does not possess the knowledge, capabilities and circumstances to exercise those freedoms. For instance, do they have the subject and/or pedagogic knowledge, the technological capabilities and support structures to create educational works, to learn from such works, or to add new knowledge to those works? In particular, this also raises issues about the knowledge, capabilities and circumstances of a lone learner or teacher as opposed to a team or community, with many possible social restrictions arising from their circumstances.

The sociality of education is part of the underpinning philosophy of sharing and collaboration that OER represent and as spelled out in the Cape Town Declaration:[12]

> We are on the cusp of a global revolution in teaching and learning. Educators worldwide are developing a vast pool of educational resources on the Internet, open and free for all to use. These educators are creating a world where each and every person on earth can access and contribute to the sum of all human knowledge. They are also planting the seeds of a new pedagogy where educators and learners create, shape and evolve knowledge together, deepening their skills and understanding as they go.
>
> This emerging open education movement combines the established tradition of sharing good ideas with fellow educators and the collaborative, interactive culture of the Internet. It is built on the belief

---

12   http://www.capetowndeclaration.org/read-the-declaration

that everyone should have the freedom to use, customize, improve and redistribute educational resources without constraint. Educators, learners and others who share this belief are gathering together as part of a worldwide effort to make education both more accessible and more effective.

In effect this declaration seeks the emancipation of education as well as emancipation through and within education, although the emphasis to date has been more on the emancipation of teachers than of learners (Murphy, 2013; Orr *et al.*, 2015). This is changing as more research is done (Weller *et al.*, 2015) and new mechanisms are put in place to gain recognition for informal study (Law, 2015) although the majority of these developments are an augmentation of formal and non-formal educational activities at established (educational) institutions rather than radical non-academic, community-led initiatives (Coughlan and Perryman, 2015).

In contrast to MOOCs, OER have directly impacted on the politics of education with a number of governments passing laws and developing policies supportive of OER (Orr *et al.*, 2015) and through international agreements such as the UNESCO sponsored Paris OER declaration.[13] Thus certain political restrictions are being addressed in relation to OER, centred mostly on encouraging governments to openly license publicly funded educational materials for public use thus adding to the stock of material in the global OER commons, but also in encouraging open educational practices wherever possible, although the dispersed nature of OER repositories acts as a deterrent to broader engagement as indicated by several surveys of educators (e.g. Karunanayaka *et al.*, 2015). In that sense OER offers more scope than open universities or MOOCs in transforming education from within, by changing the overall culture of education as a human activity system as much as offering new routes to education for disenfranchised groups, such as women in developing countries (Perryman and De los Arcos, 2016). However, the dominance of formal education within this system can still easily crowd out these developments which are gaining most traction (so far) within non-formal and informal education.

---

13 http://www.unesco.org/new/fileadmin/MULTIMEDIA/HQ/CI/CI/pdf/Events/Paris OER Declaration_01.pdf

Concluding Remarks

The recently approved Sustainability Development Goals explicitly apply to all countries, whatever their deemed state of development (defining development as the process of economic and social transformation that is based on complex cultural and environmental factors and their interactions). Notwithstanding the concerns over language framing debates, as noted earlier for education for sustainability, discussing education through the notion of education for development may help us better understand issues of emancipation within education and the role that open education can play. Education is then about the personal and professional development of people, learners and teachers alike; it is also about the intellectual and practical development of everyone as expressed through organizations and societies. Within the field of development, Sen (1999) has written extensively on development as freedom and also introduced the notion of a capability approach. Saito (2003) has more explicitly set this out for education:

> The human capital received from education can be conceived in terms of commodity production. However Sen argues that education plays a role not only in accumulating human capital but also in broadening human capability. This can be through a person benefitting from education "in reading, communicating, arguing, in being able to choose in a more informed way, in being taken seriously by others and so on". (p. 24).

While, in principle, open education in its various guises can help people benefit from learning who may not have otherwise had the opportunity, in practice it may not be doing much more to emancipate people than closed education is doing. This is because prevailing social, cultural and economic norms still place greater value on education arising through the existing physical, political and legal infrastructures. The development of more recent digital infrastructures has been crucial to any expansion of open education and, overall, open licensing (a legal instrument) has done most to challenge those existing structures. But in the end it will probably be the development of capabilities through an even wider framing of educational open practices that will do most to provide emancipation through, within and from education; and to do so in an evolutionary rather than revolutionary way. So, in my view, the rhetoric is way ahead of the reality and the reality will be less profound than the rhetoric suggests.

References

Benkler, Y. (2006), *The Wealth of Networks: How Social Production Transforms Markets and Freedom*, New Haven and London: Yale University Press, http://dx.doi.org/10.1177/0894439307301373

Cannell, P., Macintyre, R. and Hewitt, L. (2015), Widening Access and OER: Developing New Practice, *Widening Participation and Lifelong Learning*, 17(1), pp. 64–72, http://dx.doi.org/10.5456/WPLL.17.1.64

Checkland, P. (1999), *Systems Thinking, Systems Practice*, 2nd edn., London: Wiley.

Chowdry, H., Crawford, C., Dearden, L., Goodman, A. and Vignoles, A. (2010), *Widening Participation in Higher Education: Analysis Using Linked Administrative Data*, IFS working paper W10/04, http://www.ifs.org.uk/wps/wp1004.pdf

Coughlan, T. and Perryman, L. (2015), Learning from the Innovative Open Practices of Three International Health Projects: IACAPAP, VCPH and Physiopedia, *Open Praxis*, 7(2), pp. 173–189, http://dx.doi.org/10.5944/openpraxis.7.2.188

Daniel, J. (2012), Making Sense of MOOCs: Musings in a Maze of Myth, Paradox and Possibility, *Journal of Interactive Media in Education*, 3 (p. Art. 18), http://dx.doi.org/10.5334/2012-18

De Lissovoy, N. (2011), Pedagogy in Common: Democratic Education in the Global Era, *Educational Philosophy and Theory*, 43: 1119–1134. doi:10.1111/j.1469-5812.2009.00630.x

Farnes, N. (1988), Open University Community Education: Emancipation or Domestication?, *Open Learning: The Journal of Open, Distance and E-Learning*, 3(1), pp. 35–40, http://dx.doi.org/10.1080/0268051880030107

Freire, P. (1970), *Pedagogy of the Oppressed*, New York: Continuum.

Ferguson, R. and Clow, D. (2015), Consistent Commitment: Patterns of Engagement Across Time in Massive Open Online Courses (MOOCs), *Journal of Learning Analytics*, 2(3), pp. 55–80, http://dx.doi.org/10.18608/jla.2015.23.5

Gulati, S. (2008), Technology-Enhanced Learning in Developing Nations: A Review, *The International Review of Research in Open and Distributed Learning*, 9(1), pp. 1-16, http://dx.doi.org/10.19173/irrodl.v9i1.477

Gunawardena, C. and LaPointe, D. (2008), Social and Cultural Diversity in Distance Education, in Evans, T., Haughey, M. and Murphy D. (Eds.), *International Handbook of Distance Education*, pp. 51–70, Bingley: Emerald Publishing.

Grau-Valldosera, J. And Minguillón, J. (2014), Rethinking Dropout in Online Higher Education: The Case of the Universitat Oberta de Catalunya, *The International Review of Research in Open and Distributed Learning*, 15(1), pp. 290–308.

Hilton, J., Wiley, D., Stein, J. and Johnson, A. (2010), The Four R's of Openness and ALMS Analysis: Frameworks for Open Educational Resources, *Open Learning: The Journal of Open, Distance and E-Learning*, 25(1), pp. 37–44, http://dx.doi.org/10.1080/02680510903482132

Jordan, K. (2014), Initial Trends in Enrolment and Completion of Massive Open Online Courses, *International Review of Research in Open and Distributed Learning*, 15(1), pp. 133–160.

Kahn, P. (2014), *Critical Perspectives on Methodology in Higher Education Research*, SRHE Annual Research Conference 10–12 December 2014, https://www.srhe.ac.uk/conference2014/downloads/SRHE_Conf_2014_abstracts.pdf

Karunanayaka, S. P., Naidu, S., Rajendra, J. C. N. and Ratnayake, H. U. W. (2015), From OER to OEP: Shifting Practitioner Perspectives and Practices with Innovative Learning Experience Design, *Open Praxis*, 7(4), pp. 339–350, http://dx.doi.org/10.5944/openpraxis.7.4.252

Kelly, A. P. (2014), *Disruptor, Distracter, or What? A Policymaker's Guide to Massive Open Online Courses (MOOCS)*, Bellwether Education Partners, p. 39, http://bellwethereducation.org/sites/default/files/BW_MOOC_Final.pdf

Lane, A. (2012), A Review of the Role of National Policy and Institutional Mission in European Distance Teaching Universities with Respect to Widening Participation in Higher Education Study Through Open Educational Resources, *Distance Education*, 33(2), pp. 135–150, http://dx.doi.org/10.1080/01587919.2012.692067

Lane, A. (2013), Social and Economic Impacts of Open Education, in Squires, L. and Meiszner, A. (Eds.), *Openness and Education, Advances in Digital Education and Lifelong Learning*, Vol. 1, pp. 137–172, Bingley: Emerald Publishing, http://dx.doi.org/10.1108/s2051-2295(2013)1

Lane, A. (2015), Open Universities, in Peters, M. A. (Ed.), *Encyclopaedia of Educational Philosophy and Theory* (Springer online).

Lane, A., Caird, S. and Weller, M. (2014), The Potential Social, Economic and Environmental Benefits of MOOCs: Operational and Historical Comparisons with a Massive "Closed Online" Course, *Open Praxis*, 6(2), pp. 115–123, http://dx.doi.org/10.5944/openpraxis.6.2.113

Law, P. (2015), Recognising Informal Elearning with Digital Badging: Evidence for a Sustainable Business Model, *Open Praxis*, 7(4), pp. 299–310, http://dx.doi.org/10.5944/openpraxis.7.4.247

Loeckx, J. (2016), Blurring Boundaries in Education: Context and Impact of MOOCs, *International Review of Research in Open and Distributed Learning*, 17(3), pp. 92–121, http://dx.doi.org/10.19173/irrodl.v17i3.2395

Murphy, A. (2013), Open Educational Practices in Higher Education: Institutional Adoption and Challenges, *Distance Education*, 34(2), pp. 201–217, http://dx.doi.org/10.1080/01587919.2013.793641

Newell, C. (2008), Distance Education: Enabling and Disabling, in Evans, T., Haughey, M. and Murphy D. (Eds.), *International Handbook of Distance Education*, pp. 87–107.

Nkuyubwatsi, B. (2016), Positioning Extension Massive Open Online Courses (xMOOCs) Within the Open Access and Lifelong Learning Agendas in a Developing Setting, *Journal of Learning for Development*, 3(1), pp. 14–36.

Nunan, T. (2008), The Business of Distance Education: Whose Profit, Whose Loss?, in Evans T., Haughey, M. and Murphy D. (Eds.), *International Handbook of Distance Education*, pp. 855–868.

OECD (2015), *Education at a Glance 2015*, http://www.oecd-ilibrary.org/education/education-at-a-glance-2015_eag-2015-en

OECD (2016), *Recognition of Non-formal and Informal Learning*, http://www.oecd.org/edu/skills-beyond-school/recognitionofnon-formalandinformallearning-home.htm

Open University (2015). *Fact and Figures*, http://www.open.ac.uk/about/main/strategy/facts-and-figures

Orr, D., Rimini, M. and Van Damme, D. (2015), *Open Educational Resources: A Catalyst for Innovation, Educational Research and Innovation*, Paris: OECD Publishing, http://dx.doi.org/10.1787/9789264247543-en

Peters, O. (2008), Transformation through Open Universities, Evans T., Haughey, M. and Murphy D. (Eds.), *International Handbook of Distance Education*, pp. 279–302.

Pitman, T. (2015), Widening Access in a Fee-Deregulated System: Exploring Contemporary Ideals of "Fair" Access to Higher Education, *Widening Participation and Lifelong Learning*, 17(3), pp. 17–31, http://dx.doi.org/10.5456/wpll.17.3.17

Ritzer, G. and Jurgenson, N. (2010), Production, Consumption, Prosumption: The Nature of Capitalism in the Age of the Digital "Prosumer", *Journal of Consumer Culture*, 10(1), pp. 13–36, http://dx.doi.org/10.1177/1469540509354673

Rohs, M. and Ganz, M. (2015), MOOCs and the Claim of Education for All: A Disillusion by Empirical Data, *International Review of Research in Open and Distributed Learning*, 6(6), pp. 1–19, http://dx.doi.org/10.19173/irrodl.v16i6.2033

Saito, M. (2003), Amartya Sen's Capability Approach to Education: A Critical Exploration, *Journal of Philosophy of Education*, 37(1), pp. 17–33, http://dx.doi.org/10.1111/1467-9752.3701002

Sen, A. (1999), *Development as Freedom*, New York: Oxford University Press.

Simpson, O. (2009), Open to People, Open with People: Ethical Issues in Open Learning, in Demiray, U. and Sharma, R. C. (Eds.), *Ethical Practices and Implications in Distance Learning*, IGI Global.

Suoranta, J. (2015), Jacques Rancière on Radical Equality and Adult Education, in Michael A. Peters (Ed.), *Encyclopaedia of Educational Philosophy and Theory*.

Tait, A. (2013), Distance and E-Learning, Social Justice, and Development: The Relevance of Capability Approaches to the Mission of Open Universities, *International Review of Research in Open and Distributed Learning*, 14(4), pp. 1–18.

Wals, A. and Jickling, B. (2002), "Sustainability" in Higher Education: From Doublethink and Newspeak to Critical Thinking and Meaningful Learning, *International Journal of Sustainability in Higher Education*, 3(3), pp. 221–232, http://dx.doi.org/10.1108/14676370210434688

Weller, M. (2015), MOOCs and the Silicon Valley Narrative, *Journal of Interactive Media in Education*, 2015(1), pp. 1–7, http://dx.doi.org/10.5334/jime.am

Weller, M., de los Arcos, B., Farrow, R., Pitt, B. and McAndrew, P. (2015), The Impact of OER on Teaching and Learning Practice, *Open Praxis*, 7(4), pp. 351–361, http://dx.doi.org/10.5944/openpraxis.7.4.227

Wiley, D. (2014), *The Access Compromise and the 5th R*, Iterating toward Openness, http://opencontent.org/blog/archives/3221

Wiley, D. and Green, C. (2012), Why Openness in Education?, in D. Oblinger (Ed.), *Game Changers: Education and Information Technologies*, pp. 81–89, Educause, https://net.educause.edu/ir/library/pdf/pub72036.pdf

Winn, J. (2012), Open Education: From Freedom of Things to the Freedom of People, in Neary, M., Stevenson, H. and Bell L. (Eds.), *Towards Teaching in Public: Reshaping the Modern University*, pp. 133–147, New York: Continuum.

Winn, J. (2015), Open Education and Emancipation of Academic Labour, *Learning, Media and Technology*, 40(3), pp. 385–404, http://dx.doi.org/10.1080/17439884.2015.1015546

Wright, C., Dhanarajan, G. and Reju, S. (2009), Recurring Issues Encountered by Distance Educators in Developing and Emerging Nations, *International Review of Research in Open and Distributed Learning*, 10(1), pp. 1–25.

3. Technology Strategies for Open Educational Resource Dissemination

Phil Barker and Lorna M. Campbell

This chapter addresses issues around the discovery and use of Open Educational Resources (OER) by presenting a state of the art overview of technology strategies for the description and dissemination of content as OER. These technology strategies include institutional repositories and websites, subject specific repositories, sites for sharing specific types of content (such as video, images, ebooks) and general global repositories. There are also services that aggregate content from a range of collections, these may specialize by subject, region or resource type. A number of examples of these services are analyzed in terms of their scope, how they present resources, the technologies they use and how they promote and support a community of users. The variety of strategies for resource description taken by these platforms is also discussed. These range from formal machine-readable metadata to human readable text. It is argued that resource description should not be seen as a purely technical activity. Library and information professionals have much to contribute, however academics could also make a valuable contribution to open educational resource (OER) description if the established good practice of identifying the provenance and aims of scholarly works is applied to learning resources. The current rate of change among repositories is quite startling with several repositories and applications having either shut down or having changed radically in the year or so that the work on which this contribution is based took. With this in mind, the chapter concludes with a few words on sustainability.

   http://dx.doi.org/10.11647/OBP.0103.03

Introduction

In the fourteen years since MIT's OpenCourseWare launched, the scale
of the open educational resources (OER) movement has exploded in
terms of projects, money invested and resources released. There have
been many benefits, including a gradual shift to greater openness in
educational practice and increasing awareness of licensing issues in
education but, in spite of this investment, resource discovery is still
cited as being a significant barrier to finding, using and repurposing
open educational resources (Wiley, Bliss and McEwen, 2014; Dichev
and Dicheva, 2012). This chapter will address the issue of resource
discovery by presenting an overview of technology strategies for OER
dissemination of relevance to individuals, groups and institutions that
are releasing educational content under open licenses. The technology
strategies we focus on include repositories, content management
systems, aggregators and metadata. While these technologies also play
an important role in managing the development, curation and licensing
of OERs, dissemination and resource discovery are of paramount
importance as people cannot use and repurpose resources unless they
can find them, and without reuse OER cannot reach its full potential.

The technologies that can be used to disseminate OERs include
institutional repositories and websites, subject specific repositories,
sites for sharing specific types of content (such as video, images, ebooks)
and general global repositories. There are also services that aggregate
content and descriptions of content from other collections; these may
specialize by subject, region or resource type. We will present a number
of examples of these services and then analyze how they present
resources, how they promote and support communities of users, and
the strategies they have adopted for resource description. Though the
specific services cited may be discontinued or morph into something
new, there is much to be learned from their characteristics.

The following sections describe a variety of approaches employed
by educational practitioners and institutions to developing and using
repositories and aggregators for managing and disseminating OERs,
classified under headings which reflect their scope: institutional, subject
specific, content type specific and general or global. This selection
of repositories and aggregators is not intended to be systematic or

comprehensive, however it serves to illustrate the range of technical approaches employed to disseminate open educational resources.[1] The second half of the chapter presents a synthetic analysis of strategies drawn from these examples, looking at what lessons can be drawn about strategies for presentation, community support or resource description. Sustainability is also discussed briefly.

Repositories and Aggregators

For the purposes of this contribution, the term "repository" is used to mean any service hosting a collection of resources, especially one that is organized thematically and facilitates resource discovery through structured resource descriptions. As well as making resources available, repositories may disseminate resource descriptions in machine-readable formats. The term "aggregator" is used for services that collect resources and resource descriptions automatically from multiple sources in order to facilitate resource discovery.

The role that repository and aggregator services play in education will depend primarily on whether one is focusing on resource creation or use. From the point of view of a creator of learning resources, repositories can be used to disseminate these resources widely. There are many factors that may motivate individuals and institutions to disseminate open educational resources including personal promotion, funded projects, showcasing courses (i.e. marketing) and a philanthropic desire to make resources more widely available for the general good. One would expect that whatever the motivation is, it should lead to a desire to see the resources widely disseminated. Services that aggregate metadata and resources from a number of OER providers can be used to amplify this dissemination. Making information and resources available through a wide range of sites and services that people use regularly improves the discovery process because it does not expect users to come to a dedicated site to find content.

---

1   Disclosure: the authors have acted in an advisory or consultancy role for some of the services described below. Specifically, Lorna M. Campbell was a member of the Jorum Steering Group; Phil Barker was a consultant to the development of Core Materials and Kritikos. The authors have no ongoing financial association with any of these projects.

A frequent starting point for teachers and learners who are looking for educational resources is Google. However, repositories and aggregators can provide more specific information about the educational properties and use of resources and also play a useful role as a focal point for communities of users, including academics, students, learning technologists and instructional designers. To this end, it may be useful for an educational institution to curate collections of resources used in its courses regardless of where they were created.

Institutional Repositories and OER Websites

The projects highlighted here represent a range of approaches developed by educational institutions to managing and disseminating OER, and they illustrate a variety of different purposes and priorities. Nearly all have some means of syndicating information about their resources to aggregators, but the emphasis placed on syndication varies.

MIT OpenCourseWare

MIT OpenCourseWare (MIT OCW) comprises a wide range of resources derived directly from MIT courses, e.g. syllabuses, recordings, notes and slides from lectures, reading lists, assessment questions and assignments (Massachusetts Institute of Technology, [n.d.]). These are presented as used at MIT with no modification to make them more generally applicable or aesthetically pleasing. Some resources are hosted on external platforms, e.g. video on YouTube, and content is also made available via iTunes U. Metadata is exported from OpenCourseWare to aggregators such as OER Commons and iTunes U and a variety of RSS feeds are available which can be ingested by aggregators such as Solvonauts.

MIT OCW has a well-established initiative with good engagement with the OER community. It provides an attractive view of the institution's resources, based on a mix of its own technology and external services. MIT OCW is a "top-down" initiative (as is the next initiative, U-Now, and OpenLearn, below) that focusses on a single type of OER, i.e. Open CourseWare.

University of Nottingham, U-Now

The U-Now repository (The University of Nottingham, [n.d.]) contains resources, or links to resources, used in University of Nottingham courses. Most are released under Creative Commons licenses, however some have no formal license associated with them. The amount of material available from each course varies greatly from the basic syllabus through to video and text representing the bulk of a course. There are also links to third party resources related to the course. Tools to support the creation of resources (Xerte Community, [n.d.]), their discovery (Xpert, [n.d.]) and attribution (Xpert Image Attribution, [n.d.]) have also been developed. Data is syndicated via RSS feeds to aggregators such as iTunes U (a proprietary service with some extensions to the RSS specification) for further dissemination.

The significant aspect of U-Now is its role in supporting the institution's longstanding commitment to open education in the context of other institutional strategic objectives such as internationalization by facilitating the provision of the same resources across multiple campuses.

University of Oxford, OpenSpires, etc.

The University of Oxford has a number of open education initiatives, including podcasts and projects focusing on specific topics (for example Great Writers Inspire, [n.d.], and World War I Centenary, [n.d.]). There are also more general open content initiatives that are relevant to education, such as digital archives of library and museum content (see OpenSpires, [n.d.]). Notable among the technology approaches adopted by the various Oxford initiatives is the use of podcasts, i.e. the syndication of recordings and metadata by RSS feeds. Several services aggregate these podcasts, including Apple's iTunes U, giving them wider circulation than would otherwise be the case.

To some extent, Oxford illustrates the challenges of managing the disparate views on open education that will arise from initiatives across a large institution, however it also shows the wealth of innovation and resources that can be surfaced in this way.

Open University, OpenLearn

OpenLearn [n.d.] brings together several aspects of the UK Open University's "external" activities, i.e. those that are not restricted to people enrolled on OU courses. This includes material linked to BBC TV series as well as course materials that have been released as OER.

The Open University has engaged with OER since 2006, but clearly has a much wider commitment to open education. Their OpenLearn website uses OER to draw people in from casual interest to enrolled student. The content differs from the OER released by most other institutions in that it constitutes a fairly comprehensive treatment of a topic rather than a selection of resources used on a course. OpenLearn content is arguably more akin to an ebook than a collection of course materials. This clearly reflects the nature of the OU's distance learning resources compared to materials used by other institutions for face to face learning. The OU also provide tools for the creation and remixing of content through their OpenLearn Works platform.

MOOCs

MOOCs are not repositories in any conventional sense of the word, and are rarely open in the OER sense, however it is useful to consider them here as examples of widely disseminated collections of learning resources. What many MOOC platforms lack, however, is the means to provide access to or disseminate information about their resources outside the context of the platform. Normally, the content in a MOOC is only accessible for the duration of the course; if the content remains available after the course has ended, it tends to be available to registered users only. However this is not always the case, for example content from the University of London International Programmes' MOOC on English Common Law [n.d.] is both openly licensed and available to all. Some institutions may also make their MOOC resources available through other platforms including course blogs and services such as YouTube.

Subject Specific Repositories and Aggregators

Subject specific repositories and aggregators are generally designed to engage with and support subject discipline communities across multiple institutions. They may host particular domain specific resource types and use specialized resource descriptions and vocabularies.

HumBox

HumBox [n.d.] contains open educational resources for humanities education, drawn from about a dozen UK HEIs. Resource formats include slide decks, text documents, images, audio and video recordings, mostly single file resources which are not arranged as courses. The repository hosts about 2000 resources, and though the project ended in 2010, new resources continue to be added. HumBox is built on the EdShare [n.d.] platform from the University of Southampton, which is based on the open source ePrints repository with extensions for education-related functions.

HumBox is a good example of a formal repository with extensions to serve a subject domain community of educators. From a wider open education perspective, this approach could also be used to encourage engagement from learners with shared interests.

CORE-Materials

CORE-Materials [n.d.] is essentially a catalog of Materials Science and Engineering OERs that are hosted elsewhere on the web. The materials come from a variety of sources mostly associated with UK HE, but including some industry, third sector and overseas organizations and are hosted on a variety of platforms including Flickr, YouTube and creators' own websites. The resources include images, interactive resources, texts, videos/animations, equations and data sets.

The project that developed this collection has now ended, but when it was collecting material, a resource submitted to the project would be catalogued and the description held in a local database; where appropriate a local copy was made (e.g. for images, but not for websites). This information was then used to syndicate the resource via API to suitable third party hosts, including Flickr, SlideShare, YouTube, Vimeo, Scribd and others. The central database enables local resource discovery and syndication of information about the resources to other discovery services, while hosting the resources on third party sites exploits the ability of these platforms to get resources "out there".

Kritikos

Kritikos [n.d.] was originally developed to aid the discovery of visual resources for engineering education, but now has a more general scope; it is not limited to openly licensed resources and does not attempt to identify the licensing terms of the resources described. It attempts to enable learners to support their own learning by allowing communities of learners to contribute to the resource base and by having a strong focus on user (student and teacher) comment, rating and recommendation.

Kritikos is based on two technologies: the Google Custom Search Engine API, which is used to perform filtered searches of the whole web or searches of selected sites (e.g. those that host videos), and the Learning Registry [n.d.], which aggregates data about online learning resources, in this case ratings, reviews and recommendations submitted by users of the resources. The Learning Registry API allows these recommendations to be presented in other systems, e.g. recommended third party resources can be displayed for specific courses.

Content Type Specific Repositories

Some of the most successful "repositories" of learning materials are the popular online resource hosting platforms such as YouTube, Flickr, etc. By definition, these platforms focus on a single more-or-less well defined media type, as listed in Table 1. They tend to make resources available for all to view (some allow for more restricted sharing as a premium feature), rather than making them available under open license, though some will allow Creative Commons licenses to be associated with resources and provide functionality around this.

While these platforms are not repositories in the conventional sense, they fulfil the role of hosting materials while allowing structured information about those materials to be disseminated via their APIs. Most of these platforms will be familiar to readers so we will not describe them individually; instead we will analyze them as a class and list some significant examples.

As a result of their popularity and ubiquity, these sites set user expectations for the dissemination and delivery of resources on the web; expectations that are difficult to meet for educational repositories

Table 1: examples of popular online resource hosting platforms listed
by media type. Countless others exist.

Scope	Site	Notes
Images	Flickr	Allows CC licenses. Used by some large heritage organizations. Of especial note is *The Commons* https://www.flickr.com/commons
Images	Wikimedia Commons	"A database of ca. 30 million freely usable media files to which anyone can contribute" ~98% of the media files are images. Allows CC and other open licenses.
Video	YouTube	Allows CC BY license, but this is not displayed prominently, no ability to download other people's resource which limits value of this license. YouTube Edu for educational resources.
	Vimeo	Allows range of CC licenses.
	Wikimedia Commons	See above
	iTunes U	Not open, but a useful dissemination channel for audio and video podcasts and ebooks.
Audio	SoundCloud	Allows CC licenses, mostly music.
	Wikimedia Commons	See above
	iTunes U	See above
Text, articles, books etc.	Google Docs	Strong on editing/content creation, various options for dissemination.
	SlideShare	See under presentations, also allows upload of pdf and Word docs.
	OpenStax	Openly licensed resources from the Rice Connexions project, specializing in textbooks.
	iTunes U	For eBooks, see above.
	Github	See below under source code, also useful for documentation.
Presentations	SlideShare	Allows CC licenses.
	Google Slides	Strong on editing/content creation, various options for dissemination.
Source code	Github	Allows a range of open licenses.

that do not have access to commercial revenue streams or the luxury of being able to focus exclusively on a single resource type. These sites are popular, ubiquitous and effective and generate significant revenue streams. Institutions cannot be expected to replicate the level of functionality they offer, therefore many are increasingly using these platforms alongside institutional repositories to disseminate resources. Clearly there are risks associated with using these platforms as they may change their policies or technical approach or, in rare cases, disappear altogether, with little notice. However, it should also be noted that these commercial platforms are arguably more sustainable than education sector services and institutional repositories.

General and Global Repositories and Aggregators

As open education has global reach and is not limited by subject or resource type, there is a strong argument for using services that have the widest possible scope. However, in doing so there is a risk of losing some of the advantages of specialization, for example the ability to focus on the needs of a particular community or to develop technology solutions appropriate to a single resource type. Below we consider examples of effective general and global repositories and aggregators.

MERLOT

MERLOT [n.d.] includes links to tens of thousands of resources with associated comments. All subjects and levels of education are covered but it should be noted that not all resources are openly licensed. Resources are classified by type, including simulations, assignments, online courses, open textbooks and other repositories. The scope is global, however there is a preponderance of material from the US and some of the resource descriptions are couched in US terminology and reference US educational frameworks. All of these items have been contributed by the MERLOT member community, who have either authored the materials or who have found them sufficiently useful to share with others. All the materials in MERLOT are reviewed to ensure they are suitable for retention in the collection and many undergo more extensive "peer review".

Solvonauts

Solvonauts.org [n.d.] aggregates metadata about openly licensed resources to provide an OER search service. It includes over 110,000 resource descriptions from over 1,400 sites. The service aggregates metadata syndicated by RSS, ATOM and and provides specialist search services for pictures, videos and audio. Solvonauts is an open source software project and the code can be downloaded and installed locally.

OER Commons

OER Commons (OER Commons, [n.d.]) includes links to resources in all subjects and levels and many resource types; in total over 100,000 resources are listed. Not all resources are open, some have limited re-use rights. The geographic scope is global, however there is a preponderance of material from the US and, as with MERLOT, some of the resource descriptions reference US terms with an emphasis on alignment to US school curricula. OER Commons also includes content creation tools and community facilities for teachers.

Strategies for Presentation

Having outlined a range of repository and aggregation services, we now discuss the strategies they adopt for presenting and describing resources, and the support they provide to communities of users. Institutional OER repositories frequently aim to present materials in such a way as to showcase the institution's course materials or to align with the institution's strategic aims with respect to open education. MIT OCW, for example, provides a highly visual interface to resources organized with reference to MIT's course structures and topics, with secondary organization by resource type. Landing pages are "course home pages" with the denser content (e.g. lecture notes) available one click deeper. The Open University goes further and presents a journey from casual exploration of the OU's material, through to greater engagement with course material to becoming an enrolled OU student, with little reference to OER as a concept. Nottingham's U-Now repository adopts an alternative approach, being more of a back-end system to manage content that is used and exposed through the University's other services. Consequently, the interface is rather plain with an emphasis on browse and search functionality, presented in a text-oriented interface, and with the browse function emphasizing the courses on which resources are used.

Continued access to openly licensed MOOCs offers some benefits in terms of the presentation of learning resources in comparison to depositing individual resources in repositories. Most importantly, the educational context of the resource is preserved, making it more useful for both teachers and learners. This contextualization is particularly useful for non-textual resources as they are presented in the context of a course which includes information about educational subject and level.

In contrast to institutional repositories, aggregators take their descriptions from a diverse range of sources, each potentially using a different categorization scheme, which impedes the creation of a coherent browsing interface. They therefore tend to use free text search rather than browse by category. As an example, Solvonauts' presentation is entirely based on search, the results pages simply provide a list of resource descriptions under a link to the resource. OER Commons' search and browse facilities are similarly clear and uncluttered, with results pages showing basic metadata and enabling filtering of results and onward browsing to similar resources. It is notable that both of these aggregators emphasize license information in the presentation of resources, which is an understandable consequence of them drawing on a range of sources with a variety of licensing regimes. Subject-specific repositories that require manual deposit of resources from a specific community of users are able to request that depositors provide metadata to categorize the resource against a relevant scheme, enabling them to provide more sophisticated browse functionality (see, for example, Core Materials). However, the extra effort required to provide this additional information may inhibit users from depositing resources. An alternative approach is to divide the content into collections, for example, Humbox's Oral History collection (Humbox, [n.d.]), and link the collections to individual sources or communities of users.

The presentational strategies of popular online content sharing platforms typically have a strong focus on viewing and previewing resources. One strength of these platforms is that the homogeneity of resource type means that preview and display can be handled consistently. Most also promote social sharing, with user profiles and groups, which enables collections of resources to be displayed either from a single user or from groups of contributors.

Strategies for Community Support

Some repositories and aggregators aim to serve preexisting communities (e.g. an institution or subject community), while others create communities from their users. Whether the community builds the service or vice versa, the importance of communities in ensuring that the repository or aggregator can engage with and meet user needs has long been recognized (Margaryan and Littlejohn, 2007). While they are not mutually exclusive, it is useful to consider engagement with the following range of communities: the host institution, resource depositors and users (educators and learners).

One way to achieve sustainable backing is to address institutional strategic objectives. Some institutional repositories have a clearly articulated internal role in supporting the efficient reuse of learning materials while others may have an external focus. For example, within the University of Nottingham, Open Nottingham is integrated with institutional learning technology support and the delivery of courses at international campuses. By contrast, many of the University of Oxford projects, e.g. Politics in Spires (OpenSpires, [n.d.]), explicitly focus on outreach and several have active blogs aimed at engaging the public at large.

Another way to sustain a service is to build a wide-reaching community and user base. For repository and aggregator services that draw their content from a wide pool of contributors, features for community building often replicate those that are familiar from social sharing sites. For example, registered users of HumBox have profile pages which show the resources they have added and links to these pages appear in the resource metadata. OER Commons includes the ability to rate and discuss content, and to form groups for sharing and discussion. Users of OER Commons can contribute resources from the web using a bookmark button or combine content using OER Commons' open author tool. Both OER Commons and Humbox allow users to join groups and the resources they deposit can be associated with these groups.

One effective way to build communities of users is to enable them to work together to create or improve resources, an approach that is exemplified by GitHub. An interesting, but seemingly underused feature in Humbox is that registered users may clone resources, i.e. make their own copy in the repository which can be modified. The Open University's OpenLearnWorks [n.d.] allows users from outside the OU to create courses either by modifying and remixing OpenLearn material or by creating resources from scratch. Although the extent of external contributions seems modest, OpenLearnWorks illustrates OpenLearn's attempts to go beyond simply disseminating the OU's own resources.

Community engagement features such as comments, ratings and recommendations are staple functionalities of popular social sharing sites, however these features are not always appropriate for academic resources. For example, while comments on GitHub can exemplify in-depth community engagement, albeit within the specific context of software development, YouTube comment streams are not a great place to discuss the academic content of a video. Kritikos demonstrates an attempt to replicate this type of functionality for educational resources by enabling recommendations to be displayed within Kritikos and shared with other environments used by teachers and learners.

Given the limited success of many OER repository services in building features that promote community engagement, it is worth considering MERLOT separately. MERLOT is significant as it is one of the longest running collections of online learning resources (the project began in 1997) and has developed a considerable community of users. All resources are either created or recommended by users and many have been peer reviewed and commented on by others. MERLOT actively supports its user community by highlighting community facilities on its homepage, organizing conferences, publishing newsletters and presenting awards for individual resources and community members. It also permits institutions to design custom pages/portals for curated content from within the larger collection.

Strategies for Resource Description

Resource description is important for managing the development, curation and dissemination of all learning resources, however it is particularly important for OER as it is one way of ensuring that licensing and copyright information is recorded. Arguably, however, the primary function of resource description is to facilitate resource discovery; people cannot use/reuse resources unless they can find them, and without discoverability OER will not function and succeed in its aims. Consequently, some understanding of resource description for discovery purposes is important for any individual, group or organization wishing to make their resources discoverable.

The description of resources in order to facilitate discovery is obviously a core function of libraries; many well-established standards and procedures exist, and over the last two decades there have been various attempts to extend these strategies to deal with online learning resources, with varying degrees of success. It is important to ask from the outset if there is anything unique about OER description that is different from the description of other types of resources. The answer is yes, in relation to both the resources' openness and their educational value. Ideally, open resources should be made available on the open web in such a way that their text content can be fully viewed by indexing services. This means that resource discovery will not be reliant on associated abstracts or metadata. For some resource types, which are of particular value to education, e.g. images, audio, video, computer simulations, etc., it is clearly not possible to index text from the resource itself. However, such resources are frequently presented in some form of educational context, e.g. as part of an online course, so full text indexing of the associated pages and resources is often possible. Even where the educational context is lost, for example when resources are hosted on a content sharing site such as YouTube or Vimeo, it is possible to retain some context about the resource creator and the collection from which the resources are drawn. A second important factor is that traditional library approaches generally do not address the description of a resource's educational value. Library catalogs tend to focus on the inherent properties of a resource (e.g. title, author, publication date), however many aspects of a resource that make it educationally useful (e.g. pedagogic approach, educational context) are not actually inherent properties of the resource itself, rather they are dependent on how the resource is used. Some educational aspects can be identified as properties of the resource itself, for example educational level, typical age of the learner, learning resource type (e.g. is it an assessment, a lesson plan, a tutorial?), but many of these are difficult to define or are inter-related. These factors make the creation of formal metadata difficult. In terms of describing online learning resources, context is key and shared experience within a community is important.

Description, Self-description and Metadata

Resource description can refer to both human readable textual descriptions and formal machine readable metadata. Metadata is defined by the National Information Standards Organization as

> [the] structured information that describes, explains, locates, or otherwise makes it easier to retrieve, use, or manage an information resource. Metadata is often called data about data or information about information (NISO, 2004).

The significance of "structured information" in this definition is that it is used "to refer to machine understandable information" (NISO, 2004). So, metadata is information that is formally structured and encoded according to a technical specification. While resource creators may not be well-versed in these technical specifications, some form of semi-structured description should be achievable. It is well accepted academic practice that resources should contain a certain amount of information to describe their content and provenance. As Robertson (2008) highlighted, academic papers follow a pattern of presenting the title, authors' names, authors' affiliations, date of submission and an abstract of their subject matter; if they are published in a journal they would also include information about the journal name, issue and date of publication. In many institutions, student coursework or assignments must be submitted with a cover sheet identifying the student and the course or module for which the work is submitted. Outside of academia, and with non-textual resource types, similar conventions are common, for example we would expect a professionally produced video to include titles and credits. Such resources can be considered to be *self-describing*. It seems a reasonable assumption that academics, students and institutions that wish to be associated with the OERs they create and publish should include certain descriptive information that is agreed by general community convention. In parallel with basic bibliographic information, it seems reasonable that this basic descriptive information should include Title, Author, Date (e.g. of creation or publication), Institution, Abstract, Keywords, Course Code or name. Although few would argue against the value of providing such basic information, in reality the provision of descriptive information as part of online educational resources has always been much more haphazard than for scholarly works or even student assignments.

A number of formal metadata standards have emerged over the last decade which attempt to address the issue of educational resource description by formalizing the encoding of this information. A comprehensive description and analysis of learning resource metadata standards is presented in Barker and Campbell (2010). There are two broad strategies behind learning resource metadata: 1) the "traditional" approach of creating catalog records which separate the metadata from the resource, creating a self-contained stand-alone metadata record that fully describes the resource; 2) augmenting web resources with semantic information to assist the discovery of resources based on their content and the links between them.

The IEEE 1484.12 Standard for Learning Object Metadata (the LOM, IEEE, 2002) is an example of the record based approach. The LOM's conceptual data schema is a hierarchy of elements, the first level is composed of nine categories, each of which contains sub-elements; these sub-elements may simply contain data, or they may themselves be aggregate elements that contain further sub-elements. Taken as a whole, the set of elements in the LOM defines a stand-alone record based on a data schema which covers all education-specific and generic aspects of a resource.

Sitting somewhere between textual description and metadata is schema.org, an initiative launched by the search engines Google, Yahoo!, Bing and Yandex. This initiative arose from the difficulty of identifying the semantic meaning of text found on web pages, e.g. which text is the author's name and which is their affiliation? Schema.org seeks to address this problem by embedding information into web pages that identifies the meaning of the text. This is achieved either by adding tags to the HTML markup or by including islands of structured metadata (Barker and Campbell, 2014). With this information it is possible for a search engine to associate text in the page with key properties or characteristics of the resource. The URLs of the hyperlinks identify associated entities (e.g. authors and publishers) and allow further information about them to be obtained. The Learning Resource Metadata Initiative (Learning Resource Metadata Initiative, 2013) has added properties to schema. org that allow the markup of educationally significant information. It is broadly compatible with the IEEE LOM and should facilitate the indexing of textual descriptions of learning resources by Google and other big search engines.

Metadata describing the inherent properties of resources tends to be static (e.g. the author of a resource is unlikely to change), whereas educational resource descriptions benefit from being dynamic, with users adding information about how they used a resource and whether that use was effective (see Campbell, 2008, for a description of Jennifer Trant's concept of "tombstone metadata"). Structured data describing how and in what context a resource has been used and how the user rates or recommends a resource has been termed paradata (Campbell and Barker, 2013). Paradata is generated as learning resources are used, reused, adapted, contextualized, favorited, tweeted, retweeted or shared. This type of information tends not to be captured by more traditional cataloguing methods which aim to describe what a resource is, rather than how it may be used. Paradata can complement metadata by providing an additional layer of contextual information, capturing the user activity related to the resource and helping to elucidate its potential educational utility.

All these approaches to resource description and metadata have been used to describe open educational resources. IEEE LOM has been used to facilitate interoperability between repositories where agreement can be reached on common cataloguing standards, for example the ARIADNE Foundation's standards-based technology infrastructure (Ariadne, [n.d.]). LRMI/schema.org is a useful way to share information about learning resources with big search engines and paradata, stored in a Learning Registry node, is used to enhance the services provided by Kritikos.

While all these approaches have their value, none are entirely unproblematic and we would suggest that whatever approach is taken to creating metadata to describe OER, this should not be seen as an alternative to the provision of basic information so that resources are self-describing and discoverable by major search engines.

A Final Word on Sustainability

Some of the research on which this chapter is based was originally undertaken for a report written in late 2014 and it is startling that in the space of twelve months, several repositories and applications have either shut down or have changed radically. Sustainability is clearly a key issue facing OER initiatives (Rolfe, 2012). It is inevitable that grant funded programmes and projects will come to an end, so it is incumbent on those who are committed to open education to ensure that the resources created by such initiatives remain available even when programmes end. While project outputs may be deposited in a dedicated repository or platform, there is greater likelihood that they will remain available if they are deposited in multiple locations. For an example of this approach, see the Core Materials project described above. Syndicating resources (not just metadata) via aggregators and global OER repositories is another positive step that projects can take to ensure their resources continue to remain available. Consequently, we suggest that, currently, the best way forward to ensure the continued availability of OERs is to describe them in such a way that makes them discoverable by major search engines, to reduce reliance on a single point of deposit and explore what may be learned from preservation and syndication approaches employed in other domains.

References

Ariadne [n.d.], http://www.ariadne-eu.org

Barker, P. and Campbell, L. M. (2014), *What is Schema.org?* (Cetis Briefing No. 2014:B01), http://publications.cetis.org.uk/2014/960

Barker, P. and Campbell, L. M. (2010), Metadata for Learning Materials: An Overview of Existing Standards and Current Developments, *Technology, Instruction, Cognition and Learning, 7*(3–4), pp. 225–243, http://www.icbl. hw.ac.uk/publicationFiles/2010/TICLMetadata

Campbell, L. M. (2008), *Sharks, Tombstones and Timewarps at Dublin Core*, http://blogs.cetis.ac.uk/lmc/2008/10/04/sharks-tombstones-and-timewarps-at-dublin-core

Campbell, L. M. and Barker, P. (2013), *Activity Data and Paradata* (Cetis Briefing No. 2013:B01), http://publications.cetis.ac.uk/2013/808

CORE-Materials [n.d.], http://core.materials.ac.uk

Dichev, C. and Dicheva, D. (2012), *Open Educational Resources in Computer Science Teaching*, Proceedings of the 43rd ACM Technical Symposium on Computer Science Education, pp. 619–624, New York: ACM, http://doi. org/10.1145/2157136.2157314

EdShare [n.d.], https://www.edshare.soton.ac.uk

English Common Law [n.d.], http://lawsfolio.londoninternational.ac.uk/eclmooc

Great Writers Inspire [n.d.], http://writersinspire.org

HumBox [n.d.], http://humbox.ac.uk

IEEE (2002), *1484.12.1-2002, Standard for Learning Object Metadata. The Institute of Electrical and Electronics Engineers, Inc.* (Standard).

Kritikos [n.d.], https://kritikos.liv.ac.uk

Learning Registry [n.d.], http://learningregistry.org

Learning Resource Metadata Initiative (2013), *LRMI Metadata Terms* (Specification), http://dublincore.org/dcx/lrmi-terms/1.1

Margaryan, A. and Littlejohn, A. (2007), Repositories and Communities at Cross-purposes: Issues in Sharing and Reuse of Digital Learning Resources, *Journal of Computer Assisted Learning,* 24(4), pp. 333–347, http://doi.org/10.1111/j.1365-2729.2007.00267.x

Massachusetts Institute of Technology [n.d.], *MIT OpenCourseWare*, http://ocw.mit.edu/index.htm

MERLOT [n.d.], https://www.merlot.org/merlot/index.htm

NISO (2004), *Understanding Metadata*, http://www.niso.org/publications/press/UnderstandingMetadata.pdf

OER Commons [n.d.], https://www.oercommons.org

OpenLearn. [n.d.], http://www.open.edu/openlearn

OpenLearn Works [n.d.], http://www.open.edu/openlearnworks

OpenSpires [n.d.], http://openspires.it.ox.ac.uk

Robertson, J. (2008), *Open Educational Resources, Metadata, and Self-description*, http://blogs.cetis.org.uk/johnr/2008/12/08/open-educational-resources-metadata-and-self-description

Rolfe, V. (2012), Open Educational Resources: Staff Attitudes and Awareness, *Research in Learning Technology*, 20, http://www.researchin learningtechnology.net/index.php/rlt/article/view/14395

Solvonauts [n.d.], http://solvonauts.org

University of Nottingham, The [n.d.], *U-Now Open Courseware*, http://unow.nottingham.ac.uk

Wiley, D., Bliss, TJ and McEwen, M. (2014), Open Educational Resources: A Review of the Literature, in J. M. Spector, M. D. Merrill, J. Elen, and M. J. Bishop (Eds.), *Handbook of Research on Educational Communications and Technology*, pp. 781–789, New York: Springer.

World War I Centenary [n.d.], http://ww1centenary.oucs.ox.ac.uk

Xerte Community [n.d.], http://www.xerte.org.uk

Xpert [n.d.], http://www.nottingham.ac.uk/xpert

Xpert image attribution [n.d.], http://www.nottingham.ac.uk/xpert/attribution

4. Identifying Categories of Open Educational Resource Users

Martin Weller, Beatriz de los Arcos, Rob Farrow,
Rebecca Pitt and Patrick McAndrew

The Open Educational Resource (OER) movement has been successful in developing a large, global community of practitioners, in releasing high quality learning material and influencing policy. It now stands at the cusp of mainstream adoption, which will require reaching different audiences than previously. In this contribution the findings of the OER Research Hub are used to identify three categories of OER user: OER active, OER as facilitator and OER consumer. These groups have different requirements of OER and thus varying strategies would be required to meet their needs if mainstream adoption was to be realized.

http://dx.doi.org/10.11647/OBP.0103.04

Introduction

Open Educational Resources (OER) have been part of the open education movement since 2002, with the advent of MIT's OpenCourseWare project. The history of OER goes back further than this if one considers the Learning Object developments of the 1990s and emergence of openly licensed software as precursors. Their premise is a relatively simple one, and has remained largely unchanged since the initial MIT project: creating educational content with an open license so it can be accessed freely and adapted. The Hewlett Foundation's definition of an OER is:

> [...] teaching, learning, and research resources that reside in the public domain or have been released under an intellectual property license that permits their free use and re-purposing by others. Open educational resources include full courses, course materials, modules, textbooks, streaming videos, tests, software, and any other tools, materials, or techniques used to support access to knowledge. (Hewlett Foundation, [n.d.])

This gives a clear definition of OER, but for many practitioners this becomes blurred in practice, and overlaps with any online resource, regardless of licence. Although this chapter is concerned primarily with OER as defined here, this mixed economy is part of the practice of users, and so is reflected in some of the later discussion.

The OER movement has been something of a success story compared with many educational developments, for instance the aforementioned learning objects, which gained a good deal of initial attention. There is a global OER movement, with repositories in most major languages. Funding has been provided by foundations such as Hewlett and national bodies such as JISC in the UK, and sustainable models that do not require external funding have begun to emerge, for example the Open University's OpenLearn project (Perryman, Law and Law, 2013). It is difficult to quantify OERs by time or projects, since it will vary depending on definition, but Creative Commons have estimated there are over one billion CC licensed resources (Creative Commons, 2015). For example, should online collections from museums be included? Or more general resources such as YouTube videos, SlideShare presentations, iTunes U downloads? Even if the focus is solely on university based OER projects then there is considerable output, with the Open Education Consortium listing over 200 institutional members, all of whom have a commitment to open education and releasing OERs (OE Consortium, 2015). MIT has now made over 2,000 courses freely available (MIT OCW, 2015) and the Open University's OpenLearn site has released over 10,000 hours of learning resources.

One major development in OERs over this period has been the advent of open textbooks, although these represent just one form of OER. The premise of open textbooks is relatively simple — create electronic versions of standard textbooks that are openly licensed and freely available and can be modified by users. The physical versions of such books are available at a low cost to cover printing, for as little as $5 USD (Wiley, 2011). The motivations for developing open textbooks are particularly evident in the US, where the cost of textbooks accounts for 26% of a four-year degree programme (GAO, 2005). This creates a strong economic argument for their adoption in higher education, and a similar case can be made at K12 level.[1]

There are a number of projects developing open textbooks using various models of production. A good example is OpenStax, who have funding from several foundations to develop open textbooks targeting the subject areas with large national student populations, for example "Introductory Statistics", "Concepts of Biology", "Introduction to Sociology", etc. The books are co-authored and authors are paid a fee to work on the books, which are peer-reviewed. The electronic versions are free, and print versions available at cost. The books are released under a CC-BY license, and educators are encouraged to modify the textbooks to suit their own needs. In terms of adoption, the OpenStax textbooks had been downloaded over 120,000 times and 200 institutions had decided to formally adopt OpenStax materials, leading to an estimated saving of over $30 million in a little over two years (OpenStax College, 2014).

The OER movement has managed to grow substantially over the past decade. It has released a vast amount of educational material, and seen diverse implementation projects across the globe. The OER movement has gone through different phases, from startup, to growth and, in places,

---

1   K12 is a term for the sum of primary and secondary education sectors. The expression is a shortening of kindergarten (K) for 4- to 6-year-olds through twelfth grade for 17- to 19-year-olds, the first and last grades of free education in a number of countries including Australia and the US.

sustainability. This has happened in parallel with a number of related developments in the open education movement, namely the success of open access publishing, particularly through national mandates (SPARC, 2015), and the more recent popular attention garnered by MOOCs. Education policy has also started to recognise the potential of OER, for example the US Department of Labor launched a $2 billion programme, Trade Adjustment Assistance Community College and Career Training (TAACCCT), aimed at improving workforce and employability training. All new material produced through these grants was mandated to release their content under a Creative Commons licence (Allen, 2016). This has created a context in which the OER movement views the next phase as one of becoming mainstream in educational practice. For example, the Hewlett Foundation White Paper (2013) on OERs states that its goal is "to pave the way towards mainstream adoption of OER in a manner that promotes greater, sustainable educational capacity", and the theme of the 2015 OER conference in the UK was "mainstreaming open education" (OER conference, 2015).

In order for OERs to enter the mainstream of educational practice, their use by learners, educators and policy makers would need to become common practice; the default option. The broad approach of the OER movement thus far has been to increase OER awareness and to grow the OER community. However, for mainstream adoption it may be that other approaches are now required and what was a successful strategy in one stage of development may not be successful in another. This may not have been an overarching, or deliberate strategy, but reflects the manner in which movements develop. This contribution will examine different forms of engagement with OER, using the research of a project based at the Open University, the OER Research Hub, as the basis for proposing three forms of engagement. By understanding these types of engagement, strategy for OER adoption can be influenced.

The OER Research Hub

The OER Research Hub (http://oerhub.net) was a project funded by the Hewlett Foundation, which commenced in 2012. The aim of the project was to create an evidence base for the OER community. Much of the initial phase of the OER movement can be characterized as being belief-driven about the potential benefits of OERs. These beliefs might be stated as obvious, undeniably true or based on anecdote, but rarely backed up by evidence. This was because the movement had to gain sufficient momentum to have evidence to investigate whether this potential was realized. The OER movement may now have realized this critical mass of evidence needed to investigate these more fully. The OER Research Hub set out to establish this evidence base, using 11 hypotheses which represented the commonly stated beliefs and claims in the OER community:

A. Performance: Use of OER leads to improvement in student performance and satisfaction.

B. Openness: The Open Aspect of OER creates different usage and adoption patterns than other online resources.

C. Access: Open education models lead to more equitable access to education, serving a broader base of learners than traditional education.

D. Retention: Use of OER is an effective method for improving retention for at-risk students.

E. Reflection: Use of OER leads to critical reflection by educators, with evidence of improvement in their practice.

F. Finance: OER adoption at an institutional level leads to financial benefits for students and/or institutions.

G. Indicators: Informal learners use a variety of indicators when selecting OER.

H. Support: Informal learners adopt a variety of techniques to compensate for the lack of formal support, which can be supported in open courses

I. Transition: Open education acts as a bridge to formal education, and is complementary, not competitive, with it.

J. Policy: Participation in OER pilots and programs leads to policy change at an institutional level.

K. Assessment: Informal means of assessment are motivators to learning with OER.

Methodology

The project adopted a mixed methods approach. As well as gathering existing evidence onto an evidence map (oermap.org), the project worked with fifteen different collaborations, across four sectors: K12,[2] community college, higher education and informal learning. Interviews, case studies, and quantitative data were gathered, but this paper mainly reports on responses to surveys. A set of survey questions was created, addressing the eleven hypotheses. Although slight variations were permitted depending on context, the same pool of questions was used across a wide range of respondents. These included students in formal education, informal learners, educators at K12, community college and higher education level and librarians. In total, twenty-one surveys were conducted, with nearly 7,500 responses.

The collaborations were as follows:

1. The Flipped Learning Network (FLN) — a community of teachers whose mission is "to provide educators with the knowledge, skills and resources to successfully implement flipped learning" (Flipped Learning Network, [n.d.]).

2. Vital Signs — a citizen-science programme for middle-school children run by the Gulf of Maine Research Institute. The aim is for 7th and 8th grade kids to learn science by doing science "using inquiry, peer review and scientific tools to investigate genuine research questions about invasive species" (Vital Signs, [n.d.]). Community College Consortium for OER (CCCOER) — a coalition of more than 240 colleges across 11 states in the US, who are starting to use OER.

3. Open Course Library (OCL) — a collection of shareable learning materials, including syllabi, course activities, readings, and assessments designed by teams of experts in the Washington area.

4. OpenLearn — the OU's web-based platform for OER. It hosts hundreds of online courses and videos and is accessed by over three million users a year.

5. TESS-India — a project developing OERs for teacher training in India.

6. Bridge to Success — a project that developed and piloted whole course OER in math and learning/personal development skills (*Succeed with Math* and *Learning to Learn,* respectively).

---

2   For a definition of K12 please see Chapter 4, fn 1 in the present volume.

7. OpenStax CNX (formerly Connexions) — a repository of OER, which have been shared and peer-reviewed by educators. The OpenStax CNX platform also enables users to remix and create their own resources. OpenStax College are providers of a range of open textbooks.

8. School of Open — an initiative of Creative Commons and Peer to Peer University (P2PU) which provides facilitated and non-facilitated open courses on different aspects of "openness" (e.g. copyright and licensing, OER, Wikipedia etc.).

9. BCcampus Open Textbook Project — this aims to create 40 open textbooks for use in HE institutions in British Columbia, Canada.

10. MERLOT — an OER repository and community.

11. ROER4D — a project investigating the impact of OER in the Global South.

12. The Saylor Academy — a non-profit organization offering free courses.

13. Siyavula — math and science open textbook providers based in South Africa.

14. Project Co-PILOT (Community of Practice for Information Literacy Online Teaching) — this project promotes OER on digital and information literacy in the higher education sector.

Each of the collaborations had a researcher from the Research Hub assigned to work with them. Three or more of the 11 hypotheses were also allocated to each collaboration, with hypotheses A (Performance) and B (Openness) being relevant to all. In addition, one fellow from each collaboration visited the Open University to focus on a specific area of research.

Supplementary to the evidence acquired from these targeted collaborations, the project also incorporated evidence from the OER community and published research which was added to the evidence map. The team adopted an agile methodology adapted from software development. This was focused around week-long sprints which targeted particular hypotheses. One such sprint focused on populating the evidence map from research repositories and through regular review of academic journals.

The overall survey data was gathered across the collaborations, with 7,498 respondents in total, and the frequencies analysis of this data constitutes the main evidence basis for this chapter. The breakdown of respondents from each of the collaborations was as follows:

Flipped Learning Network (n=118); CCCOER (n=128); Saylor (n=3213); OpenLearn (n=1668); OU iTunes U (n=1114); Siyavula (n=89); Librarians (n=218); General Survey (n=147); School of Open (n=129); BCCampus (n=85); Open Stax (n=400) and OU YouTube (n=189).

A detailed analysis of the evidence is given for the following: each hypothesis (Weller *et al.*, 2015); open textbook use (Pitt, 2015); K12 teacher adoption (de los Arcos *et al.*, 2016); informal learners (Farrow *et al.*, 2016). The aim of this contribution is to use this data to identify different types of OER users, which can be classified by different forms of engagement with OERs. This analysis focuses on identifying categories of OER engagement that will inform the intention of making OER use mainstream practice, and is based on the authors' interpretation of the OER data set.

Types of OER Users

Open education in general, and OERs specifically, form a basis from which many other general teaching practices benefit, but often practitioners in those areas are unaware of OERs explicitly. The focus in the OER community thus far has largely been to expand this group of "OER aware" users, but mainstream adoption will see OER usage by new audiences. Analyzing the findings of the OER Research Hub reveals three main categories of OER users: OER active, OER as facilitator, and OER consumer. The categories include users from different sectors, including educators, formal and informal learners, higher education and K12. However, some categories may see higher representations of some user types, for instance the OER active category may have a higher proportion of educators than learners, since it is focused on engagement with the OER movement, but it will not be exclusive to educators.

OER active

This category of user is aware of OER issues, in that the term itself will have meaning for them, they are engaged with issues around open education, are aware of open licenses and are often advocates for OERs. This group has often been the focus of OER funding, conferences and research, with the aim of growing the size of this audience. An example of this type of user might be the community college teacher who adopts an openly licensed textbook, adapts it and contributes to open textbooks.

Much of the OER Research Hub work focused on this group, and the findings highlight the positive benefits for this community, for instance increased confidence from learners, reflection by educators and cost savings. However, the findings also highlight the difficulties in expanding this group, for instance in terms of their awareness of OER and the significance of licenses.

With regards to the positive aspects, there is a strong claim concerning the benefits of OERs for both learners and educators, for example 62.1% of educators and 60.7% of formal learners reported that using OER improved student satisfaction, and 44.1% of educators and 38.9% of formal learners agreed that OER use resulted in better test scores. It must be remembered, however, that these results are self-reported and may not accord with actual performance.

However, the research also revealed that knowing where to find resources is one of the biggest challenges to using OER and that awareness of well-established OER repositories, such as MERLOT, is low compared with free resource sites such as the Khan Academy and TED.[3] There was also a disparity in belief and practice that suggests that there may be practical barriers in expanding this group of users. For example, only 14% of informal learners (i.e. those learners not currently enrolled in a formal study programme) selected OER with an open license allowing adaptation, despite the fact that 84% of all informal learners said they adapted the resources they found to fit their needs (although what "adaptation" means here may vary, as discussed in the next category). Similarly, only 14.8% of educators created resources and published them with a Creative Commons license despite the fact that a majority of educators (70.4%) considered open licensing important and 58.9% were familiar with the Creative Commons logo.

While the OER active group has continued to expand and has established a successful community, it is unrealistic to assume that every educator will become interested and active in the OER movement. It

---

3 For a discussion of TED see Chapter 4 in this volume: Situated Learning in Open Communities: The TED Open Translation Project by Lidia Cámara de la Fuente and Anna Comas-Quinn.

may not be necessary for every educator to engage with OER for it to be considered mainstream, but as with eLearning in general, it would need to impact upon the majority of educational practice. A recent survey of educators in US higher education found that awareness of OER was low, but that awareness was not a requirement for adoption (Allen and Seaman, 2014). This leads to the second category of OER user.

OER as facilitator

This group may have some awareness of OER, or open licenses, but they have a pragmatic approach toward them. OERs are of secondary interest to their primary task, which is usually teaching. OER (and openness in general) can be seen as the substratum, which allows some of their practice to flourish, but their awareness of OER issues is low. Their interest is in innovation in their own area, and therefore OERs are only of interest to the extent that they facilitate innovation or efficiency in this. An example would be a teacher who uses Khan Academy, TED talks and some OER in their teaching.

One of the collaborations on the OER Research Hub was the Flipped Learning Network. Flipped Learning moves the direct instruction element away from the face-to-face component and into the individual's learning space (Flipped Learning Network, 2014). The face-to-face time is then spent on dynamic, interactive group learning. The claim is that the flipped model reverses the traditional approach as class time is spent doing tasks where students exercise critical thinking and homework is used to support understanding and knowledge acquisition. In practice, this often means giving students videos and other online resources to view at home. OERs are therefore of relevance, in that they can help these educators realize their main aim, which is "flipping" their classroom. They are not absolutely necessary, however, for instance many educators use YouTube videos without paying attention to the license it has been released under. As well as this, flipping a classroom could be achieved by using licensed materials from content providers, for example the commercial publisher Pearson offer a course on the "Foundations of Flipped Learning" (Pearson, [n.d.]), and could presumably offer all of the resources to "flip" a classroom for a subscription fee.

However, the OER Research Hub found that adaptation was a key requirement for educators, with 79.4% of all OER users adapting resources to fit their needs. As stated above, though, people's interpretation of adaptation varies. For some users it means using the resources as inspiration for creating their own material, as this quote illustrates:

> What I do is I look at a lot of free resources but I don't usually give them directly to my students because I usually don't like them as much as something I would create, so what I do is I get a lot of ideas.

This is particularly relevant for those in the Flipped Learning network as they are seeking new ideas to teach their subject. While this is an important use of OER, it arises principally as a result of their online availability rather than openness, and so does not necessarily require OER in order to be realized. However, the freedom to reuse ideas is encouraged by an open license and users feel able to do so without fear of infringing any copyright.

For other users, adaptation is more direct, e.g. editing or re-versioning the original or aggregating elements from different sources to create a more relevant one, as this quote demonstrates:

> The problem where I teach now is that we have no money; my textbooks, my Science textbooks are 20 years old, they're so out-dated, they don't relate to kids [...] so I pick and pull from a lot of different places to base my units; they're all based on the Common Core; for me to get my kids to meet the standards that are now being asked of them, I have no choice, I have to have like recent material and stuff they can use that'll help them when they get assessed on the standardised test.

And for others, adaptation may be taking an existing resource and placing it in a different context within their own material. The resource is not adapted, but the manner in which it is used is altered.

What this suggests is that there may be a continuum of adaptation in practice, ranging from adapting ideas for their own material to full re-versioning of content. The degree to which OER are required to realize this adaptation also increases along that continuum. At the "inspiring ideas" end, they are not required for simple reuse in a different context; the open license is useful, but many educators will ignore rights issues if the material is only being accessed by their class. At the full adaptation end of the continuum, open licensing is required.

It is likely that teachers will not remain static on this continuum, one of the findings of the OER Research Hub was that the more educators used OER, the more willing they were to share. For example, high numbers of both OpenStax College using educators and Siyavula educator survey respondents report being "more likely" to use other free educational resources/open educational resources for their teaching as a result of using Siyavula/OpenStax (Siyavula: 90.2%, n=55 and OpenStax: 79.5%, n=58). Sharing content is made much easier if there are no concerns around licenses.

In the example of Flipped Learning, then, OERs are useful for realising a different aim, they are a related topic of interest, but not the primary one. However, the open aspect leads to developments which are not possible with resources that are merely digital and online.

Cost savings for students can also be viewed as a goal, which OER can help achieve. Much of the motivation for the open textbook movement relates to the financial burden of buying proprietary textbooks. The potential savings here are one area of OER impact that has seen rigorous, quantitative research. Hilton *et al.* (2014) found an average saving of $90.61 USD per student per course, across a wide range of community and stage college courses. In the OER Research Hub study, 79.6% of formal students (i.e. those enrolled in a programme of study at a higher education institute) reported that they saved money by using OER, primarily open textbooks. Cost savings also have other positive impacts on study, for example in student retention, and immediate access to content, as this quote demonstrates:

> I sure think that if the institution more fully made use of open educational resources that we could benefit financially: by retaining more students who otherwise have to drop out because of the high cost of textbooks; by providing higher quality and more diverse and accessible learning and teaching resources which would be a great financial benefit.

However, if cost savings were the only goal, then OERs are not the only answer. Materials could be made free, or subsidized, which are not openly licensed. The intention behind the OER approach is that it has other benefits also, in that educators adapt their material, and it is also an efficient way to achieve the goal of cost savings, because others will adapt the material with the intention of improving its quality, relevance or currency. As with the Flipped Learning Network, OERs are, in this instance, one means of achieving a related objective.

OER consumer

This group will use OER amongst a mix of other media and often not differentiate between them. Awareness of licences is low and not a priority. OERs are a "nice to have" option but not essential, and users are often largely consuming rather than creating and sharing. An example might be students studying at university who use iTunes U materials to supplement their taught material.

For this type of user, the main features of OERs are their free use, reliability and quality. One under-reported use of OERs is by formal learners to sample study in their topic before entering formal study, with 52.7% of formal learners accessing OER indicated that they were using OER to supplement their formal studies. Similarly, 32.4% of learners stated that their interest in using OER was a chance to try university-level content before signing up for a paid-for course. Similarly, many learners were using OERs to supplement study whilst currently in formal education, with 46.9% of all formal learners in our sample stating that OER had a positive impact in helping them complete their course of study. For these users, the OERs need to be freely available, at the appropriate level of study and from a reputable institution. The open license is not a primary concern for this group, although there may be circumstances when they wish to adapt, or share them. This was reflected in the importance learners placed on the factors that influence their selection of OER, the top three of which were: relevance to their particular needs; a good description of learning objectives and outcomes; ease of download. The presence of a Creative Commons license was ranked fourteenth out of a possible seventeen options.

A related use of OER is that for informal learners it can function as an alternative to formal study. For these learners, the quality and zero cost were important, with our study showing that 89% of learners using OER say that the opportunity to study at no cost influenced their decision to use OER.

These learners are studying for personal interest predominantly: 86.3% state this as the main reason over improved job opportunities or mandated requirements. For these learners, the quality of the content is of prime interest, and the lack of formal support is not seen as significant for their goals, with only 18.7% stating that not having the support of a tutor/teacher to help them was a barrier to their use of OER.

For this category of OER user, open licensing is at best an additional bonus, over the quality and usefulness of the resource. This is captured in this quote referring to the Siyavula open textbook project in South Africa:

> OER *per se* does not excite learners. Good content does — free or paid, legal or pirated. Siyavula's stuff works because it is GOOD. Being CC makes it legal to download, not fun to use. There are 100's of free/CC Geogebra resources. 98% are useless to me.

Discussion

Three categories of OER use have been identified through the work of the OER Research Hub: OER active; OER as facilitator; OER consumer. In expanding the OER community over the past twelve years, the focus has largely been on growing the first of these groups, that is, making people aware of the benefits of OER use and adaptation. This has been a successful strategy in establishing a sufficiently large OER community globally such that OER projects can be developed, funding can be secured and advocacy can be conducted. All of these actions are required to establish a sustainable community, and represent the necessary foundation for a movement to enter the mainstream. However, in order for OER to become part of mainstream practice in education, additional strategies are required in order to meet the needs of the other two categories of users identified here.

(2009) has talked of "Dark Reuse", that is when reuse is happening in places that cannot be observed, analogous to dark matter, or simply it is not happening at all. Wiley challenges the OER movement about its aims:

> If our goal is catalyzing and facilitating significant amounts of reuse and adaptation of materials, we seem to be failing. [...] If our goal is to create fantastically popular websites loaded with free content visited by millions of people each month, who find great value in the content but never adapt or remix it, then we're doing fairly well.

Wiley contrasts creating popular websites and the reuse of content, but by considering these three perspectives of OER engagement, it is possible to see how both elements of Wiley's goals are realizable, as they represent different aims for each category. The main focus of OER initiatives has often been the OER active group. It is this group that creates open resources and advocates the movement. For example, Wild (2012) suggests three levels of engagement for HE staff that progress from piecemeal to strategic to embedded use of OER. The implicit assumption is that one should encourage progression through these levels, that is, the route to success for OER is to increase the population of what we have here labelled the OER active group. Perryman and Seal (2016) expand on this model which incorporates inhibitors and enablers (such as internet access) to account for uptake in developing nations.

Whilst expanding the OER active group is undoubtedly a requirement for the mainstream adoption of Open Educational Resources, it may not be the only approach. Another strategy may focus on increasing penetration of OER into the other categories of users identified here. As awareness of OER repositories was very low amongst these users, a way of improving uptake for these groups is to increase the visibility, search engine optimization and convenience of the resources themselves, without presuming a specific knowledge of open education. This might be realized through creating a trusted brand to compete with resources such as TED. If this was desirable then the funding and ownership of such an open brand would then be a focus for development.

Similarly, a strategic aim to engage with the second two groups would influence both the formats of OER and the content. For instance, the popularity of content varied across users' groups, with educators favoring science and maths, formal learners preferring science, psychology and philosophy, and computer science, economics and business preferred by informal learners. Video was the preferred format across all groups, but if the OER community were to target the OER consumer directly, then shorter content that is more viral in nature may be preferable. The community would then be focusing on promoting the development of these types of OER.

These categories of OER users are not exclusive, nor does an individual remain fixed within a category. Once users have encountered OER they are keen to access more of it, with 84.5% of informal learners stating that they are more likely to take another open course or study a free open educational resource. Educators in particular often become advocates, with 95% saying they share OERs. This quote from a K12 teacher was typical of the increase in sharing practice brought about by exposure to OERs:

> Free online resources have virtually opened up my world for sharing resources. Our district will never be able to pay, nor will I, so sharing was just a chance thing before now. Now, it is a daily occurrence most times.

There may be some progression, therefore, from either OER consumer or OER as facilitator into the OER active category. However, it is not necessary for this progression and increased OER awareness to occur for OERs to achieve mainstream adoption. Within one project or institution it is possible to witness all three types of user in operation. For example, Tidewater Community College embarked on the Z-degree programme (to make zero cost textbooks available to students) with two aims (DeMarte and Williams, 2015):

- To improve student success through increased access and affordability
- To improve teaching efficiency and effectiveness through the ability to focus, analyze, augment, and evolve course materials directly aligned to course learning outcomes

OER was seen a facilitator of these aims, but the project required its adopters to be OER aware. As the project expands to more courses in the college, it may be that the instructors are more interested in OER as a facilitator that allows revised course design and improved retention.

Although the OER Research Hub survey represents one of the most comprehensive studies of OER usage, it has its limitations; further investigation is needed in order to validate these categories and to assess some of the finer detail within each. The first of these limitations is geographical coverage. There were 180 different countries in the respondents but a concentration in the United States (35.8%) and United Kingdom (21%). In considering the strategies to realize mainstream adoption of OER, it is likely that the needs of these three categories of users will differ by region, so more focused studies in specific areas are needed. Similarly, the needs of users across different demographic groups within these categories are likely to vary. The respondents in the OER Research Hub surveys tended to be well qualified with a majority holding a postgraduate (34.4%) or undergraduate degree (27.5%), and a very small percentage declaring that they have no formal qualification (4.3%). Lastly, these surveys looked at users who were already accessing OERs through one route, even if they were unaware of the term "OER". In order to gain mainstream adoption it will be necessary to study how other, casual users can gain access to OERs.

Notwithstanding these limitations the Research Hub survey represents the best cross section of OER users currently available and as such it provides a useful means of considering the next phase of OER strategy. If the intention to become part of mainstream practice is to be realized then an expansion of usage beyond the current OER active group is required. As well as attempting to grow the community that constitutes this OER active group, different approaches will be required to meet the needs of the OER as facilitator and OER consumer groups.

Conclusion

The OER movement has seen steady growth and development since its inception, and elements are now being accepted into the mainstream of educational practice. In order to achieve widespread adoption it is likely that new strategies will be required by the OER community, whether researchers, funders, practitioners or policy makers. In order to inform this work, it will be necessary to develop a better understanding of how different communities use Open Educational Resources and the problems OER solves for them.

The work of the OER Research Hub provides a basis for this analysis as it provides a large data set of attitudes and perceptions of OER users. The three categories outlined in this paper of OER active, OER as facilitator and OER consumer represent an initial, but not exhaustive attempt, to rationalize these different forms of OER engagements. This analysis highlights that different strategies will be required to suit the expectations of these users, and thus a coordinated, directed vision may be necessary. This will present a challenge for a loose, open community but can be realized through open discussion and targeted funding and projects.

References

Allen, N. (2016), U.S. Labor Department Adopts Open Licensing Policy, http://sparcopen.org/news/2016/dol-open-licensing-policy

Allen, I. E. and Seaman J. (2014), Opening the Curriculum: Open Educational Resources in U.S. Higher Education, 2014, *Babson Survey Research Group*, http://www.onlinelearningsurvey.com/oer.html

de los Arcos, B., Farrow, R., Pitt, R., Weller, M. and McAndrew, P. (2016), Personalising Learning Through Adaptation: Evidence From a Global Survey of K-12 Teachers' Perceptions of their Use of Open Educational Resources, *Journal of Online Learning Research*, 2(1), pp. 23–40.

Association for the Advancement of Computing in Education (AACE), http://www.editlib.org/p/151664

Creative Commons (2015), State of the Commons Report, https://stateof.creativecommons.org/2015

DeMarte, D. and Williams, L. (2015), The "Z-Degree": Removing Textbook Costs as a Barrier to Student Success through an OER-Based Curriculum, http://www.scribd.com/doc/256908260/Z-Degree-Final-Report

Farrow, R., de los Arcos, B., Pitt, R. and Weller, M. (2015), Who are the Open Learners? A Comparative Study Profiling non-Formal Users of Open Educational Resources, *European Journal of Open, Distance and E-Learning*, 18(2), http://oro.open.ac.uk/4496

Flipped Learning Network (2014), Definition of Flipped Learning, http://fln.schoolwires.net//site/Default.aspx?PageID=92

Green, C. (2013), The Impact of Open Textbooks at OpenStax College, http://creativecommons.org/weblog/entry/38890

Government Accounts Office (2005), College Textbooks: Enhanced Offerings Appear to Drive Recent Price Increases, http://www.gao.gov/assets/250/247332.pdf

William and Flora Hewlett Foundation [n.d.], Open Educational Resources, http://www.hewlett.org/programs/education/open-educational-resources

William and Flora Hewlett Foundation (2013), White Paper: Open Educational Resources — Breaking the Lockbox on Education, http://www.hewlett.org/library/hewlett-foundation-publication/white-paper-open-educational-resources

Hilton III, J., Robinson, T., Wiley, D. and Ackerman, J. (2014), Cost-savings Achieved in Two Semesters Through the Adoption of Open Educational Resources, *The International Review of Research in Open and Distributed Learning*, 15(2), http://www.irrodl.org/index.php/irrodl/article/view/1700/2833

MIT OCW (2015), About MIT OpenCourseWare, http://ocw.mit.edu/about

OER Conference (2015), 14–14 April 2015, Cardiff, UK, https://oer15.oerconf.org

Open Education Consortium (2015), Open Education Consortium members, http://www.oeconsortium.org/members

OpenStax College (2014), Our Textbooks Have Saved Students $30 Million, https://www.openstaxcollege.org/news/our-textbooks-have-saved-students -30-million

Pearson [n.d.], http://www.pearsonschool.com/index.cfm?locator=PS2244

Perryman L.-A., Law P. and Law A. (2013), *Developing Sustainable Business Models for Institutions' Provision of Open Educational Resources: Learning From OpenLearn Users' Motivations and Experiences,* Proceedings: The Open and Flexible Higher Education Conference 2013, Paris, http://www.eadtu. eu/images/stories/Docs/Conference_2013/eadtu annual conference 2013 - proceedings.pdf

Perryman L-A. and Seal T. (2016), Open Educational Practices and Attitudes to Openness across India: Reporting the Findings of the Open Education Research Hub Pan-India Survey, *Journal of Interactive Media in Education*, 1 (15), pp. 1–17, http://oro.open.ac.uk/46370/1/JIME Pan-India.pdf; http://doi. org/10.5334/jime.416

Pitt, R. (2015), Mainstreaming Open Textbooks: Educator Perspectives on the Impact of OpenStax College Open Textbooks, *The International Review of Research in Open and Distributed Learning (IRRODL)*, 16(4), pp.133–155, http:// www.irrodl.org/index.php/irrodl/article/view/2381

SPARC (2015), Analysis of Funder Open Access Policies around the World, http://sparceurope.org/analysis-of-funder-open-access-policies-around-the- world

Weller, M., de los Arcos, B., Farrow, R., Pitt, B. and McAndrew, P. (2015). The Impact of OER on Teaching and Learning Practice, *Open Praxis*, 7(4), pp. 351–361, 10.5944/openpraxis.7.4.227

Wild J. (2012), OER Engagement Study: Promoting OER Reuse among Academics SCORE Research Report, https://ora.ox.ac.uk/objects/ uuid:eca4f8cd-edf5-4b38-a9b0-4dd2d4e59750

Wiley, D. (2009), Dark Matter, Dark Reuse, and the Irrational Zeal of a Believer, http://opencontent.org/blog/archives/905

Wiley D. (2011b), The $5 Textbook, http://www.slideshare.net/opencontent/the- 5-texbook

5. Situated Learning in Open Communities: The TED Open Translation Project

Lidia Cámara de la Fuente and Anna Comas-Quinn

Online communities where users can engage as both consumers and producers of content offer increasing opportunities for teachers and learners to connect formal and informal learning, often through open practice.

TED Translators, an online community of volunteers involved in the crowd-sourced translation of audiovisual open content, provides a good opportunity for teachers to involve their students in completing authentic tasks that make a real contribution to society, in this case, disseminating ideas across languages and cultures whilst practicing the skill of translating video subtitles.

Using a qualitative approach based on the analysis of participants' narratives, we explored the experiences of situated learning within a community of practice as part of a pedagogy that seeks to exploit the intersection between learning in formal and informal contexts. We focused on students' perceptions of the learning derived from participation in TED Translators, and the role of this activity in the training of translators, and found that participants valued the learning of a new skill and the often serendipitous knowledge they gained about other topics, and were mostly positive about the role of this kind of activity in translator education.

Introduction

The democratizing effect of the internet has blurred the lines between experts and non-experts in many fields, and changed the concept of knowledge and how and where learning takes place (Tapscott and Williams, 2008). An increasing number of online communities, where users can engage as both consumers and producers of content, offer extensive opportunities for teachers and learners to connect formal and informal learning, often through open practice (Beetham, Falconer, McGill and Littlejohn, 2012) as exemplified by the Wikipedia Education Programme.[1]

In the field of translation, technology is shaping content (web, app and games), but also substantially altering the landscape of practice (post-editing of machine translation and online volunteer translation). Exploring the boundary between online volunteer translation and translation education may yield important insights into how pedagogy responds to these changes in practice.

This chapter explores the relationship between learning and participation in an online volunteer community, TED Translators, involved in the crowd-sourced translation of audiovisual open content. Translation graduates were introduced to the translation of subtitles to develop subtitling, digital and collaborative learning skills. This research set out to capture and describe the experiences of participants undertaking an authentic, experiential, situated activity (Kiraly, 2015), and to explore the feasibility of using online volunteer translation communities as part of translators' training, possibly as an intermediate step between classroom-based instruction and graduate placements or internships.

The next section outlines the main theoretical principles on which authentic, experiential and situated learning is based, including the conceptualization of learning that underpin different views of education practice. The context section describes the setting for the study, TED Translators, and what research on TED Translators tells us about volunteer motivation.

The methodology section describes the study undertaken by the researchers, its design, methodology, participants, data collection tools

---

1   https://outreach.wikimedia.org/wiki/Education

and analytic method. The findings are then presented and discussed in relation to theories of learning in formal and informal contexts, and to how individuals conceptualize the learning they derive from different activities.

The contribution closes with some reflections on the significance of the investigation, its limitations, and ideas for further research in this area.

Theoretical Framework

Efforts have been made in translation education to replace traditional instructivist teaching methods, where the teacher prepares and serves the information for the student to "absorb", with pedagogies that are more in line with current research on learning and teaching (Orrego Carmona, 2013: Mitchell-Schuitevoerder, 2014, Kiraly, 2005, 2012). These are often project-based and driven by the need to keep up with technological change and its effects on translation. They are also typically anchored in a constructivist paradigm, based on the notion, crystallized in the metaphor of learning as participation (Sfard, 1998), that knowledge is subjective and constructed through participation in social and cultural settings.

Understanding learning as a situated experience, that is, one that arises from involvement and co-participation in a social context and with the community that generates and uses that learning (Lave and Wenger, 1991), underpins this socio-constructivist approach to translator education advocated by some scholars (Risku, 2010; Kiraly, 2012).

Situated learning focuses on participation in groups and situations that allow learners to become aware of, and eventually contribute to, the generation of knowledge relevant to them. Lave and Wenger (1991) called these "communities of practice", groups described by Wenger (1998) as sharing an interest in improving how they carry out an activity, whether they intentionally set out to learn or not. Learning in a community of practice is a dynamic concept linked to the relations within the community and to individuals' drive to becoming a full member of that community.

Research on communities of practice has evolved to explore how these interact with each other in full "landscapes of practice", a metaphor used to describe "a complex system of communities of practice and the boundaries between them" (Wenger-Trayner and Wenger-Trayner, 2015, p. 13). Professional occupations fit well into this description with their many communities of practitioners, researchers, managers, associations, educators, etc. that are linked in different ways to each profession. Landscapes of practice are dynamic and contested, as different communities compete for power and the control of resources or legitimate discourse and gatekeeping. Still, landscapes are diverse, and each practice has its own culture and its own knowledge, although "[w]hether the competence of a community is recognized as knowledge depends on its position in the politics of the landscape". (*ibid.*, p. 16). The practices developed by online volunteer translation communities are a good example of this, given the controversial nature of volunteer translation viewed by some scholars as a practice that reinforces the notion that translation can be free (O'Hagan, 2012) and hence is damaging to the profession.

The boundaries between practices and communities can cause tension and misunderstanding but can also function as triggers for reflection and innovation for those communities. More importantly these boundaries can be used in learning if educators can fathom the kinds of objects and activities that will help learners explore a boundary productively to trigger reflection on the practice of a community.

Beyond learning as participation, the metaphors of learning as becoming, and learning as expansion or transformation (Hager and Hodkinson, 2009) have also been associated with situated, authentic learning, and are applied to the process of generating knowledge whilst carrying out an activity, a process that transforms participants, activity and context, and creates new understandings that result in new ways of doing things (Engeström, 1987).

Similarly, in their theory of enactivism, Davis and Sumara (1997) propose that "cognition does not occur in minds or brains, but in the possibility for shared action" (p. 117). They consider thought as "dynamic and always in flux [...] always caught up in new learning" (p. 106) and therefore regard "student learning as dependent on, but not determined by, the teaching" (p. 115). Learning within the enactivist framework is seen as being "'occasioned' rather than 'caused' [...] dependent on, but not determined by, the teaching" (p. 115) and leading to transformation both in the agent (the learner) and the context. Building on Davis and

Sumara's work, Kiraly's research on translator education also presents learning as "the result of the complex interplay of processes and only incidentally and occasionally the direct result of teaching" (2015, p. 28).

Some consideration must be given here to defining informal learning, understood as "all forms of intentional or tacit learning in which we engage either individually or collectively without direct reliance on a teacher or externally organized curriculum" (Livingston, 2006, p. 204). Informal learning can occur in multiple contexts (Bekerman, Burbules and Silberman Keller, 2006) and has been considered fundamental for existing formal learning in educational establishments (Coffield, 2000).

Vavoula (2004) offers the following typology of learning (see Figure 1), distinguishing according to whether the goals and processes are determined by the teacher or the learner, or not determined at all. This investigation focuses on the intentional and unintentional learning derived from participation in an open online volunteer community.

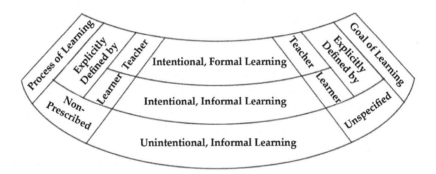

Figure 1. Typology of learning, based on the presence of, and control over, the object and the process of learning. Image from Vavoula (2004),

TED and TED Translators

TED stands for Technology, Entertainment and Design and "is a nonprofit devoted to spreading ideas, usually in the form of short, powerful talks".[2] The official talks are given in English at conferences organized by TED, where experts share their knowledge in an engaging

---

2   http://www.ted.com/about/our-organization

way. The short lectures are recorded, edited and published online by TED, making them accessible globally to a large audience.[3] Local TEDx events following the same format are organized around the world, and also recorded and published through the TED platform.

As a public engagement initiative, TED's enormous reach and popularity has been attributed to the successful harnessing of technology to reduce the gap between experts and the public. Recent studies using bibliometric and webometric indicators have concluded that TED appears to be "one of the most prominent science popularization initiatives in history" (Sugimoto and Thelwall, 2013, p. 673).

To a large extent, the reach and impact of TED Talks can be attributed to the contribution of its volunteers, around 16,000, who transcribe the talks and translate the subtitles into more than 100 languages. Subtitles are essential to make the content accessible to those with hearing impairments, and can further benefit the one billion worldwide for whom English is a second or foreign language (Graddol, 2000). Providing subtitles in multiple languages is central to achieving TED's aspiration to "[reach] out to the 4.5 billion people on the planet who don't speak English",[4] and making digital content available in multiple languages is key in promoting social inclusion (Helsper, 2008).

TED volunteers are the archetypal "prosumers" (Ritzer and Jurgenson, 2010) — consumers of content who also contribute to its production. Launched by TED in 2009 in response to user demand, TED Open Translation Project (TED OTP), later rebranded TED Translators, aimed at coordinating and facilitating the translation of subtitles by harnessing volunteers' enthusiasm. In that TED Translators easily fits Wenger's (1998) definition of a community of practice: it shares a very specific domain of interest, the translation of subtitles for TED talks; many of its members interact and support each other through the associated Facebook groups, local translatathon events, or by attending face-to-face translation workshops at the annual TEDGlobal conferences. As a result of such close interactions members have developed a well-defined

---

3   "In the fall of 2012, TED Talks celebrated its one billionth video view [...] TED Talks continue to be watched around the world, with an average of 17 new page views a second". https://www.ted.com/about/our-organization/history-of-ted

4   http://blog.ted.com/2009/05/13/ted_open_trans

shared practice and codified shared resources, such as guidelines made available through a wiki and video channels.

Volunteers' profile

There is no protocol for screening volunteers wishing to participate in the project. However, the skills shown in Figure 2 are a pre-requisite to participate as a translator or transcriber in TED Translators.

Language and subtitling skills:

- Volunteer translators should be fluently bilingual in both source and target languages.
- Volunteer transcribers should be fluent in the transcription language.
- Volunteer translators and transcribers should be knowledgeable of subtitling best practices.

Figure 2. Pre-requisite to participate as a translator or transcriber in TED Translators

Cámara (2014) reported on the profile of volunteers after placing her survey of participants (N=178) in the main Facebook TED Translators support group. The majority of respondents were aged 18–35, and the ratio of male to female was fairly balanced, except in the 18–25 segment, where there were twice as many men as women, and a high proportion of students, and in the 36–45 segment, where two thirds of respondents were female translators. A large number of professionals were working as translators, teachers, scientists, researchers, and engineers, or in the information sciences. The majority had some kind of academic qualification, and around a sixth were students. A third of respondents had professional translation skills, and three-quarters of all respondents had no qualification in subtitling before joining TED Translators. Amongst the quarter of respondents who claimed previous experience in subtitling, 86% had less than one year of experience in the field, and the majority had acquired that experience through other volunteering opportunities.

Volunteers' roles

Volunteers can undertake several tasks including transcription, translation, revision and final approval before publication. Transcribers work in the original language of the talk, creating the subtitles that translators use as the basis for generating subtitles in other languages. Anyone can become a transcriber or translator in TED Translators, but it is recommended that only experienced volunteers, those who have already translated or transcribed at least ninety minutes of talks, undertake the revision phase, which consists of checking the transcript or translation for linguistic and technical accuracy.

The final check and approval for publication of the translation or transcript is carried out by volunteers who have applied for and been selected to the role of Language Coordinators on account of their experience and willingness to commit further to the project. Language Coordinators have an additional mentoring role and provide support to less experienced translators through language-specific Facebook groups. Quality control is thus inbuilt into the workflow (O'Hagan, 2012) and valuable feedback and support is provided by reviewers and language coordinators to translators and transcribers, in an apprenticeship style model (Lave and Wenger, 1991).

Knowledge management

TED has recognized the need for knowledge management tools to support and facilitate the work of volunteers. From 2011, the community has developed its own wiki, OTPedia,[5] and a video tutorial channel, the TED Translators Learning Series, to collect and disseminate training material, style guides and best practice on all aspects of TED Translators work.[6] Language Coordinators play a major role in capturing and shaping best practice, and providing feedback and suggestions to improve workflows and technical aspects (including the subtitle editor provided by the open source audiovisual translation platform Amara).[7] There are also opportunities to meet at annual international workshops

---

5   http://translations.ted.org/wiki/Portal:Main
6   https://www.youtube.com/channel/UC6b3FWOn0YwVq0MHy0DtfBg
7   http://www.amara.org

where Language Coordinators consolidate and extend their work, and strengthen the community.

Research on TED Translators

Learning and practising subtitling and the possibility of receiving feedback from more experienced translators are some obvious attractions for volunteers. In one of only two studies to date on translators' motivations in TED Translators, Cámara's (2014) respondents reported three main drivers to volunteering in TED Translators (% who chose this answer):

- playing an active and interactive role in the expansion of the TED mission (75%).
- making the most of their free time while enjoying themselves (53%).
- acquiring subtitling skills and experiencing inter-cultural interactions in an informal learning context (53%).

In another study, Olohan (2013) analyzed the discourse of volunteers through eleven posts published in the TED Translators blog in which volunteers explain why they translate for TED Translators. Acknowledging the limitations of her work, and in particular the bias in the data — as the posts are published by TED Translators and therefore likely to have been chosen because they chime with the mission of the organization — she nevertheless concluded that drivers for participation could be grouped into six categories:

- contributing to the TED mission of enabling others to benefit from TED and the sharing of ideas;
- effecting social change and "changing the world";
- altruistic behavior and the satisfaction derived from it (the "warm glow");
- the desire to be part of a community and connect with others;
- enhancing learning and knowledge (although not of translation skills but of the content of the talks); and
- the "fun" and "excitement" derived from translating and understanding.

Both studies concluded that learning is part of what motivates TED Translators volunteers to take part in this activity. The research presented in this chapter set out to find out what participants perceive they learned from the experience and how they view this learning. The results of this investigation will hopefully contribute to an understanding of the way the practices of online informal learning communities can be adopted in formal learning environments.

Methodology

In this study we set out to answer two questions:

- What do students learn from their engagement with TED Translators, and how do they learn?
- What benefits can translation students and translation professionals derive from participation in TED Translators?

This research is grounded in a constructivist paradigm, based on a view of knowledge as embodied and constantly changing, as the individuals and the complex ecology of relations they are part of also change (Davis and Sumara, 1997).

Given that only few studies on online volunteer translation communities have been carried out to date, an exploratory, qualitative approach anchored in a constructivist paradigm and based on the examination of subjective experience is appropriate to gain a better understanding of how learning is experienced and perceived by participants.

Context and task

For this investigation a self-paced supported six-week activity,[8] subsequently shared as an Open Educational Resource, was designed and offered on a voluntary basis to a small group of Translation Studies graduates from a Spanish university. The tasks and supporting materials were posted in a dedicated, "private"[9] Facebook group, and the researchers provided individual support to participants through

---

8   The activity can be found at http://loro.open.ac.uk/4802
9   Membership and content available by invitation only. See "What are the privacy settings for groups?" https://www.facebook.com/help/220336891328465

the Facebook group, as they worked through the learning materials. These educational resources had been gathered from existing content (OTPedia and Learning Series videos) in a wrap-around learning design intended to promote learner autonomy and the efficient use of distributed resources. Participants were also encouraged to join the relevant Facebook TED Translators language groups for further support from regular TED Translators volunteers.

Both researchers are TED Translators volunteers (one a Language Coordinator since the role was established in 2011), and as such are aware that the interpretation of the findings may be colored by their insider status. Additionally, although their role in this study was that of facilitators and researchers, their status as academics in higher education institutions may have influenced the narrative constructions of participants, who had very recently finished their undergraduate studies (one participant was still a university student).

Participants

Participants were recruited by an English Lecturer at a Spanish university who leads a collaborative teaching innovation project. The self-selected group of students and former students participating in the study were given the opportunity to practice their English while acquiring translation, digital and online collaboration skills. Having been informed about the objectives and timeline for this project, six participants volunteered to take part in the activity, five recent graduates and an undergraduate. The group comprised six females and one male aged between eighteen and twenty-five, three of them based in Spain and three in the US. Four participants were still studying (one at undergraduate and three at postgraduate level), and two described themselves as professional translators, although indicating that they had not yet had experience as paid translators. Only one participant had some experience of translating subtitles, but not professionally. Out of the original six participants one female graduate participant dropped out early on in the study and five completed the task.

As the questionnaire revealed all participants showed high levels of familiarity with technology and social media both to seek and create information, and as effective tools to enhance their learning.

Data collection: instrument and procedure

As both participants and researchers were spread across four countries in two continents online methods of data collection were adopted. Participants were asked to fill in a questionnaire at the start of the activity to provide general demographic data and to determine their previous experience with textual and audio-visual translation, as well as their self-reported attitudes towards technology and learning.

Given the pressures on participants' time and the fact that they had already devoted a substantial amount of time to completing the tasks, conducting individual interviews at the end of the activity was unfeasible. For this reason, the investigators devised an asynchronous method of data collection, inspired by the tool known as narrative frame (Barkhuizen and Wette, 2008), a method that provides "guidance and support in terms of both the structure and content of what is to be written", and ensures "that the content will be more or less what is expected (and required to address the research aims) and that it will be delivered in narrative form" (p. 376).

In this case, three sets of questions, encouraging a response in the form of a structured textual narrative, were posted in the Facebook group. Additional feedback was also requested in personal emails to allow individual participants to make further comments privately.

The three sets of questions, posted several days apart, addressed: 1) feedback on the activity itself, particularly views on how feasible it was to carry out the different tasks independently; 2) assessing participants' perceptions on what they had learnt; and 3) their views regarding the role of volunteer translation in relation to translator education and the practice of professional translation. The Findings and Discussion section is based on the last two groups of questions.

Analytic method

Participants' contributions to the final discussion were assembled into a textual corpus and analyzed thematically. Thematic analysis focuses on pinpointing, examining, and recording patterns (or "themes") within data. Themes are patterns across data sets that are important to the description of a phenomenon and are associated to a specific research question. Braun and Clarke (2006) describe this methodology as a two-step process: a first assessment of the data on a semantic level, that is, at the explicit or surface level of the information, followed by the identification of latent themes, "the underlying ideas, assumptions, and conceptualizations — and ideologies" (p. 84), their interpretation and their further investigation.

Thus a thematic analysis requires that the researchers identify themes that are either mentioned by several participants or are substantially developed by a single participant. Determining what is significant and constitutes a theme is one of the key challenges of the process, as researchers will inevitably bring their own agendas and biases to the analysis. In this case, both authors carried out the thematic analysis independently, and agreed the main themes within each set of questions. The following section contains the analysis and interpretation of the data illustrating the main themes identified with the most relevant quotes, and relating back the themes to the research questions and the literature.

Findings and Discussion

Participants were asked about their experience of the systems, procedures and instructions they used to complete the tasks. Most participants found the instructions clear and easy to follow, and reported that the experience of taking part in the activity had been good. Almost all of them also commented on how user-friendly the subtitle editor was, and how helpful they found the videos in preparing them to tackle the subtitling task. Two of them, however, did find the creation of an account difficult, and for one of them the technical issues marred the whole experience, leading to feelings of frustration:

> The video did not help me [...] I tried over and over again, but I could not register. I contacted the Support Desk, and I asked for help in this Facebook group. [...] I spent more time trying to fix them [the registration problems] than actually translating the task. [...] the experience wasn't good and is still being confusing and frustrating. (P2)[10]

---

10 Here and hereafter each quote is attribute to a participant number in the study.

Learning

The second set of questions probed participants' learning experiences, and their perceptions of what it was that they had learnt through their participation in this activity.

The skill of subtitling emerged strongly as the most easily recognized and fundamental aspect of the learning gained through participation in the activity. With one exception, this was the first subtitling task participants had ever attempted, and comments were overwhelmingly positive, with participants describing subtitling as "interesting" and "enjoyable". Still, the complexity of the task was acknowledged, with different aspects being identified, such as the difficulty in compressing text, regarded as "an interesting challenge that tested my imagination and resourcefulness" (P3), synchronizing the subtitles, "I think that was the part I enjoyed the most and Amara is a really great software for that" (P4), and "the importance of subtitling guidelines with regard to subtitle duration, line-breaking, etc". (P2). The experience also resulted in a new critical appreciation for the work involved in subtitling: "Having seen the work that goes behind good subtitles, I do now appreciate them more and I criticize them more every time I see bad ones" (P3).

It is interesting to note that the popular concept of learning as the acquisition of skills, what Hager and Hodkinson (2009) call the skills lens[11] dominates participants' understanding of learning, a stance congruent with prevalent translation training models based on competences (PACTE, 2005; EMT, 2009).

Joining a community of practice and engaging in a dialogue with more experienced participants was valued, and participants commented on the benefits of having their work checked by more experienced translators and of engaging in a dialogue with them. For instance: "Knowing that my subtitles would be proofread by a professional[12] translator before being published gave me confidence" (P2), and,

---

11   Hager and Hodkinson (2009) identify four conceptual lenses, or ways of understanding learning: the propositional learning lens, the skill learning lens, the learning through participation in human practices lens and the learning as transformation or reconstruction lens.

12   Although the participant uses the word "professional", the review is undertaken by a more experienced volunteer translator, who is not necessarily a professional translator (understood as one who translates for payment and commercially).

"Best part has been the exchange of opinions with my reviewer and proofreader" (P5).

However, for one participant there were conflicting pressures between wanting to do well in order to receive praise from the reviewer, and being more relaxed about accuracy in the knowledge that quality was not entirely her responsibility:

> ... the fact that a proofreader is going to check your translation releases some of the pressure of translating. It is weird, if you do not have a proofreader you try to do it well because you don't want anything with mistakes published with your name on it. (P3)

On the one hand, the value of the quality control system inbuilt into the TED Translators workflows (O'Hagan, 2012) is acknowledged, but on the other hand, the limitations imposed by the rules and practices of the community are sometimes resented, as novice participants have not been part of their generation. This is the case with the requirement to use Global Spanish[13] (referred to as "neutral Spanish" in the quote below), which caused most of the errors in participants' work. The Spanish TED Translators community agreed that communication should be favored over the claims of any particular Spanish variety, and guidelines were drawn to that effect. Several participants ignored these guidelines and translated into Peninsular Spanish (choosing *"vosotros"* instead of the more widely used *"ustedes"*), causing reviewers to send back translations for amendment.

Still, disagreements with reviewers are not uncommon, and the system is set up to facilitate knowledge creation through dialogue between translator and reviewer, using the comments and personal message features in the platform as seen in this example of a participant challenging the reviewer's decisions: "I've written [to] him today about the last changes because I don't agree 100% and the translation seems to be already 'published'" (P5).

Finally, the value of incidental learning was also mentioned, alongside the learning of different topics that took place while translating or whilst

---

13   Global Spanish is understood in the TED Translators community as "that which seeks unity in diversity", by favoring communication and intelligibility, and denying the right of speakers of any variety of Spanish to impose their variety above others http://translations.ted.org/wiki/Spanish

watching the videos to select one for translation, as exemplified by this comment on public speaking from one of the participants: "I realized how important is to control the way you talk when you do it in public specially controlling the pace and pauses" (P3).

Motivation and Benefits

The last set of questions asked participants to identify the advantages that engaging in this online volunteering activity might have for students of translation and for professional translators. Even though the question was phrased in positive terms, that is, participants were not asked to identify the disadvantages, it is worth noting the long list of advantages that were mentioned for students in particular, and the almost entire absence of disadvantages.

Developing translation skills and a first taste of subtitling as well as experiencing the pressures of professional translation were mentioned as positive outcomes of the activity. Exploring the content of the videos was also a positive for participants, allowing them to discover new fields, and to "learn about the world, hear different perspectives and events they never heard of, and hopefully open their minds a little bit more" (P3). Being able to learn without having to read was also mentioned as an advantage of continuing with this activity.

A valued and motivational aspect of contributing to TED Translators was the fact that the students' work would be reaching a global audience, for example:

- It was very motivating and rewarding the fact of knowing that my translation would be published and read by a great number of users world-wide (P2).
- Because we just finished our translation degree (some of us) and being given the opportunity to develop our skills in such an world-wide context is encouraging and exciting (P4).

Given their short experience in the field of translation, it appeared to be harder for participants to name possible advantages of contributing to TED Translators for professional translators — who in Cámara's (2014) survey of TED Translators volunteers accounted for 10% of respondents. Having a "relevant social role" (P2), broadening their knowledge and making "contacts that may help them with their professional life"

(P3) were the only benefits mentioned. However, one participant had strong views on the undesirability of encouraging the perception that translation is something that is done for free, noting that "the same way the guy who sets up the microphone gets paid, the translator should as well" (P3). In that respect, her views are aligned with some in the profession who worry that the existence of online volunteer translation legitimizes the notion of free translation (O'Hagan, 2012)

There were also polarized views on the desirability of volunteering as a translator. Some highlighted the creation of civic value (Shirky, 2010) made through online volunteering, and the need for translation to transcend linguistic barriers (Beaven, Comas-Quinn, Hauck, de los Arcos and Lewis, 2013) to make knowledge more accessible globally:

- Within the globalization era we are living in, it is important to have all the information available and to spread it in a comprehensible way (P4).

- I believe that volunteering can have a positive impact on the community (P2).

However, one participant likened volunteering to internships as an unavoidable form of exploitation most graduates will experience before they can establish themselves professionally.

> I've learned that I don't want to translate for free anymore even if it's a non-profit organization. [...] This is the second time I volunteer as a translator and I guess it's something we all go through, in other fields they get bad paid internships with which they have to live, as translators we get nothing but we can live anywhere and do it on our free time; in both cases it adds up to our resume. However, I think volunteer translation is devaluating our already highly devaluated profession [...] (P3).

Conclusion

This investigation has, in our view, generated useful insights into the opportunities and challenges of developing and implementing a Translation learning activity using an open online community, TED Translators. From our point of view as educators we have gained a better understanding of how some learners may perceive an activity based on volunteering negatively, in a context where some Translation scholars and professionals see volunteer translation as a threat to the profession. Conversely, feedback from participants "suggests that engaging in an authentic task and having their work published to the world is highly motivating, as is the opportunity of learning from a community of more experienced translators. Several also appreciated the civic value created by their work and their contribution to transcending linguistic barriers to make knowledge available more widely. On balance, there are more positive aspects in participants' feedback, and this leads us to believe that it is worth persisting in developing an open pedagogy (Wiley, 2013) using online volunteer translation communities and open tools. However, there are challenges inherent in combining informal and formal learning contexts, such as the ethics of mandating students to participate in volunteering activities or create open content (Martínez-Arboleda, 2014).

Beyond the learning derived from the experience, participants' feedback will also be used to improve systems and guidelines, reflecting the expansive learning model where shared action leads to changes in activity, agents, context and knowledge. The registration process in the subtitling platform is atypical and confused some participants, in spite of the comprehensive instructions, video tutorial, etc. This has an implication for learning design and the development of support and learning materials, given that learners are likely to expect technology to behave in the way they are used to from experience, rather than as described in the instructions. Robust technical support needs to be in place to ensure that technical problems do not mar the learners' experiences.

For the authors and for other Translation educators, the feedback received from participants will contribute to improve further iterations of this activity, for example, in ensuring that more guidance is given on how to establish a dialogue with reviewers. For Spanish, in particular, the need to use Global Spanish needs to be highlighted, and some discussion and critical engagement with this notion before the task could help learners understand the importance of this decision. A similar approach could be used to explore the place of volunteer translation in the landscape of practice, and its potential for translator education.

There are limitations in a study that has engaged a very small number of participants in a new type of learning activity that capitalizes on an existing online community of practice and its learning resources. However, as a means of exploring how education can harness informal learning systems, existing online communities and open tools, this project has helped us understand some of the challenges as well as the benefits it can bring to learners. It has also reinforced our belief that further research is needed on the intersection between formal and informal learning where using open tools and practices can provide learners with authentic, situated learning opportunities that make a contribution to society.

References

Barkhuizen, G. and Wette, R. (2008), Narrative Frames for Investigating the Experiences of Language Teachers, *System*, 36, pp. 372–387, http://dx.doi.org/10.1016/j.system.2008.02.002

Beaven, T., Comas-Quinn, A., Hauck, M., de los Arcos, B. and Lewis, T. (2013), The Open Translation MOOC: Creating Online Communities to Transcend Linguistic Barriers, *Journal of Interactive Media in Education*, 3 (p. Art. 18), http://jime.open.ac.uk/jime/article/view/2013-18

Beetham, H., Falconer, I., McGill, L. and Littlejohn, A. (2012), JISC Open Practices: Briefing Paper, https://oersynth.pbworks.com/w/page/51668352/OpenPracticesBriefing

Bekerman, Z., Burbules, N. C. and Silberman Keller, D. (2006), *Learning in Places — The Informal Education Reader*, New York: Peter Lang, http://dx.doi.org/10.1111/j.1548-1492.2010.01070.x

Braun, V. and Clarke, V. (2006), Using Thematic Analysis in Psychology, *Qualitative Research in Psychology*, 3(2), pp. 77–101, http://dx.doi.org/10.1191/1478088706qp063oa

Cámara de la Fuente, L. (2014), Multilingual Crowdsourcing Motivation on Global Social Media, Case Study: TED OTP, *Sendebar*, 25, pp. 197–218.

Coffield, F. (2000), *The Necessity of Informal Learning*, Bristol: The Policy Press.

Davis, B. and Sumara, D. (1997), Cognition, Complexity, and Teacher Education, *Harvard Educational Review*, 67(1), pp. 105–125, http://dx.doi.org/10.17763/haer.67.1.160w00j113t78042

EMT Expert Group (2009), Competences for Professional Translators, Experts in Multilingual and Multimedia Communication.

Engeström, Y. (1987), *Learning by Expanding: An Activity-Theoretical Approach to Developmental Research*, Helsinki: Orienta-Konsultit.

Graddol, D. (2011), *The Future of English?*, The British Council, https://www.teachingenglish.org.uk/article/future-english

Hager, P. and Hodkinson, P. (2009), Moving Beyond the Metaphor of Transfer of Learning, *British Educational Research Journal*, 35(4), pp. 619–638.

Helsper, E. (2008), *Digital Inclusion: An Analysis of Social Disadvantage and the Information Society*, London: Oxford Internet Institute, http://dx.doi.org/10.1080/01411920802642371

Kiraly, D. (2005), Project-Based Learning: A Case for Situated Translation, *Meta*, 50(4), pp. 1098–1111, http://dx.doi.org/10.7202/012063ar

Kiraly, D. (2012), Growing a Project-Based Translation Pedagogy: A Fractal Perspective. *Meta*, 57(1), pp. 82–95.

Kiraly, D. (2015), Occasioning Translator Competence, *Translation and Interpreting Studies*, 10(1), pp. 8–32.

Lave, J. and Wenger, E. (1991), *Situated Learning: Legitimate Peripheral Participation*, Cambridge: Cambridge University Press, http://dx.doi.org/10.1017/cbo 9780511815355

Livingston, D. (2006), Informal Learning: Conceptual Distinctions and Preliminary Findings, in Bekerman, Z., Burbules, N. C. and Silberman-Keller, D. (Eds.), *Learning in Places: The Informal Education Reader*, New York: Peter Lang.

Martínez-Arboleda, A. (2014), *The Ethics of Student Digital Publication*, Presentation given at the OER14 Conference, 29 April 2014, University of Newcastle, UK, https://oer14.oerconf.org/archive/14/oer14/92/view/index. html

Mitchell-Schuitevoerder, R. (2014), *A Project-Based Syllabus Design Innovative Pedagogy in Translation Studies*, PhD Thesis, Durham University, http:// etheses.dur.ac.uk/10830/1/R.E.H.Mitchell-Schuitevoerder_thesis_2014. pdf?DDD36+

O'Hagan, M. (2012), From Fan Translation to Crowdsourcing: Consequences of Web 2.0 Empowerment in Audiovisual Translation, in A. Ramael, P. Orero and M. Carroll (Eds.), *Audiovisual Translation and Media Accessibility at the Crossroads*, pp. 25–41, Amsterdam, NY: Rodopi.

Olohan, M. (2014), Why do you Translate? Motivation to Volunteer and TED Translation, *Translation Studies*, 7(1), pp. 17–33, http://dx.doi.org/10.1080/14 781700.2013.781952

Orrego Carmona, D. (2015), Using Non-Professional Subtitling Platforms for Translator Training, *Rivista internazionale di tecnica della traduzione*, 15, pp. 129–144.

PACTE (2005), Investigating Translation Competence: Conceptual and Methodological Issues, *Meta*, 50(2), pp. 609–619, http://dx.doi. org/10.7202/011004ar

Risku, H. (2010), A Cognitive Scientific View on Technical Communication and Translation. Do Embodiment and Situatedness Really Make a Difference?, *Target*, 22(1), pp. 94–111, http://dx.doi.org/10.1075/target.22.1.06ris

Ritzer, G. and Jurgenson, N. (2010), Production, Consumption, Prosumption: The Nature of Capitalism in the Age of the Digital "Prosumer", *Journal of Consumer Culture*, 10(1), pp. 13–36, http://dx.doi.org/10.1177/1469540509354673

Sfard, A. (1998), On Two Metaphors for Learning and the Dangers of Choosing Just One, *Educational Researcher*, 27(2), pp. 4–13, http://dx.doi. org/10.3102/0013189x027002004

Shirky, C. (2010), *Cognitive Surplus. Creativity and Generosity in a Connected Age*, London: Penguin.

Sugimoto C. R. and Thelwall M. (2013), Scholars on Soap Boxes: Science Communication and Dissemination in TED Videos, *Journal of the American Society for Information Science and Technology*, 64(4), http://dx.doi.org/10.1002/asi.22764

Tapscott, D. and Williams A. D. (2008), *Wikinomics. How Mass Collaboration Changes Everything*, London: Atlantic Books.

Vavoula, G. (2004), *KLeOS: A Knowledge and Learning Organisation System in Support of Lifelong Learning*, PhD Thesis, University of Birmingham, UK, http://www2.le.ac.uk/departments/museumstudies/about-the-school/people/dr-giasemi-vavoula/Publications/downloads/publicationpreprints/Thesis-GVavoula.pdf

Wenger, E. (1998), *Communities of Practice: Learning, Meaning and Identity*, Cambridge: Cambridge University Press.

Wenger-Trayner, E. and Wenger-Trayner, B. (2015), Learning in a Landscape of Practice: A Framework, in E. Wenger-Trayner, M., Fenton-O'Creevy, S., Hutchinson, C., Kubiac and B. Wenger-Trayner (Eds.), *Learning in Landscapes of Practice: Boundaries, Identity, and Knowledgeability in Practice-based Learning*, pp. 13–29, London: Routledge.

Wiley, D. (2013), *What is Open Pedagogy?*, http://opencontent.org/blog/archives/2975

6. Educational Policy and Open Educational Practice in Australian Higher Education

Adrian Stagg and Carina Bossu

Open Educational Policy has become increasingly the subject of government attention globally, primarily with a focus on reducing educational costs for tax payers. Parallel to, yet rarely convergent with, these initiatives is an espoused sector-wide commitment to broadening participation in higher education, especially for students of low socio-economic backgrounds. Criticism of both open education and social inclusion policy highlights a deficiency in both the metrics used by policy-makers and the maturity of conceptual understanding applied to both notions. This chapter explores the possibilities afforded to social inclusion in universities by open education, and the case for an integrated approach to educational policy that recognizes the impact of a multi-causal foundation on the broader educational ecosystem.

http://dx.doi.org/10.11647/OBP.0103.06

Introduction

The scope and extent of the relationship between Open Educational Practice (OEP) and national educational policy has been subject to varying degrees of interest internationally. Whilst countries such as the UK, the US and Canada have supported open education through a range of policy initiatives (McKerlich, Ives, and McGreal, 2013), Australia lacks a consolidated approach for higher education. Recent Australian policy is underpinned by a need to build social capacity, widen participation and inclusion, and to create an educational system that is internationally competitive — goals that align ideologically with not only democratic society but also open educational systems. These open systems recognize a role in catalyzing change to meet the future demands on tertiary education foreshadowed by current trends. Despite this alignment, open educational practice has yet to be explicitly recognized in Australian educational policy due to governmental predisposition to focus on open research and open access to government information and research.

This contribution explores the conceptual underpinnings of educational systems in a democratic nation and how open educational practice supports the development of learners who are societally participative, collaborative and critical consumers of information. The dialogue focuses on the intersection of policy and social inclusion in higher education and further explores how OEP actively contributes to goals, but tempers this with the understanding that the inherent measurements for social groups are fundamentally flawed. Secondly, it recognizes that OEP is only one component in a much-needed holistic and multi-causal approach to describing Australian higher education.

Whilst an explicit integration of Australian policy and an awareness of the affordances of open education has yet to occur, foundational research has resulted in a Feasibility Protocol for higher education that explores multi-level policy implications for open education systems (Bossu, Bull and Brown, 2015). An examination of the protocol yields policy recommendations that — if pursued — can support Australian higher education to be an internationally-competitive offering founded in the principles of a democratic nation.

Defining Open Education in Context

James and Bossu (2014, p. 81) assert that open education is not a new term as it was adopted by open universities approximately 100 years ago to represent "learning "anywhere, anytime", open entry and [alternative] exit points, which were the foundations of open universities and their correspondence and distance education models". Currently, there are a wide range of open approaches and movements to "open up" education. These approaches include not only OER and OEP, but also open access (research and data), open learning design, open technologies, open policies, open governance and so forth. The implicit philosophy of open education is to reduce barriers to increase access to education. For the purpose of this chapter, open education will be used as a broad concept in which all the above will be included. For the same outcome of conceptual clarity, "open education systems" is used to describe an educational institution that authentically practices openness in not only educational terms, but in administrative, transactional, and strategic actions. A systemic adoption of open practice, therefore is a complex, multi-faceted proposition. This contribution, however, confines the scope to the relationship between open education and national educational policy.

An explicit understanding of the complexity of the OEP adoption makes this a "problematic space", compounded by a lack of evidence, especially in learning design literature. As such, it currently lacks a foundational research-led evidence base at the practitioner level and a theoretical under-pinning. Additionally, OER research has been criticized for a broad inability to generalize beyond the immediate context of individual studies. This hampers the Open Educational Resources (OER) community as there are practical issues (such as staff development, organizational policy, and business models) that need to be concurrently addressed. Furthermore, awareness of OER and issues surrounding locating, evaluating, repurposing and attributing still require attention. One critique (Glennie, Harley, Butcher, and van Wyk, 2012) points to a lack of "critical perspective", offering the explanation that it is "perhaps unsurprising when the concept of OER presents itself as such a self-evident social "good" (p. 7).

This "self-evident good" manifests in research that suggests the use of OER can allow previously disadvantaged students to engage with degree programs by lowering educational costs, reduce costs for course development, improve global-level collaboration in teaching and learning, make teaching resources readily available in a range of languages, raise educational resource quality, and act as a further catalyst for learner-centred pedagogy.

These goals seem admirable, but the weakness in open rhetoric is practicality (or a lack thereof). There is evidence to also suggest that OEP is, after ten years, neither widespread, nor well-known, and that learner and educator use of OER is far from mainstream practice (Conole, 2013).

Educational Policy and the Democratic Nation

Post-industrial educational systems need to acknowledge the macro-economic environment into which graduates must enter, and thus provide students with competitive skills for the workforce (especially life-long and life-wide learning), opportunities for social mobility, and the ability to effect social change (Chesters and Watson, 2013). As the global demand for university credentialing has (and continues to) grow at a rapid rate, current educational systems will need to change to meet the demand. Whilst the number of domestic student places available continues to grow in Australia, the higher education sector has historically sought to actively grow their international cohorts based on an inverse relationship with the value of the Australian dollar. The international demand for higher education, especially in regions with high economic growth (such as India) is even greater. The paradox faced by universities is that whilst demand continues to rise, the barriers to successfully engaging with tertiary education have not lowered (Chesters, 2015).

The notion of social inclusion has been of interest to Australian higher education for decades, and is underpinned by the conceptual understanding of the role of education in a western democracy. John Dewey (1916, p. 87) held that democracy is "characterised by a widening of the area of shared concerns and the liberation of a greater diversity of personal capacities". Democracy is therefore more than simply building a participatory society, but rather constructing a society with decision-making based on a foundation of justice that is demonstrated by a commitment to fairness, freedom, and respect (Olsen, Codd, and O'Neill, 2004).

"Social justice" is at the heart of university policy and priorities (as a reflection of national priorities) when the focus is on social inclusion, student equity and diversity, and student support. If one takes a whole-of-life perspective of a university education then it becomes "the way in which citizens are or should be empowered to influence the education that in turn shapes the political values, attitudes, and modes of behavior of future citizens" (Gutmann, 1987, p. 14). Gutmann's point on empowerment underscores that a democratic society should not be reduced to a rule of majority. Therefore, the attitudes and priorities of the state need to be a collective expression of the society it represents (Olssen, 2012, p. 264), having a clear reciprocal relationship with the nation's educational systems.

The Challenge of Inclusion

Whilst it has already been noted that international demand for higher education has increased, the lack of equity in gender, socio-cultural and socio-economic representation continues. Internationally, governments have set targets (as has Australia) through mechanisms, studies and reports such as A Fair Chance for All (Department of Employment, Education and Training, 1990) and the Bradley Report (Bradley, Noonan, Nugent, and Scales, 2008) and is reflected in the more recent Keep It Clever (Universities Australia, 2015) statement. The evidence base for the focus on target setting for various groups differs as much by country as do the targets set. Australia has made progress increasing university admission, retention, and progression for many under-represented groups, but widening access for students from rural and remote communities and low socio-economic backgrounds remains "one of the persistent and seemingly intractable equity issues in Australia" (James, 2012, p. 85).

To provide context and clarity for these terms, it is necessary to articulate the measures and indices used by the Australian Bureau of Statistics (ABS) to determine whether a student is of low socio-economic status (SES), or from a rural or remote background. The Australian definition of a low socio-economic status is reliant on a combination of four indices that examine socio-economic advantage and disadvantage, education and occupation, and economic resources based on five-yearly cycles of national census data (ABS, 2013).

These measures are not without criticism. A review of these indices conducted by Universities Australia (2008) recommended major improvements to the instrument, classification, and rigor of the data that supported this index. In particular, it highlighted that a key factor of the classification was the postcode of each student's origin (not their current residence) and that classifications were predicated on parental occupation rather than educational attainment. It also noted that the current data collection methods were inadequately provided, with evidence of causal factors influencing behaviors and attitudes to education among those categorized as low socio-economic status students.

Furthermore, there is little empirical evidence to suggest that providing access to education alone addresses social inclusion, social integration, or social mobility; rather existing studies describe a complex situation which requires a "multi-causal understanding of the factors underlying under-representation" (James, 2012, p. 99). A more mature and holistic view of the student ecology is required; one that is not solely guided by government targets at predetermined deadlines.

The available data shows that students from a low socio-economic background enrolled in university education rose from 41,457 to 70,598 between 2001 and 2014; this segment now represent 17.5% of the total student population, an increase of only 1.29% (Australian Department of Education and Training, 2015). This data is even more striking if we consider that the total number of "freshers", or first-year students, has increased by 63% over the same years. As a segment of the total number of domestic enrolments over the same period of time, the number of students of low-socioeconomic status has increased from 16.4% (2001) to 16.53% (2014).

As a percentage of total enrolled higher education students, regional student representation has risen from 15.4% (2001) to 19.3% in 2014 (*ibid.*), whilst remote students decreased from 1.3% (2001) to 0.95% (2014). Commencing remote students now comprise only 1.08% of commencing students (2014), decreasing from 1.5% in 2001.

The outcomes of widening participation across Australian society aim to lead to greater levels of social integration and social mobility, and so has both the aforementioned justice-based democracy approach, but also has national economic benefits. As such, it can potentially enable the dual outcome of economic growth and civic cohesion (Giddons, 2000). Across the Australian higher education landscape, though, institutions have diverse localized views of "social justice". Whilst a "focus on social justice may be explicit in many universities' missions (whether through implicit practice, or overt policy), the scope of initiatives will vary. The definition of "social justice" through higher education of most interest to open education practitioners, however, is "that the principle of individual social justice [means] access to higher education and success in higher education should not be determined by class, ethnicity, geographical location or other personal characteristics" (Universities Australia, 2008).

Australia has the challenge of widening participation in higher education whilst both domestic and international enrolments experience growth. The sustainability of current educational practices and systems are therefore questionable. Internationally, on-campus higher education systems will be unable to meet the demands of university placements.

Additionally, the reality is that higher education reform is more often a stratified social segregation based on university placements exacerbated by the competitive nature of university student numbers (James, 2012). Students compete to attend those universities whose credentials are most valued in the work marketplace, whilst universities compete for the students whose future achievements will reflect well on the *alma mater*. The commercial nature of the higher education sector and the ideological and philosophical underpinnings of the "university education" are apparently at cross-purposes in terms of addressing the issue of social inclusion.

Open Education, Democracy, and Social Inclusion

Current open education systems have not only had a role in widening participation as they had previously, but also a role in lowering the costs of education, providing opportunities for raising the quality of learning and teaching, and aligning with sustainable education systems. The open education movement is ideologically aligned with the notions of democracy and social inclusion discussed previously. Potentially, Open Educational Practice could reduce the costs of higher education (especially in the provision and purchase of educational resources such as textbooks), provide opportunities for cross-institutional collaboration and peer-review of teaching materials (and a possible increase in the quality of university courses), and provide access to low- or no-cost materials that will be still be accessible to students post-graduation (unlike subscribed databases, and closed journal and data sets) (D'Antoni, 2008).

However, as resources and teacher-focused approach (sometimes exemplified by the "textbook as course" educational design) are still pervasive in the Australian higher education sector, some universities see the teaching resources — rather than the teaching presence — as the "competitive advantage". This perceived advantage is indicative of a commercialized world view of some educational institutions in Australia and a predisposition to value artefacts of teaching as tangible proof that learning is occurring.

Like social inclusion, though, setting targets for the adoption of open resources (such as percentage of open texts, or an "open first" institutional policy) rarely examines the attainment of educational and societal outcomes. There are further claims of cost-savings in reusing open content, but little empirical evidence has been found. Whilst there are *potential savings* for students demonstrated by open textbook adoption, these figures are predicated on the notion that every student in a course purchases the set text — which evidence dispels to a great extent (Senack, 2014).

In addition, Open Educational Practice requires a more rigorous evidence base to inform policy makers. In the current environment, open educational policy is hampered by a lack of awareness and evidence— which could result in an inconvenient and fruitless partnering between evidence-poor statistics and a problematic, emerging open education system. If these issues could be addressed concurrently, however, the intermingling of research-informed, empirically based decision making and national educational policy could be a catalyst for change in Australian higher education that is able to purposefully meet the demand for education in the future.

Rather, Open Educational Practice becomes one mechanism woven into the institutional ecology. It needs to align with, support, and enable institutional priorities through a mature symbiotic relationship with institutional policy that recognizes, rewards, and influences local learning and teaching culture. However, the awareness and integration of open education and open educational practices in Australia have yet to reach a level where they can effectively provide an evidence-base for national policy makers. Despite the lack of awareness and support for evidence-based research, there have been policy developments directly and indirectly related to open education in Australia. In the following section, we attempt to discuss some of these developments and their potential impact on open practices.

Open Policy: The Australian Experience

As with other developed countries such as the UK, US, Canada and some European countries, the Australian government has been investing in open access policies since 1998 through programs and initiatives designed to raise awareness, build infrastructure, metadata standards and guidelines. A more recent government initiative is the Australian National Data Service (ANDS, 2014) which was created in 2008 and is currently "the major government funded initiative to provide the infrastructure necessary to support an open data environment". ANDS is a large database containing research resources from educational and research institutions in Australia. One of the aims of ANDS is to create an Australian Research Data Commons where research information, including data and researchers' contact details, can be easily accessible to all. These and other programs have played an important role in making open access policies successful in higher education in Australia. Today, most Australian universities have an open access repository where research data and outputs from government funded projects are made available, typically using open licenses, including Creative Commons licenses, for other researchers to use and re-use (Picasso and Phelan, 2014). In addition, major research funding bodies have also responded positively to the government position on open access and have encouraged these practices through their own regulations (*ibid.*).

Still following global trends, the Australian government itself has implemented some open policies in order to make government documents available to the public under an open license, to increase transparency, and as a support for openness through informing and engaging the public with the government in a diverse range of activities (Bossu, 2016). It is interesting to note that educational policies that consider open education seems to be taken more seriously at state levels. For example, in Victoria, the Department of Education and Early Childhood Development is increasingly applying licenses to educational content with a focus on OER. The government of South Australia's Department for Education has gradually been developing resources that will be distributed under Creative Commons Attribution Non-Commercial (CC-BY-NC) licenses, and Creative Commons Attribution Share-Alike (CC-BY-SA) licenses.[1] The Western Australian Department of Education has been encouraging teachers to find and use OER through their preferred search engines, and is considering applying open licenses to materials developed with public funds (Butcher and Hoosen, 2012). Despite the fact that these open policies and initiatives at federal and state levels are only in their initial phases and not widespread, and some are also not directly related to education, they certainly demonstrate the government's commitment to transparency, sharing of information, and open access to publicly funded resources. This commitment could be translated into encouragement to other publicly funded organizations, such as higher education institutions, to follow.

However, the lack of a dedicated government policy or regulation that clearly supports the adoption of open education and practices in higher education in the country has not stopped some Australian universities from getting involved in the open education movement that is gaining momentum around the world. In the last decade, advocates, practitioners and their institutions have sought funds and opportunities to undertake projects, develop national and international collaborations, conduct research, and make policy recommendations at national and institutional levels so that the open education movement in Australia can advance. These efforts seem to have been realized as several Australian universities are having their intellectual property policies currently

---

1   http://creativecommons.org.au/learn/licences

being reviewed or re-developed. Other institutions have encouraged the adoption of open education through supporting documentation, such as university strategic plans or teaching performance reviews (Bossu, 2016).

The growing interest of Australian universities to develop new institutional open policies or review existing ones to include reference and elements of open education is evident in more recent studies conducted on the adoption of open educational resources across the Australian higher education system (Bossu, 2016). These studies have shown that not only are universities' intellectual property policies being revised, but also that open education is an active element of many current universities' strategic plans. One example of such a development is the Technology Enhanced Learning and Teaching White Paper 2014–18, developed by the University of Tasmania.[2] It was through this White Paper that the conceptualization and dialogue on how the University might start incorporating and implementing open education within its mainstream activities began. This was the first of a series of documents that recognized the University's willingness to engage in open education. Likewise, the University of Southern Queensland began a process of annual grants from 2015 that support, recognize, and fund open educational initiatives.[3] These include open textbooks, open courses, open technical approaches to collaborative resource authoring and open learning experiences that support the transition of students to the tertiary environment. These grants have the tri-fold purpose of raising awareness, building staff capacity, and providing an evidence base for institutional policy (Partridge and Stagg, 2016).

The development of such institutional policies has major implications for open practitioners. Firstly, research has demonstrated that Australian practitioners believe that institutional open policies could play an important role in promoting the effective use and adoption of open education (Bossu *et al.*, 2014a). In addition, by including open education within institutional strategies, practitioners would feel secured and

---

2   http://www.teaching-learning.utas.edu.au/__data/assets/pdf_file/0003/439014/ Technology-Enhanced-Learning-and-Teaching-White-Paper_Background-papers-Academic-Senate-15-November-2013.pdf

3   http://www.usq.edu.au/learning-teaching/excellence/2016landtgrants/opened

comfortable in getting actively engaged with these activities instead of being concerned and overwhelmed regarding additional open education activities. Practitioners also believe that institutions should invest and develop mechanisms to raise awareness and understanding regarding open licenses, intellectual property and quality assurance issues. Most importantly, institutions need to formally recognize and promote individuals' and group engagement with open education (Bossu *et al.*, 2014a). Such open policies have the potential to reconnect practitioners who often feel the divide between policy and practice, exacerbated by a feeling that policy makers rarely have the time to invest in gaining in-depth knowledge of the issue or topic (Crosnoe, 2012). The two-way relationship between policy and research is of particular interest to the Australian political landscape due to its emergent nature and the potential for establishing an empirical evidence base for policy makers and practitioners alike.

The Feasibility Protocol

As discussed previously, in despite of the limited direct developments in educational policy for open education, some of the opportunities and benefits of open education have been recognized by the Australian government through investments in open access and open government. However, it was only in 2010, almost ten years after open education — mostly through OER — emerged in other parts of the world (i.e. MIT Open Courseware Consortium in 2001), that it started getting some popularity in higher education in Australia. It was during this period that the Australian Government Office for Learning and Teaching (OLT), funded a two-year research project to investigate the adoption, use and management of open educational resources in Australian higher education. This was an important project for the progress of OER in Australia because it represented the recognition by the Australian government (through the OLT) that investigation in this new and underexplored field needed to be conducted in Australia. It was also a great opportunity for the researchers involved in this project to uncover the state of play about OER across the country.

The project findings were based on an online survey distributed to a wide group of stakeholders across the higher education sector in

Australia including practitioners, senior executives, copyright officers, librarians and so forth, and on interviews with key stakeholders (Bossu *et al.*, 2014a). The findings revealed that most respondents were aware of the open education movement, mostly OER, and rated their knowledge of OER as intermediate. However, the majority of participants had either rarely or never used OER. As for those who had used them, learning objects were the most preferred type of resources utilized. Encouragingly, a large number of participants stated that they would like to be more involved in OER activities. Perhaps one of the reasons why participants were not engaged with OER could have been due to the lack of institutional strategies and policies to support OER and open education projects and initiatives at that time (the project's data was collected in late 2011) (Bossu *et al.*, 2014a).

One of the main deliverables of this project was the Feasibility Protocol, a set of guiding principles that prompts questions and raises issues to be considered by educational institutions wishing to experiment with open education. The protocol attempts to assist higher education leaders and policy makers to make informed decisions about the adoption of open education at several levels within the institution, from management to practitioner levels, including academics and students (Bossu *et al.*, 2014b). The Feasibility Protocol addresses four aspects which include:

- *Opportunities* that open education could bring to institutions and broader society;

- *Challenges* associated with the adoption of open education;

- *Strategic Directions* for an effective adoption of open education; and

- *Policy Recommendations* for higher education institutions in Australia (Bossu *et al.*, 2014b).

Opportunities of open education

As discussed previously, open education can bring many opportunities to the higher education sector, educational institutions, practitioners and students. Some of these benefits have also been identified in the Feasibility Protocol. At a sector level, open education can assist to bridge the gap between formal and informal education; support the diverse student cohort across the higher education sector in Australia (for example, remote and rural students, adult and distance learners and national, international, refugee and imprisoned students) etc.; and can assist to position the Australian higher education sector on the global stage (for example, by adopting the 2012 Paris OER Declaration) (Bossu *et al.*, 2014b).

At institutional levels, open education has the potential to:

- Increase institutional reputation through showcasing of educational content and learning and teaching innovations;
- Create opportunities for national and international collaboration with other institutions;
- Increase access to education by assisting the alignment of an institution's agenda for social inclusion and widening participation;
- Create economies of scale by developing more effective ways to create, use, re-use and remix open content, and
- Promote innovations and quality in teaching and learning

The Feasibility Protocol also revealed many opportunities for practitioners. Some of them are:

- Increase collegial and subject level collaboration
- Create more opportunities for learning
- Enrich practitioners' teaching experiences
- Enhance existing pedagogical approaches to learning and provide the basis for new ones

As for the students, opportunities arising from the adoption of open education could be:

- To enhance learning through networked and collaborative learning;
- To promote richer learning experiences through access to learning resources available outside institutional boundaries;
- To meet students' different needs and learning styles; and
- To promote and enhance lifelong learning

Challenges

Despite the wide range of opportunities that can emerge from the adoption of open education, many challenges remain. According to the Feasibility Protocol, the main challenge for the Australian higher education system is perhaps the incorporation of open education into mainstream education through the national regulatory frameworks for learning and teaching (e.g. TEQSA). Perhaps one of the most significant challenges at institutional level is the persistence of a traditional academic culture and mindset that represents barriers for the adoption of open education. Such traditions are steeped in history and may be slow to evolve and embrace a new approach to educational content creation or use re-use, re-mix and storage techniques. Other challenges faced by educational institutions are:

- The need to develop and revise current institutional business models to ensure the sustainability of open education initiatives; and

- Develop policy enablers to promote open education institution wide

The Feasibility Protocol noted that some of the challenges faced by practitioners are:

- The lack of skills and knowledge required by individuals to adopt open education;

- The lack of understand regarding copyright and intellectual property issues, which could limit and concern practitioners; and

- Increase workload (mostly in institutions where open education is not recognized and/or not incorporated into learning and teaching activities).

Some factors that might pose challenges for students to adopt open education are:

- Poorly contextualized resources;

- Inadequate access to the internet for remote and rural students;

- Limited digital literacy skills; and

- Open content that does not meet students' needs

Strategic Directions

Strategic Directions is the third and perhaps the most important element of the Feasibility Protocol. Even though it is important to recognize the opportunities and challenges that open education brings to stakeholders, it is believed that having a well thought-out plan and/or a detailed strategy are much more important elements for a successful open education initiative. Below are some questions and issues posed by the Feasibility Protocol at sector, institutional and practitioner levels. The strategic directions questions at the sector level are:

- To what extent could open education assist the revitalization of the higher education sector in Australia?
- How can government incentives, priorities and funding encourage the adoption of open education across the sector?
- How can educational policies promote and sustain open education across the sector?

At an institutional level, three main strategic directions emerged: resourcing, innovation and planning. Resourcing is an umbrella definition covering additional investments, such as infrastructure, technology, and personnel (including academic staff development) required for the implementation of an open education initiative. Innovation focuses on the adoption of open education as a way to promote an institution's "uniqueness and distinctiveness" amongst other higher education institutions. It also looks at ways in which open education can be used to meet lecturers' and students' expectations about the use of innovative technologies for learning. Under the rubric of innovation also feature ways in which open education could be integrated into institutional processes, such as Prior Learning and Assessment Recognition (PLAR). Finally, strategies related to planning include institutional consultations with stakeholder groups, investigating the scope and purpose of open education initiatives, identifying the OE champions within each institution, and developing dedicated open education policies.

Most importantly the key to success of open education initiatives is the development of strategies that chime with practitioners' needs and aspirations. In order to increase awareness and uptake of open education amongst practitioners, institutions need to increase capacity and provide the technical and human support needed for lecturers to adopt an innovative way of devising and delivering education. Another strategy to successfully engage this cohort in open education is by offer recognition and reward (e.g. via promotion and awards) to those who have included aspects of open education into their teaching.

Policies Recommendations for Higher Education Institutions

The Feasibility Protocol also looked at studies of Intellectual Property (IP) policies of Australian universities (which are publicly available online) to determine how these documents address the ownership of course content and educational resources created and developed by their employees (Scott, 2014). As a result, the Protocol highlights some points for consideration by universities tackling the issue of intellectual property and copyright policies of open education content created by their staff:

- Extoll the value of open education as part and parcel of university policy;

- Embed in current and future employment contracts a reward mechanism to support the development of content for open education;

- Establish a mechanism to verify that university content intended for OER release is not already subject to university commercialization or other agreements;

- Develop a set of guidelines and recommendations for lecturers on the types of open licenses available for OER content; and

- Create university guidelines and procedures to ensure the quality of the open education material and its copyright compliance.

The engagement from this project also led to further initiatives, including collaboration based initiatives with national and international institutions, and institutionally based ones. Some of these initiatives are externally funded, while others are funded internally, still others have not received any funding but are progressing nonetheless. This project, its deliverables, the stakeholder engagement and network that emerged as a result of interactions during the time of this project have led to the realization that much more is needed to be done for Australian higher education to fully benefit from OER and open education. Many believe that for open educational practice to become one mechanism woven into the institutional ecology, it needs to be aligned with support and enable institutional priorities through a mature symbiotic relationship with institutional policy that recognizes, rewards, and influences innovative learning and teaching.

Final Considerations

Open education systems have no doubt played an important role in assisting higher education sectors and governments worldwide to meet their current and future educational targets of widening participation, lowering costs, improving the quality of learning and teaching and promoting social inclusion and democracy. However, contemporary open education systems are still relatively new approaches to learning and teaching and pose many challenges to the accepted norms of the Western higher education system. In order to learn more and take full advantage of these new systems, many countries have attempted to trial, develop and implement educational policies that incorporate elements of open education (Bossu *et al.*, 2014a).

In Australia, despite some important initiatives, the absence of explicit educational policies and incentives appear to be limiting the adoption of open education. To date, there have been few internal institutional strategies and policy enablers to encourage universities to pursue open education to better support current students, attract new ones, and compete against as well as collaborate with other Australian and international institutions. Thoughtfully designed educational policies that encourage and promote innovative learning and teaching can facilitate the sector's realization of the full potential of open education and place Australia amongst the leading countries in this field.

Also discussed here was an example of a sector-wide research in open education, which led to the development of a Feasibility Protocol. Despite the fact that the Protocol was developed in late 2012, most of its recommendations are still valid today as developments in open education in Australia have been limited since then. The Feasibility Protocol still remains a valuable instrument and has the potential to assist senior executives and policy makers to make informed decisions about open education, including the issues and questions that they should consider regarding the opportunities, challenges, strategic directions and policies issues involving open education in Australia. Nevertheless, it is important to highlight that the Feasibility Protocol is not a rigid instrument. It can be adapted, changed, and further developed to meet individual university needs, as each institution has unique structures, agendas, cultures, and strategic plans for future and current activities. Ultimately, the usefulness of the Feasibility Protocol will depend on individual institutions and the way that their senior executives make use of it.

References

Australian National Data Service (2014), Our Approach: The Australian Research Data Commons, http://www.ands.org.au/about/approach.html#ardc

Benn, S. and Peters, R. (1959), *Social Principles of the Democratic State*, London: Allen & Unwin.

Bossu, C. (2016), Open Educational Practices in Australia, in F. Miao, S. Mishraand R. McGreal (Eds.), *Open Educational Resources: Policy, Costs and Transformation*, Paris and Burnaby, Canada: UNESCO and Commonwealth of Learning, http://oasis.col.org/handle/11599/2306

Bossu, C., Brown, M. and Bull, D. (2014a), *Adoption, Use and Management of Open Educational Resources to Enhance Teaching and Learning in Australia*, Sydney: Australian Government Office for Learning and Teaching, http://www.olt.gov.au/system/files/resources/CG10_1687_Bossu_Report_2014.pdf

Bossu, C., Brown, M. and Bull, D. (2014b), *Feasibility Protocol for OER and OEP: A Decision Making Tool for Higher Education*, Sydney: Australian Government Office for Learning and Teaching, www.olt.gov.au/system/files/resources/CG10_1687_Bossu_Feasibility Protocol_2014.pdf

Bossu, C., Bull, D. and Brown, M. (2015), Enabling Open Education: A Feasibility Protocol for Australian Higher Education, in C. Bonk, M. Lee, T. Reeves and T. Reynolds (Eds.), *MOOCs and Open Education around the World*, London: Routledge.

Bradley, D., Noonan, P., Nugent, H., and Scales, B. (2008). *Review of Australian Higher Education: Final Report*, Canberra: DEEWR, http://hdl.voced.edu.au/10707/44384

Butcher, N., and Hoosen, S. (2014), *A Guide to Quality in Post-traditional Online Higher Education*, Dallas: Academic Partnerships, https://icde.memberclicks.net/assets/NEWS/2014/guide2.pdf

Chesters, J. (2015), Within-generation Social Mobility in Australia: The Effect of Returning to Education on Occupational Status and Earnings, *Journal of Sociology*, 51(2), pp. 385–400.

Chesters, J. and Watson, L. (2013), Understanding the Persistence of Inequality in Higher Education: Evidence from Australia, *Journal of Education Policy*, 28(2), pp. 198–215, http://dx.doi.org/10.1080/02680939.2012.694481

Conole, G. (2013), *Designing for Learning in an Open World*, Vol. 4. New York: Springer, http://dx.doi.org/10.1007/978-1-4419-8517-0

Crosnoe, R. (2012), Opportunities for and Challenges of Translating Educational and Developmental Research into Policy and Intervention, in E. Wethingtonand and R. Dunifor (Eds.), *Research for the Public Good: Applying the Methods of Translational Research to Improve Human Health and Well-being*, pp. 53–72, Washington: American Psychological Association.

D'Antoni, Susan (2008), Open Educational Resources: The Way Forward, Deliberations of an International Community of Interest. Reviewing Initiatives and Issues, *Open Learning: The Journal of Open, Distance and e-Learning*, 24(1), pp. 3–10, http://dx.doi.org/10.1080/02680510802625443

Department of Education and Training (2015), *Selected Higher Education Statistics: 2014 Student Data*, https://www.education.gov.au/selected-higher-education-statistics-2014-student-data

Department of Employment, Education and Training (1990), *A Fair Chance for All: National and Institutional Planning for Equity in Higher Education: A Discussion Paper*, Canberra: Australian Government Publishing Service.

Dewey, J. (1916), *Democracy and Education: An Introduction to the Philosophy of Education*, New York: MacMillan.

Giddons, A. (2000), *The Third Way and its Critics*, Cambridge: Policy Press.

Glennie, J. Harley, K. Butcher, N. and T. van Wyk (2012), *Open Educational Resources and Change in Higher Education: Reflections from Practice*, Vancouver: Commonwealth of Learning.

Gutmann, A. (1987), *Democratic Education*, Princeton: Princeton University Press.

James, R. (2012), Social Inclusion in a Globalised Higher Education Environment: The Issue of Equitable Access to University in Australia, in T. Basit and S. Tomlinson (Eds.), *Social Inclusion and Higher Education*, pp. 83–108, Bristol: Policy Press.

James, R. and Bossu, C. (2014), Conversations from South of the Equator: Challenges and Opportunities in OER across Broader Oceania, *RUSC Universities and Knowledge Society Journal*, 11(3), pp. 78–90, http://dx.doi.org/10.7238/rusc.v11i3.2220

McKerlich, R., Ives, C. and McGreal, R. (2013), Measuring Use and Creation of Open Educational Resources in Higher Education, *The International Review of Research in Open and Distributed Learning*, 14(4), pp. 1–6.

Olssen, M., Codd, J. and O'Neill, A. (2004), *Education Policy: Globalization, Citizenship and Democracy*, London: Sage, http://dx.doi.org/10.4135/9781446221501

Partridge, H. and Stagg, A. (2016), *No-cost Textbooks: Developing Low-cost Courses for Australian Higher Education*, Paper presented at HERDSA, The Shape of Higher Education Conference, 4–7 July 2016, Fremantle, Australia.

Picasso, V. and Phelan, L. (2014), The Evolution of Open Access to Research and Data in Australian Higher Education, *RUSC Universities and Knowledge Society Journal*, 11(3), pp. 122–133, http://dx.doi.org/10.7238/rusc.v11i3.2076

Scott, B. (2014), Supporting OER Engagement at Australian Universities: An Overview of the Intellectual Property Rights, Copyright and Policy Considerations for OER, http://www.olt.gov.au/system/files/resources/CG10_1687_Bossu_OER engagement_2014.pdf

Senack, E. (2014), *Fixing the Broken Textbook Market: How Students Respond to High Textbook Costs and Demand Alternatives*, Washington: Center for Public Interest Research Inc., http://www.uspirg.org/sites/pirg/files/reports/NATIONAL Fixing Broken Textbooks Report1.pdf

Universities Australia (2008), *Advancing Equity and Participation in Australian Higher Education*, Canberra: Universities Australia.

Universities Australia (2015), *Keep it Clever: Policy Statement 2016*, Australian Capital Territory: Universities Australia, https://www.universitiesaustralia.edu.au/news/policy-papers/Keep-it-Clever--Policy-Statement-2016#.WCRo9slWsoA

7. The Identified Informal Learner: Recognizing Assessed Learning in the Open

Patrina Law

Badged open courses (BOCs) were piloted on the OpenLearn platform by the Open University (OU) in the UK in 2013. These are free online course upon the completion of which, digital badges are awarded. Based on the evaluation of their impact, they now form a key strand to the OU's free learning provision, embracing Open Educational Practices at their core. The first permanent suite of BOCs was launched on OpenLearn in 2015 and evaluated for impact, both from an outreach and a business perspective. The application of a branded open digital badge, with associated assessment and feedback has provided a mechanism to motivate and reward informal learners whilst also generating a higher than expected click-through to make an enquiry about becoming a formal student.

http://dx.doi.org/10.11647/OBP.0103.07

Introduction

The Open University (OU) in the UK has long delivered a diverse range of courses to large numbers of people. The OU was established in 1969 with the aim of opening up higher education (HE) to all, regardless of circumstances, geographical location or qualifications. Currently the OU is serving some 200,000 students and is particularly concerned with reaching those who might not otherwise have access to higher education, ensuring that there are as few barriers as possible. As part of this commitment to access, the OU has freely released educational materials into the public realm. This helps to support the twin pillars of core OU activity:

- **Social mission**, that is, public awareness of, and easy access to life-long learning opportunities, including free, informal learning.
- **Business mission**, that is brand awareness, student registration, student preparedness, asset and archive exploitation/re-use in formal learning and income from fee-paying customers.

The OU has been providing free learning via its OpenLearn platform since 2006. It ensures that it provides about 5% of its course materials as free open educational resources (OER) every year on OpenLearn (www.open.edu/openlearn). It also serves as the platform through which the OU promotes its partnership with the BBC and the related free courses and articles that are created to support its co-productions with them. It does this because free learning is an interpretation of its Royal Charter which states that it will "promote the educational well-being of the community generally".

This provision of free learning is also part of one of the OU's strategic objectives: Journeys from Informal to Formal Learning (JIFL). Originally supported by a grant from the William and Flora Hewlett Foundation, the platform now hosts around 1000 free courses, short articles, activities, videos and ebooks all released under a Creative Commons license. OpenLearn is accessed by over five million users a year, of whom 100,000 are the university's own students. OpenLearn also delivers a 13% click-through rate of learners wanting to know more about becoming an OU student. Existing metrics show that as a free learning platform, OpenLearn attracts a very balanced demographic that is, its learners are less qualified overall than those attending Massive Open Online Course (MOOC) platforms.

In an attempt to demonstrate an ongoing institutional commitment to new models of teaching, learning and assessment to serve both informal learners and students alike, the development of badged open courses (BOCs) were piloted by the OU on OpenLearn and evaluated in 2013. The BOC initiative built on ongoing research on the motivations and demographic profiles of learners using OpenLearn (Law, Perryman and Law, 2013; Perryman, Law and Law, 2013). Based on the evaluation of these pilot courses and key evidence from OpenLearn surveys it was found that 80% of informal learners strongly felt that they wanted to have their informal online learning achievements recognized through the availability of free certificates. Hence a suite of free BOCs awarding an OU-branded digital badge and certificate were developed in 2014 and launched in 2015 and their impact evaluated (Law, 2015, 2016).

This chapter reports on the evaluation of the 2015 BOCs and how they build on what we now know of the strategic importance of free learning recognition in an unsupported (non-tutored) online environment. Initial results reveal that the majority of respondents declare that BOCs provide a sense of achievement despite the absence of any tutor-led instruction and that they would be sharing their achievements with their employer. In terms of impact to OU business, metrics compare favorably with informal learning *per se*, with 26% of learners visiting the BOCs choosing to click through to the OU's formal qualifications webpages. This is more than twice the percentage of the average OpenLearn learner.

Stacey (2012) identifies ten key benefits to institutions for supporting OER initiatives and provides useful criteria against which to develop and experiment with Open Educational Practices and learning design for free learning environments:

- OER increases access to education;
- Provides students with an opportunity to assess and plan their education choices;
- Showcases an institution's intellectual outputs, promoting its profile and attracting students;
- Converts students into fee paying enrolments;

- Accelerates learning;
- Adds value to knowledge production;
- Reduces faculty preparation time;
- Generates cost savings;
- Enhances quality; and
- Generates innovation through collaboration.

This initial impact of the BOCs concurs with Stacey's suggestion that OER can "lead to faster learning, greater learner success", and supports his notion that OER may subsequently generate revenue, where BOCs in particular see such high motivation and formal course sign-up (Stacey, 2012).

A Background to Digital Badging

Digital badging in educational sectors offers a new way to reward and motivate learners, providing evidence of skills and achievements in classroom or online settings. As OERs across multiple platform types and formats have continued to diversify to match learners and educators' preferences, so the notion of recognition for informal learning in these spheres has become accepted provision by some educators and philanthropic providers.

Hickey (2012) identifies three possible functions for digital badges:

1. Summative functions, that is, assessment *of* learning.
2. Formative functions for individuals, that is, assessment *for* learning.
3. Transformative functions for systems, that is, assessment *as* learning.

Models of the educational use of digital badging are wide-ranging (Hickey and Willis, 2015) though invariably have as a common theme the expectation of a motivational tool and as a form of micro-credential, that is, associated with a short course or activity undertaken to develop a skill. Gibson *et al.* (2013) simply identify digital badging as an incentive for earners to identify progress and to signify achievement and learning. Clark, Howard and Early (2006) note that motivation is key to learning and that its application with the issuing of digital badges through BOCs supports this (Law, 2016). Abramovich, Schumn and Higashi (2013) state that: "[...] the potential benefit of an assessment is determined by its ability to both maintain learning motivation and accurately communicate a student's learning". By developing summative and formative assessments using Moodle quizzes in open courses in the way that Hickey identifies above, the OU is attempting to both communicate feedback and provide motivation to learners who lack any tutorial support.

Specifically, within the context of higher education, Bixler and Layng (2013) argued that digital badges would "hold great promise" but that at the time "policies on badges for higher education institutions" did not exist. More recently, McDaniel and Fanfarelli (2015) describe the use of digital badges woven into the undergraduate curriculum as a tool for both feedback and motivation, through the issuing of badges in two different ways: by a tutor in a classroom and separately via an internal online management system.

Early detractors of digital badging were largely seen in the educational blogging community noting the mainstreaming of badging into the digital world as disruptive, dangerous if poorly employed and unlikely to have any comparative value to formal qualifications (Crotty (2012); Halavais (2012); Jenkins (2012)).

Early case studies for offering digital badges in higher education focus on concepts around the characteristics of badges as rewards. Charleer, Klerkx, Santos and Duval (2013) suggest their use is a means to feedback, encourage motivation, catalysts for discussion and being socially sharable. The drivers for offering digital badges in higher education are described by Wu, Whiteley and Sass (2015) in other contexts: within a classroom setting; as co-curricular support; as a means to fulfil graduation requirements, and as part, or all of an outreach agenda. Where case studies of digital badges to date tend to focus on a specific educational sector, the application of open badges within BOCs embraces several of these characteristics and contexts and explores their value as a strategic activity that supports social mission through the delivery of OER.

Key Features of Badged Open Courses

All learners who study a BOC participate in a number of online assessments delivered through the deployment of Moodle quizzes. The courses are designed to be as robust as any of the OU's modules in terms of quality and pedagogy: they follow strict learning design procedures, academic authoring, assessment and critical readership. Each course is structured into eight notional weeks covering twenty-four hours of learning, although a learner can take the course at his or her own pace. At the end of each week, practice quizzes are provided that count towards the assessment at the end of weeks four and eight.

Based on the evaluation of the 2013 pilots, the courses published in 2015 were largely in support of learner preparedness at an introductory level. They were entitled:

- Succeed with Maths — Part 1.
- Succeed with Maths — Part 2.
- Taking Your First Steps into Higher Education.
- Succeed with Learning.
- English: Skills for Learning.
- Succeed in the Workplace.

In order to be consistent, each BOC was developed with the same structural format in terms of the use of rich media, voice, learning design and assessment, so that any learner would come to understand what was expected of him or her when studying any BOC. This approach also supports the University to ensure quality enhancement when using the OU brand, especially in the absence of a framework for the classification of openly badged courses in higher education.

Each BOC starts with a video introducing the course content, as shown in Figure 1. This video is complemented by further, weekly videos each of which explains the learning outcomes for that section of the course and gives a "familiar face" to the learning. The pilot study showed that this "familiar face" — not necessarily the author of the content, but a subject expert or practitioner nonetheless — was appreciated by learners in the absence of any social group structure to the learning or real-time tutor.

Figure 1. Enrolment page of Succeed with Learning

Methods of Evaluation

In order to evaluate the BOCs delivered in 2015, mixed method surveys were made available at the start and end of each BOC, with participation optional. Surveys were based on those used in the pilot study and were delivered using the SurveyMonkey platform with each start of course survey and each end of course survey being identical across BOCs. Surveys comprised a combination of Likert scale, multiple choice and open questions. Data on the number of registrations and the onward journey of learners were gathered using Google Analytics and comScore Digital Analytix (DAX) software. The aim of evaluating the BOCs through surveys and data captured via platform data analytics was to examine the impact, both short and long term, of BOCs, with particular emphasis on:

- Examining demographics (in alignment with OU data collected about informal learners on OpenLearn overall);

- Tracking data to show movement of learners within the platform, where they were referred from into the platform and their onward journey;

- Gaining a profile of the types of learners who are more likely to convert to formal learning;

- Giving a picture of the types of learning methods and course elements most likely to encourage learners to progress in an open, unsupported environment; and

- Assessing the motivational aspects of badging and whether learners showed their achievements to an employer or prospective employer.

In addition, comparisons were made with data from studies undertaken by the author in 2013 and 2014 on OpenLearn (Law and Perryman, 2015) and again in 2015, in order to gain a deeper understanding of learner demographics and their motivations for study. For these studies, surveys were promoted via web-links embedded within OpenLearn and via the OpenLearn newsletter. The study included questions drawn from the OER Research Hub (OERRH, http://oerresearchhub.org) open research question base to allow for comparison with existing data collected through OER projects globally.

The OpenLearn survey received 1,177 responses in 2013, then 3,133 responses in 2014 and 1,299 responses in 2015. BOCs were not present on OpenLearn at the time the 2013 and 2014 surveys were live.

Results

Across all six BOCs during the evaluation period (March to October 2015) there were 2,804 responses to the start of course surveys and 786 responses to the end of course surveys. The project itself was reported internally through the university's strategic priority of JIFL, with the requirement that it be evaluated against anticipated benefits. These benefits are summarized in Table 1 and draw on data from surveys and internal analytics.

The surprisingly high percentage of click-throughs (26%) to make an enquiry at the OU as a result of studying a BOC (shown in Table 1) could, in part, be explained by the more favorable demographic of BOC learners compared with OpenLearn learners who then signed up for a formal higher education qualification (see Table 2).

Table 1. Summary of impact of BOCs against university metrics

	Anticipated benefit	Description	Outcome
1	**Student recruitment**	Learners participating in BOCs will be encouraged to enquire about formal learning opportunities at the OU. This could lead to equal or greater conversion to formal study for informal learners.	All learners are sign-posted to formal OU qualifications before, during and at the end of each BOC. As a direct result of learners studying BOCs there have been: • 272 formal module registrations (mostly at entry level) • 1,783 prospectus requests • 12,000 new visitors a month to OpenLearn The average click-through rate to make an enquiry at the OU as a result of using OpenLearn is 13%. For BOCs this is over 26%.
		BOCs are particularly attractive for partner organisations to promote	BOCs are being promoted through Social Partnerships Network members such as UnionLearn, Workers Education Association and Unison. BOCs will also be repurposed for the Opening Educational Practices in Scotland project and are being supported by the UK's Centre for Recording Achievement.
2	**Financial**	Experimentation with new models of producing open courses that could attract large audiences at low cost	Registration numbers for BOCs are as follows: • Succeed with maths part 1: 8,375 • Succeed with maths part 2: 1,125 • Taking your first steps in HE: 791 • Succeed with learning: 730 • English skills for learning: 7,718 • Succeed in the workplace: 875
3	**University compliance**	It is critically important that all badges are marked as "not for academic credit"	This is stated in each course description, accompanying Statement of Participation and metadata associated with the BOC.
4	**Informal learner outcomes**	Improved employability outcomes for learners	End of course surveys have shown that up to 57% of learners say that they will be sharing their achievements with an employer or prospective employer.
		A positive and valuable learning experience	Very high satisfaction rates (98%) reported in end of course surveys.

Table 2 Comparisons of demographic data for OpenLearn between 2013, 2014 and 2015 and BOCs (2015 end of course surveys)

	2013 OpenLearn	2014 OpenLearn	2015 OpenLearn	Succeed with maths part 1	Succeed with maths part 2	English skills for learning	Succeed with learning	Taking your first steps in HE	Succeed in the workplace
	n=1,177	n=3,133	n=1,299	n=235	n=79	n=155	n=130	n=85	n=102
Age (yrs)	14% 0-24 38% 25-44 38% 45-64 10% Over 65	17% 0-25 27% 26-45 39% 46-65 16% Over 66	18% 0-25 31% 26-45 39% 46-65 12% Over 66	12% 0-25 48% 26-45 32% 46-65 8% Over 66	9% 0-25 47% 26-45 32% 46-65 12% Over 66	20% 0-25 51% 26-45 26% 46-65 4% Over 66	15% 0-25 47% 26-45 36% 46-65 2% Over 66	12% 0-25 47% 26-45 35% 46-65 6% Over 66	14% 0-25 47% 26-45 38% 46-65 1% Over 66
English as a first language	81%	79%	80%	90%	91%	46%	76%	90%	82%
Highest educational qualification	16% School 9% Vocational 23% College 26% Undergrad 20% Postgrad 6% None	16% School 6% Vocational 24% College 24% Undergrad 20% Postgrad 5% None	16% School 6% Vocational 20% College 24% Undergrad 26% Postgrad 4% None	24% School 11% Vocational 23% College 20% Undergrad 14% Postgrad 8% None	27% School 4% Vocational 23% College 26% Undergrad 16% Postgrad 4% None	32% School 6% Vocational 22% College 12% Undergrad 10% Postgrad 18% None	20% School 8% Vocational 36% College 12% Undergrad 16% Postgrad 8% None	53% School 21% Vocational 6% College 10% Undergrad 0% Postgrad 10% None	15% School 20% Vocational 30% College 15% Undergrad 20% Postgrad 0% None

For example:

- The majority of respondents to the end of course survey for the Taking your First Steps in higher education BOC (53%) declare a "School leaving certificate" as their highest qualification compared to OpenLearn, where the majority of learners (44–50%) declare a "degree qualification" as their highest qualification.

- BOC learners are younger overall than OpenLearn learners. Table 2 shows that the majority of BOC learners are in the 26–45 age range; for OpenLearn they are in the 46–65 age range.

Data indicating that up to 57% of BOC learners would be sharing their achievement with an employer was of particular interest when considering the extension of the BOC courses and how these could be aligned to the formal curriculum. Hence, in September 2015, a further survey was issued to those respondents who said they would be sharing their digital badge with their employer or prospective employer and had agreed to be followed up for additional research. Initial data show that:

- 75% felt their employer valued the BOC that they had taken.

- 80% of those who had not shared their achievement still planned to do so.

- 98% felt the BOC had a positive impact on their work.

Challenges

An initial concern of the project team in defining the assessment criteria for BOCs was that the bar was being set too high — that is, applying assessments and a requirement to view each page of a BOC could act as a deterrent to, rather than a motivator for completion. Where scant research and almost no empirical data existed with regard to the impact of BOCs in an open environment at the time the BOCs were developed, developing them with such prescribed assessment criteria was considered a risk. With robust assessment becoming a key element to obtaining any university-branded digital badge, open or otherwise, the current wave of interest inspired the first conference on "Badging in Higher Education" which took place in the UK in 2016, during Open Education Week, which may have generated much-needed empirical data around the use of digital badges in education.

Another challenge was that, of the 2015 BOCs, half were developed using repurposed content; much of this had already been released on OpenLearn as OER, usually in the form of large chunks of text. This content itself was originally adapted from OU modules that had been produced for short introductory courses and withdrawn from the OU curriculum. It was felt that this approach to adapting existing content would be less time consuming than writing from scratch. However, the reality was that after developing a robust learning design and editorial approach for each BOC, there was little reduction in time spent on repurposing existing content compared with writing it anew. This can partly be explained by the proportionately large amount of time required to develop meaningful formative assessments for Moodle.

To explain the endeavor to write formative assessments for Moodle, each week of a BOC contains either a practice assessment (weeks 1–3 and 5–7) or a marked assessment that counts toward the final badge (weeks four and 8). For weeks four and 8, the author was required to write 45 questions to enable learners to repeat attempts and receive a random selection of questions and answers, up to three times (in order to form a question bank for the fiftheen quiz questions for those weeks). Each author was also required to write a further five questions for non-assessed practice evaluations required for the remaining six weeks.

Impact

The social and institutional impact on the University of delivering BOCs is being widely communicated internally and through international badging networks. Based on the impact of the 2015 BOCs, a second wave of courses is in development in 2016, ostensibly to widen the range of introductory-level BOCs. In addition, the University has decided to extend the curriculum to postgraduate level and career and professional development (CPD) courses. This notion of open badges playing a role in support of CPD is reflected in four areas of higher education that are being discussed in the author's badging networks:

1. As a method of encouraging first year students to complete.

2. As a preparedness activity between enrolment and qualification start.

3. For engaging in skills/employability courses.

4. For internal staff development.

For the OU, BOCs produced in 2016 will be in support of the higher education sector as a whole in providing a common core of CPD subjects (the courses can be re-purposed, re-badged and re-used by any institution within the terms of the Creative Commons license), to support and prepare its own students and to further extend BOCs as a vehicle for outreach. They are likely to cover the following subjects, which have been endorsed by the OU's Careers Advisory Service and are in support of the Journeys from Informal to Formal Learning strategy:

- Working in the voluntary sector.
- Working in science, technology engineering and maths (STEM).
- Digital literacy.
- Succeeding in postgraduate study.
- Digital scholarship.
- Resilience and flexibility.
- Commercial communication and negotiation.
- Leadership and followership.
- Understanding business structures.

As the OU seeks to improve the economic split-decision between new course development and repurposing existing content when it comes to building new CPD materials, it has embraced a new approach to mainstreaming the development of open content that achieves better efficiencies. Open Educational Practices are not widely embraced at the OU unless someone has been involved in the creation of an OpenLearn course or MOOC. Hence, the development of new BOCs and open courses on OpenLearn will require authors, editors and instructional designers to embed the design approach of BOCs in all open course design. Non-badged OpenLearn courses that are adapted from formal modules will now require learning design to take place at the very inception of formal module design, including the development of a BOC where this is a strategic fit.

Gaining a clearer understanding of what works best for open course design at the OU has been driven by the evaluation of the OpenLearn surveys and the BOC evaluation data overall. Based on this, the following guiding principles have been developed for University staff to consider when designing and developing OpenLearn courses:

1. Learners value recognition of their achievement (in the form of a free statement of participation and digital badge) in passing tests and completing a course of study.

2. Within all the rich media presented throughout each BOC, learners most value quizzes that include feedback.

3. Closed environments with a start and finish date — that is, MOOCs — have lower completion rates than open courses with no start and finish date.

4. The use of activities and video (especially that of a tutor, or "face" of a course) are especially valued.

5. Forced social activity encourages high drop-out rates.

Outreach

In terms of outreach to disabled learners, OpenLearn evaluations in 2013–15 have shown that the number of learners who declare a disability has been reported at around 23%. In order to put this into context, the UK national average of people of working age who declare a disability is reported at 16% (UK Department for Work and Pensions, 2014).

The 2015 OpenLearn surveys indicated that for 59% of respondents with a disability, materials on OpenLearn had improved their confidence in their ability to study. This compares well with those without a disability, for whom 58% said the materials had also improved their confidence.

Demographic data on accessibility was also gathered in both the start and end of course surveys for BOCs to ascertain completion by this group. Table 3 shows that the percentage of disabled learners varied across the BOCs:

1. For all but two BOCs (Succeed with Maths — Part 1 and English: Skills for Learning) there is a slight drop in the percentage of disabled learners completing a BOC.

2. Half of the BOCs show a higher than average percentage overall of learners declaring a disability in their start of course surveys compared to the OpenLearn overall rate.

Where this second point varies most is seen in the BOC English: Skills for Learning where only 15% declare a disability. This may be explained by a higher proportion of non-UK learners studying the course compared with the other BOCs, where figures for declaration and descriptions of disability vary compared with those figures that people in the UK have grown used to. Conversely, for Succeed with Learning, the figure for those declaring a disability (37%) is far higher than for OpenLearn overall, where the majority of learners are UK-based.

Table 3. Percentage of survey respondents who declare a disability

		Start of Course survey	End of Course survey
OpenLearn survey data 2015	**23%**		
Succeed with maths part 1 n=235		23%	18%
Succeed with maths part 2 n=79		28%	14%
English skills for learning n=155		14%	19%
Succeed with learning n=130		37%	32%
Taking your first steps in HE n=85		24%	20%
Succeed in the workplace n=102		16%	15%

One of the key comments provided by disabled learners using OpenLearn is the request to have content available in multiple formats. In response to this, and after tackling some technical difficulties in making global updates to more than 850 courses during 2015, it has now been possible to provide the following formats for all OpenLearn courses, including BOCs:

- Ebook (epub)
- IMS common cartridge
- Kindle ebook
- OU XML file
- RSS
- Word
- HTML
- Interactive ebook (epub)
- OU XML package

- PDF
- SCORM

Many of these format types are also published for free by the OU on its channels on iTunes U, Google Play and Amazon (for use on Kindle devices) and are released under a Creative Commons license, along with any new video and audio created for the courses (for iTunes U, AudioBoom and YouTube). Previously, content providers developed syndication practices as a way to make web feeds available from a website in order to provide a summary of the recently added content (such as the latest news or forum posts). In recent years at the OU, the term "syndication" has come to be used for the republishing of assets and courses — whether individually or as collections — via feeds, embedded codes or the uploading of content to third-party platforms and applications.

Table 4. Open practices incorporated by OU badged open courses

Open source	The use of Moodle, which is open source software, to host open courses and as a mechanism for delivery of open badges.
Open Educational Practices	Mainstreaming of content from module production and/or the repurposing of existing module content; understanding effective learning for the open.
Open educational resources	Freely accessibly openly licensed documents and media for teaching and learning.
Open badges	Achievement recognised and shareable through digital badges using the Open Badges Infrastructure: a recognised tool that explains a badge and the evidence behind it.
Open syndication	Educational content that is produced, commissioned and released, for free, into the public realm via branded media channels (OpenLearn) or third-party channels (e.g. iTunes U, YouTube, Audioboom, Faculti, Bibblio, Amazon and Google Play).

The term open syndication is used internally at the OU to define the distribution of OER that carries a Creative Commons license. Within it is also the activity of disaggregating a course for its parts to maximize the use of assets. For example, a BOC will be developed containing new video, audio or animations to explain key concepts. These assets are themselves released to the appropriate platform that specializes in that particular media type e.g. YouTube for video, audio and animation. In addition, the whole course will be released as an ebook. Hence, from the perspective of the University's commitment to free learning and outreach, the BOC project represents a coming together of several strands of openness in order to maximize the social and business missions of providing open learning.

Figure 2. How Badged open courses demonstrate an integration of open principles

Future Implications

With digital badging becoming established as a trend across educational sectors, it has been shown to recognize and motivate learners, providing evidence for achievements and learning in a variety of formal and non-formal settings. As the diversification of OER across multiple platform types and formats has evolved to suit different learners and educators alike, so the notion of recognition for informal learning in these spheres has become accepted provision by some educators and philanthropic providers, where it can be achieved at scale.

For MOOC providers, this recognition of participation is provided across a range of criteria (for example, passing tests or viewing part or all of a course) through the sale of certificates that carry the MOOC provider's brand. For OpenLearn, a recognition of learning is provided for free through the issuing of the open badge and OU-branded statement of participation (a PDF) in support of open principles and practice. Badge recipients progress at their own pace and not in a cohort, but have to view each page of the course and pass the assessments. Whether learners value a university-branded provision more or less than something they have paid for from a privately operating MOOC platform is yet to be evaluated.

When it comes to learning for outreach, the issuing of an open digital badge (or overarching, recognition for informal learning) for free may become an important element in the pursuit of open principles in education. This may yet also have a positive impact on employability and — as seen in the case of BOCs — reap a financial reward in the form of new student registrations that are higher than for other forms of informal learning provision thus far developed.

The use of the OpenLearn platform as a test bed for innovation in eLearning has provided some surprising data with positive implications for both the social and business missions of the OU. In addition, understanding media mix in terms of what makes an impactful and engaging OpenLearn course will have positive financial implications and enable better planning and development in an environment where around sixty new (non-badged) OpenLearn courses are being produced each year alongside formal module production. The awarding of a digital badge will also be relevant to the OU's formal students, who will see this University recognition for non-formal study on their student record and in the future, on their Higher Education Achievement Report. These particular resources could support student success in retention and completion, employability and academic excellence and, with the application of the Creative Commons license, will give other higher education providers the opportunity to share, re-badge or republish.

This last point is most likely to resonate with non-distance higher education providers more generally — especially those that do not have easy access to a production and publishing mechanism for OER but that may prefer to find a home for digital badging in support of undergraduates in their critical first year.

Conclusions

As BOCs become a business-as-usual activity for the OU and the strategy that underpins them extends from introductory to induction and from postgraduate to CPD, new goals will be set to extend their support in emerging areas across curricula. The theoretical frameworks underpinning openness in education have shown themselves to have extensive practical application: open badging is another arrow in the quiver of open applications and practices that support the goal of democratizing higher education.

The early detractors writing about digital badging, discussed earlier in this chapter, described it as dangerous if poorly employed and unlikely to have any comparative value to formal qualifications due to the fact that anyone could (and still can), issue a digital badge. What is known from the evaluation of BOCs is that learners are keen to display their achievements — to be *recognized informal learners* — but that branding is key to this desire.

Not surprisingly then, there is a move to address this notion of a lack of credibility, which is currently being spearheaded by the US-based Instructional Management Systems (IMS) organization through a working group called "Open Badge Extensions for Education (OBEE)". The group is attempting to improve and implement a consistent approach to badge taxonomy and description to:

- Augment badge metadata to provide valuable information about the credentialing institution, criteria, assessment and evidence for the awarding of an open badge

- Embed data and analytics by imposing meaningful metrics to improve badge "currency"

- Determine how badge consumers e.g. employers, will quickly discern compliant badges and therefore trust what is being represented

- Implement a "conformance certification process" to certify compliance with open badges and OBEE extensions.

Now, the spotlight of interest in digital badges is being shared by the notion that they might be a way in to educational accreditation and that this might overturn educational institutions' hold on formal credentials (Jacobs, 2012). Badges may also find themselves in the center of new developments around micro-credentialing — as a set of non-formal learning achievements verifiable to an individual to demonstrate a commitment to professional and skills development. Rather than this being interpreted as a threat to formal credit-awarding bodies, it offers a new opportunity for those developing quality-assured OERs, open badges and practices to offer an alternative route into formal education.

References

Abramovich, S., Schumn, C. and Higashi, R. M. (2013), Are Badges Useful in Education? It Depends Upon the Type of Badge and Expertise of Learner, *Educational Technology Research and Development*, 61(2), pp. 217–232, http://www.lrdc.pitt.edu/schunn/research/papers/Abramovich-Schunn-Higashi.pdf

Bixler, B. and Layng, K. (2013), Digital Badges in Higher Education: An Overview, http://tinyurl.com/PSUDBWhitePaper

Charleer, S., Klerkx, J., Santos, J. and Duval, E. (2013), Improving Awareness and Reflection Through Collaborative, Interactive Visualizations of Badges, in Kravcik, M., Krogstie, B., Moore, A., Pammer, V., Pannese, L., Prilla, M., Reinhardt, W. and Ullmann, T. (Eds.), *ARTEL13*, Proceedings of the 3rd Workshop on Awareness and Reflection in Technology-Enhanced Learning, 1103, pp. 69–81 (Paphos).

Clark, R. E., Howard, K. and Early, S. (2006), Motivational Challenges Experienced in Highly Complex Learning Environments, in Elen, J. and Clark, R. E. (Eds.), *Handling Complexity in Learning Environments: Theory and Research*, Amsterdam: Elsevier, pp. 27–43.

Crotty, J. M. (2012), Why Get a Pricey Diploma When a Bleepin' Badge Will Do? http://www.forbes.com/sites/jamesmarshallcrotty/2012/01/26/the-end-of-the-diploma-as-we-know-it/#4da9638b23f0

Department for Work and Pensions (2014), *Disability Facts and Figures*, https://www.gov.uk/government/publications/disability-facts-and-figures/disability-facts-and-figures

Halavais, A. (2012). Badges: The Skeptical Evangelist, http://alex.halavais.net/badges-the-skeptical-evangelist

Hickey, D. (2012), *Some Things about Assessment that Badge Developers Might Find Helpful*, Remediating Assessment, http://remediatingassessment.blogspot.co.uk/2012/03/some-things-about-assessment-that-badge.html

Hickey, D. T. and Willis, J. E. (2015), Research Designs for Studying Individual and Collaborative Learning with Digital Badges, in D. Hickey, J. Jovanovic, S. Lonn, J. E. Willis, III (Eds.), *Proceedings of the Open Badges in Education (OBIE 2015) Workshop*, New York: Poughkeepsie, 16 March 2015, http://ceur-ws.org

Jacobs, J. (2012), Digital Badges Threaten Colleges' Monopoly on Credentials, *US News*, http://www.usnews.com/education/best-colleges/articles/2012/01/20/digital-badges-threaten-colleges-monopoly-on-credentials

Jenkins, H. (2012), How to Earn Your Skeptic "Badge", http://henryjenkins.org/2012/03/how_to_earn_your_skeptic_badge.html

Law, P., Perryman, L-A. and Law, A. (2013), *Open Educational Resources for All? Comparing User Motivations and Characteristics across the Open University's iTunes U Channel and OpenLearn Platform*, Open and Flexible Higher Education Conference 2013, 23–25 October 2013, Paris, European Association of Distance Teaching Universities (EADTU), pp. 204–219.

Law, P. and Perryman, L-A. (2015), Internal Responses to Informal Learning Data: Testing a Rapid Commissioning Approach, *European Journal of Open, Distance and E Learning*, pp. 76 84.

Law, P. (2015), Recognising Informal Elearning with Digital Badging: Evidence for a Sustainable Business Model, *Open Praxis*, 7(4), pp. 299–310, http://dx.doi.org/10.5944/openpraxis.7.4.247

Law, P. (2016), Digital Badging at The Open University: Recognition for Informal Learning, *Open Learning: The Journal of Open, Distance and E-Learning*, http://dx.doi.org/10.1080/02680513.2015.1104500

Perryman, L.-A., Law, P. and Law, A. (2013), *Developing Sustainable Business Models for Institutions' Provision of Open Educational Resources: Learning from OpenLearn Users' Motivations and Experiences*, Open and Flexible Higher Education Conference 2013, 23–25 October 2013, Paris, European Association of Distance Teaching Universities (EADTU), pp. 204–219.

McDaniel, R. and Fanfarelli, J. R. (2015), A Digital Badging Dataset Focused on Performance, Engagement and Behavior-related Variables from Observations in Web-based University Courses, *British Journal of Educational Technology*, 46(5), pp. 937–941, http://dx.doi.org/10.1111/bjet.12272

Stacey, P. (2012), *The Economics of Open*, https://edtechfrontier.com/2012/03

Wu, M., Whiteley, D. and Sass, M. (2015), From Girl Scout to Grown Up: Applications of Digital Badges in Higher Education, *The Online Journal of Distance Education and e-Learning*, 3(2), pp. 48–52.

8. Transformation of Teaching and Learning in Higher Education towards Open Learning Arenas: A Question of Quality

Ebba Ossiannilsson, Zehra Altinay, and Fahriye Altinay

There is increasing discussion and academic debate about changing and improving learning and teaching praxis as widespread and increased digitization continues to impact life of individuals and society, both locally and globally. Widening the access to higher education is high on the global agenda not just in the field of education but also from the perspective of employment opportunities, entrepreneurship and innovation in the labor market. An open education for all learners is key to maximize the impact of education on society and to ensure its success and sustainability. Opening up education requires a change in attitudes and mindset that emphasizes flexible growth instead of fixed traditions. Enhancing quality in open education requires a system-based approach in which contingency provides for the integration of digitization and technology in both management and leadership. An open education pedagogical approach, or a more self-directed approach is likewise essential to foster openness in both praxis and culture.

This chapter analyses the role of open educational practice and culture by discussing the opportunities and dilemmas encountered in this rapidly evolving age of technology-enabled learning, as well as the key issues that must be addressed in opening up education.

Introduction

Widening the access to university education is high on the global agenda not only in terms of education-specific programme, but also as part of employment, entrepreneurship and labor market policies. UNESCO, for example, has stated that increasing access to learning is vital for our future and prosperity as the number of students in tertiary education worldwide is projected to reach over 260 million by 2025 (UNESCO, 2015). It is widely recognized that free access to learning resources is a basic requirement for education to be both successful in its reach and financially sustainable (UNESCO, 2010, 2015). Lifelong learning and increased access to higher education therefore are and must remain at the top of universities' agendas around the globe. In practice this goal is feasible only if we truly open up education and provide high-quality and easily accessible open educational resources (OER) and massive open online courses (MOOC) for all worldwide. Technologically, this is more possible today than never before because of the ever-growing access to the internet and smart devices. However, it will only be possible if the paradigm and full meaning of opening up education by offering it to anyone, anywhere, at any time, and on any device is embraced (European Commission, 2013; UNESCO, 2015). In the digital age, the diffusion of knowledge has changed fundamentally, which has led to the demand for changes in higher education practices. The diffusion of knowledge has become a strategy for open education in terms of access, processes, recognition and validation. However, the success of open education comprises several critical factors such as equity, access, and quality (UNESCO, 2015). Research has shown that additional critical factors for the success of open education are student engagement and involvement, evaluation at all levels, theoretical frameworks and codes for praxis teacher training, quality standards, learning, and content design (Aksal, 2011; Gazi, 2011).

Opening up education means rethinking the numerous dimensions that are familiar in traditional educational structures and patterns. It requires, at the very least, a changed mindset that emphasizes growth instead of fixed traditions. Enhancing quality in open education requires a system-based approach in which contingency provides the integration of digitization and technology in both management and leadership.

An open education pedagogical approach, towards self-directed learning is also essential to foster openness in both praxis and culture. Accordingly, the strengths, weaknesses, threats and opportunities involved in mainstreaming open education, open educational systems, as well as technological systems need to be evaluated. Research on the improvement of the quality of open education is a significant element of that process.

This chapter focuses on the role of open educational practice and open educational culture. The aim is to discuss the opportunities and dilemmas encountered in opening up education in this rapidly evolving age of technology-enabled learning. We will also discuss the key controversies and issues that must be addressed. Firstly, open educational practice is discussed. The following section then discusses open educational resources (OER) and massive open online courses (MOOCs), followed by a description of the transforming process. Some examples of success stories are then provided. Finally, conclusions and recommendations are suggested.

Open Educational Practices

Learning and teaching praxis has to be changed, innovated, and improved because widespread and increased digitization and opening up education continue to impact human life and society both locally and globally. According to Castaño Muñoz *et al.* (2015) and the European Commission (2013, 2014), there is an urgent need to embrace access, equity, quality, recognition, validity and entrepreneurship in learning and education in the digital society of the twenty-first century. Both argue that the main reasons are that in global society, it is necessary to foster competitiveness and collaboration in education and in the labor market. Barber, Donnelly and Riezvy (2013) predicted an "avalanche" in higher education, similar to that occurring in most areas of society where the internet has had an impact, such as in the film and music industries as well as financing and banking. They indicated that it is difficult to say exactly when this avalanche will occur, but it is sure to be sooner than many imagine. However, some researchers have argued that the avalanche has already happened (Sangra, 2014; Weller, 2014) but that the transformation and adaptation to this open paradigm in education is lacking. In addition, Barber, Donnelly, and Riezvy (2013) stated that it is essential to understand what lies ahead for the higher education sector and prepare for it in terms of theory, practice and the growth of the appropriate mindset (Dweck, 2006). Hence, today we must configure the type of higher education that we want future, new and emerging technologies to serve. Open online learning should be the means to serve great ideas rather than being an end in itself.

Opening up education requires the adoption of practices and cultures that foster academic research and collaboration to enhance learning and teaching. There are several definitions of open education, but that developed by the Open Education Consortium is the most frequently used globally and is the most relevant for the present study (Open Education Consortium, 2016). According to the Consortium, open education is:

> [...] a mode of realizing education enabled by digital technologies that are accessible to as many people as possible. It offers multiple ways of learning and sharing knowledge and a variety of access routes to both formal and non-formal education.

Furthermore, the Open Education Consortium (2016) has defined open education as comprising the "resources, tools and practices that employ a framework of open sharing to improve educational access and effectiveness worldwide".

UNESCO (2015), the Open Education Consortium (2015), and the European Commission's Institute for Prospective Technological Studies (JRC-IPTS) (Inamorato dos Santos, Punie and Castaño Muñoz, 2016) argued that open education combines the traditions of knowledge sharing and knowledge creation with twenty-first century technology to create and embed a vast pool of openly shared educational resources, thus harnessing today's collaborative spirit to develop educational approaches that are more responsive to learners' needs. However, the idea of free and open sharing in education is hardly new. The Open Education Consortium (2016) emphasized that the most basic characteristic of education is sharing, which is the foundation philosophy of education:

> [S]haring is probably the most basic characteristic of education: education is sharing knowledge, insights and information with others,

upon which new knowledge, skills, ideas and understanding can be built. Open Education seeks to scale educational opportunities by taking advantage of the power of the internet, allowing rapid and essentially free dissemination, and enabling people around the world to access knowledge, connect and collaborate. Open is key; open allows not just access, but the ability to modify and use materials, information and networks so education can be personalized to individual users or woven together in new ways for large and diverse audiences.

Because the current provision of higher education is limited by educational institutions' capacity, it is inherently available only to a portion of any society, and a significant part of any population is inevitably left out. However, education is an essential tool that individuals and society can use to solve the challenges of the present and seize the opportunities of the future. The digital revolution offers potential solutions to these limitations by giving a global audience unprecedented access to free, open and high-quality educational resources. Education and the opportunity to learn are the rights of everyone in contemporary society (Gaebel, 2014). By providing free and open access to education and knowledge, societies can enable people to fulfil these rights (Gaebel, 2014; Inamorato dos Santos *et al.*, 2016; UNESCO, 2015).

In an open world, learning needs to reflect the strengths of the institution in accessibility, design and pedagogy. Accordingly, to meet the requirements of open education, the theories and practices of learning and teaching are changing as increased digitization shapes not only how we learn and act but also how knowledge is constructed. Significantly, contextualization and interconnections affect how learners construct and relate to knowledge, and sharing knowledge through social interaction and negotiation has become crucial. The real change, according to Sangra (2015), is in the nature of knowledge. Knowledge today is created by flexible, collaborative networks in dynamic and at times unstable environments. Such collective interactive processes between individuals within frameworks of contextualization shape the process of learning, that is, how to learn, change, construct, and relate to enormous amounts of information in order to meet learners' expectations and needs in a meaningful way. Socially constructed meaning requires the incorporation of social negotiation and mediation from multiple perspectives to reach meaningful learning and the desired knowledge that is available in the large amounts of information surrounding today's learners (Courtney and Mathews, 2015).

Engaging learners in multiple perspectives and experiences through the integration of technology has become imperative (European Commission, 2014). Accordingly, in open education, learners gain skills, strategies and knowledge concurrently in a supportive and evaluative environment that develops their professional skills within the frame of lifelong and active learning. Reflective dialogues and collaborative working with others enrich the sense of self-learning. Gaining multiple perspectives on, filtering and internalizing large amounts of knowledge to shape their perspectives requires learners to be aware of changes in the strategies and construction of knowledge (Du, Xu and Fan, 2015). Keeling's study (2009) stressed that learning is a dynamic process and leads to renewal in higher education. In this respect, there is an intensified need to consider that learners today can learn anywhere at any time. This leads to a debate about the transformation of learning, inquiry and teaching. Open education calls into question changes in learning and teaching processes, while also providing learners with the confidence to construct their own knowledge as culled from a wide range of perspectives that enable learning experiences (Chen and Tsai, 2009). In this respect, the transformation of learning and teaching processes offers advantages for equity, confidence and transparency to attain alternative resources and socially constructed meaning, both of which help tap into human potential.

Compared to the traditional system of higher education, open education plays a key role in offering access, equity and adequacy to learners. Opening up education enhances the ability of education to increase social equitability by providing access to resources at any time and nearly anywhere. Because of its dramatic changes in learning and teaching patterns, open education resources favor increased social cohesion and trust, leading to an equality of access for learners. Due to the fact that equity enhances social cohesion and trust, open educational culture and pedagogy need to reform design, practice and resources to ensure the improved quality of open education. Ensuring a high standard of education for all learners through open education means their inclusion in lifelong learning processes, the attainment of human potential and achievement of meaningful knowledge (Edwards, 2015).

The adoption of open education in different educational systems raises questions about the cultural impact on the expectations and needs of learners and the possibilities for the success of open education both today and in the future. Although digitization offers both promises and perils, such as usability and financial cost, open education has already been accepted as an entrepreneurship strategy, in higher education practice, which is innovative in providing learners with access and multiple perspectives that ensure meaningful learning (Du, Xu and Fan, 2015; Gazi, 2011). Furthermore, open education offers the potential for academic collaboration through experiential and individual learning patterns that are significant for learners in constructing their own knowledge based on cooperation, negotiation and reflection.

OERs and MOOCs are part of the open education movement and will accordingly be defined and discussed in the next section.

Open Educational Resources and Massive Open Online Courses

OERs are an important tool in opening up access to education. According to the William and Flora Hewlett Foundation, OERs are defined by the following:

- Learning content: Full courses, courseware, content modules, learning objects, collections, and journals.

- Tools: Software to support the development, use, re-use and delivery of learning content including searching and organization of content, content and learning management systems, content development tools, and online learning communities.

- Implementation resources: Intellectual property licenses to promote open publishing of materials, design principles of best practice, and localization of content.

OERs include educational materials that are in the public domain or have an open license. Anyone can legally and freely copy, use, adapt and re-share these materials. OERs range from textbooks to curricula, syllabi, lecture notes, assignments, tests, audio, video, animations and even entire online courses and assessments (de los Arcos, 2013; Kanwar, Uvalić-Trumbić and Butcher, 2011; UNESCO, 2015). OERs include the open access to content and resources, such as software, audio, text, video materials and alternative resources ensuring quality and innovation. Opening up access to education has become crucial for enhancing open educational cultures.

Butcher and Moore (2015) and the Commonwealth of Learning (2015) emphasized that OERs have become very fashionable. Some see them as completely revolutionizing how learning materials are implemented in our education systems, while others view OERs from a more pragmatic perspective. The implementation of forms of OERs can reduce costs, but they also raise questions of quality, which opens the way to enhancing quality in design, development and delivery by incorporating the needs and styles of diverse learners. Hence, OERs can have a dynamic effect on both pedagogy and quality. As a form of intellectual entrepreneurship in higher education practices, the delivery of OERs can provide institutional support for open education. However, such support requires a transformation in the adoption and adaptation of open education in a competitive context to ensure its continual improvement.

The Open Education Consortium (2016) highlighted that through OER, students could obtain the following:

> Additional information, viewpoints, and materials to help them succeed. Workers can learn something that will help them on the job. Faculty can exchange material and draw on resources from all around the world. Researchers can share data and develop new networks. Teachers can find new ways to help students learn. People can connect with others they wouldn't otherwise meet to share information and ideas. Materials can be translated, mixed together, broken apart and openly shared again, increasing access and allowing new approaches. Anyone can access educational materials, scholarly articles, and supportive learning communities anytime they want to. Education is available, accessible, modifiable and free.

MOOCs offer another innovative way of opening up education to meet the dimensions of quality emphasized by the European Commission (2013, 2014), the Commonwealth of Learning (2015), and UNESCO (2015). MOOCs were first launched in 2008 by Downes and Siemens, but the term "MOOC" was developed by Cormier (2014). According to Downes (2012), every word represented in the acronym for massive open online courses is negotiable. Massive means that the courses are scalable and their participants can range from hundreds to several thousands. The degree of openness is debatable and mainly concerns access, and the so-called freemium modes, there are no prerequisites or costs, at least not in the beginning. Openness also means that MOOCs are based on freely available resources, often with open licenses as provided for by the Creative Commons (CC). Online means that the courses are delivered via the internet on any kind of device. The word "course" means that the online offering has a beginning and an end; the duration is usually four to eight weeks. The word "course" also implies that there are learning goals and a variety of forms of assessments. However, MOOCs do not provide certification or credits; nonetheless, participants are rewarded with a badge or badges. Recent developments have meant that learners can gain premium advantages, such as guidance and certification, for additional fees.

However, there is an ongoing debate about the quality of MOOCs. Some have argued that MOOCs are revolutionary educational and learning modes. Others have argued that, unlike the first MOOCs, which were based on connectivism (Downes, 2012; Siemens, 2005), the current courses are somewhat traditional, and are based on a series of video recordings.

According to Bonk *et al.* (2015), MOOCs are a relatively recent online learning phenomenon that were developed from the earliest examples nearly a decade ago. They have generated a considerable amount of media attention and attracted significant interest from higher education institutions and venture capitalists who see them as a business opportunity (Daniel, 2012; Haggards, 2013; Shan, 2015). However, many MOOCs do not always conform to the previous definition of OERs because most MOOCs are released under restrictive licenses. In addition, they are rarely available and most MOOCs are in English.

Both OERs and MOOCs extend learning alternatives beyond traditional boundaries and support the creation of opportunities to gain knowledge in the context of global education (Mapstone *et al.*, 2014; Yuan and Powell, 2013). Therefore, higher education practices should foster OER and MOOCs as initiatives to improve access and transfer knowledge based on the access and equity policies that serve diverse communities.

Transformation of Learning and Teaching in Higher Education: Theory and Practice

Higher education must play an essential role in transforming learning that it is free and open to all (The Open Educational Working Group, 2014). In this respect, professionalism is important for learning and teaching in higher education. Bucklow and Clark (2000) emphasized that changes and developments in learning and teaching in higher education must ensure the quality of students' learning experiences. Therefore, merging theory and praxis through transformation to enhance the quality of student experiences is essential in higher education. Communication and information technology allow higher education institutions to implement transformation in group learning, the global delivery of materials, and student interactions over the internet.

In the era of professionalism, what to know, how to know, and who you know play enormous roles in higher education (Siemens, 2005). Siemens argued for the importance of applying the theory of connectivism, as well as how to build and maintain professional and personal learning networks. In the changing context of higher education, accepted and traditional modes of thought need to be reconsidered. Evidence shows that linear education has failed to enhance the quality of learning and teaching. Learning and teaching are enriched through opening up a wide range of resources (Wood *et al.*, 2011). Devlin and Samarawickrema (2010) pointed out that effective teaching in the changing context of higher education demands paying attention to the quality and effectiveness of learning and teaching.

Digital media and open educational resources have extended the limits of both learners and teachers, thus renewing the context of higher education (Ponti, 2014). The use of digital media and open educational resources provide self-directed and choice-based learning (Creelman, Ehlers and Ossiannilsson, 2014; Ossiannilsson, 2016). Hence, learners can control and orchestrate their own learning (Ossiannilsson, forthcoming). Downes (2016) stressed the possibilities of personal learning and just in time learning, before striving for personalized learning in an already fixed system. Ossiannilsson has argued for the same possibilities, introducing the concept of *just for me learning* through open education. Edwards (2015) underlined the importance of openness in decreasing the barriers to education. Openness in this respect means openness in all fields of learning, that is, anyone, anytime, anywhere, and anyhow can learn with any device (Castaño Muñoz *et al.*, 2013). Focusing on openness helps prevent the monopoly of educational institutions and increases the possibility of collaborative peer learning through the co-production of knowledge.

Lifelong learning, continuous learning, upgrading skills and continuous professional development have become important in Europe because they facilitate economic growth and promote the full involvement of individuals in society. Castaño Muñoz, Redecker, Vuorikari and Punie (2013) emphasized that technological development and open education systems can create transformation in higher education. Even Weller (2011) emphasized the crucial shift towards *digital scholars* in educational settings to create an impact in terms of how technology can transform scholarly practice.

The Open Education Consortium (2015) advocates core values that enhance quality in open education including a global focus, openness, equity, collaboration and multiculturalism. The European Commission's Joint Research Centre (JRC) and the Institute for Prospective Technological Studies (Inomorates dos Santos *et al.*, 2015) summarized quality in open education as comprising the following:

- Efficacy: fitness for purpose of the object and concept being assessed.

- Impact: a measure of the extent to which an object or concept proves effective, impact depends on the nature of the object or concept itself, the context in which it is applied, and the use to which it is put by the user.

- Availability: a pre-condition for efficacy and impact to be achieved; availability is thus also an essential part of the element of quality. In this sense, availability includes concepts such as transparency and ease of access.

- Accuracy: a measure of precision and the absence of errors in a particular process or object.

- Excellence: compares the quality of an object or concept to its peers and to its maximum quality potential.

As illustrated in Figure 1, these features of quality are iterative and interrelated. If these features of quality are fulfilled, learners can orchestrate their own learning and take ownership of it. Ownership is one of the most important features of motivation and learning in open learning arenas (Ossiannilsson, forthcoming).

Figure 1. Quality dimensions in open education that enable
learners to take ownership

In addition to the movement towards increased openness, the paradigms within the educational sector need to be reconsidered. All paradigms, from curriculum design, learning pathways and styles, offers, services, delivery to assessments must be revisited. The means of recognition and validation also require reconsideration as the lines between formal and informal learning become more and more blurred. Through increased openness, linear education will give way to learning environments that facilitate, promote, and value rhizomatic learning and serendipity. Weller (2014) argued for the "battle for openness", raising the question "How open is open?" He stated that we have thus far only embraced openness inside an already close organizational structure. Hence, Wheeler (2015) argued that there is an urgent need to leave the comfort zone in teaching and learning. Cormier (2015) stated that it is time to leave the curriculum per se and have society itself serve as the curriculum to facilitate not only personalized learning but also personal learning (Downes and Ossiannilsson, forthcoming). Extending this viewpoint, Ossiannilsson (2015) argued for the need to take seriously the consequences of open learning landscapes and embrace choice based-learning so that learning is not simply available anytime, anywhere, anyhow, and to anyone, but also can include learning *just for me*. In this way, learners take ownership of their personal learning.

Examples of stories, cases, and storytelling

Latchem, Özkul, Aydin and Mutlu (2006) provided a case study of open education, in which Anadolu University was an example of e-transformation. In Turkey, the concept of open education mirrors leadership in technology development. Scholars associate increased quality with personalized and collaborative learning that is made possible by the development of convenience and flexibility in learning. Strategic planning, quality assurance, faculty development and reflective practice all play an enormous role in e-transformation. In addition, Anadolu University serves as an open education system not only in Turkey but also in Turkish communities across Europe and on the island of Cyprus. Consequently, it has one of the world's largest student bodies. It offers teamwork and research diffusion activities to provide equity and participation in online education.

Gourley and Lane's (2009) account of open education in the UK's Open University offers an insight into open educational resources and how openness can be promoted. The Open University, a pioneer in open and distance learning, now employs broadcasting in multi-directional, multiple-platform communication and collaboration, and new forms of licensing for largely digital content. The launching of open education resources as a business model for its competitive advantage explains the Open University's efforts to enhance the learning experiences of OER users, their involvement in higher education and networks, knowledge and understanding of OER delivery and the development of sustainable and scalable models of OER delivery.

Conclusions and Recommendations

This chapter has discussed the benefits of open learning and education for learners everywhere, providing them with the ability to access high-quality education and training. Education is an essential, shared and collaborative social good. We have focused on the importance of access, equity, quality, entrepreneurship, continuing professional development, learning and preparing for an uncertain future in the digital society. Research has shown that it is clear that we cannot continue to educate today's learners using yesterday's methods for a tomorrow that we do not yet understand (Sangra, 2015; UNESCO, 2015).

Open principles, such as open educational resources, free and open software, open data and open standards, are the keys to the genuine empowerment of faculty and students globally and to making education and opportunities accessible to all. How learners obtain meaningful learning has become part of the opening up debate. Accordingly, education requires new policy reforms which embrace the opening up of educational concepts and debate. Given the rapid changes in learners' needs in the digital age, there is an intensified need to focus on the renewal of innovation in learning and teaching (European Commission, 2014a, 2014b). The dissemination of learning and knowledge is essential for the reflective experience of constructing knowledge and developing skills in the process of interaction, teamwork and responsibility for personal learning within the framework of the transformation of learning and teaching (Aksal, 2011). Pedagogical innovations such as open education will also promote changes in policies to prioritize human learning and development through access to and equality in learning and teaching. In this respect, significant collaborative efforts have been made to move from a teacher-centered approach to a learner-centered approach within the framework of a lifelong learning perspective. Because of the changes in teaching and learning practices caused by digitization, pedagogical approaches need to include project-based activities, experiential learning and group dynamics to help learners reconstruct knowledge and develop skills and abilities to fulfil their potential. This chapter has reviewed how learning and teaching processes have shifted rapidly to require open education for lifelong learning. It has considered supporting theories and offered the examples of case studies in order to advocate policy and pedagogical reforms based upon open education.

In transforming lives and developing skills, education and the learning environment have important roles in ensuring inclusive and equal learning opportunities and promoting lifelong learning to an increasing number of people. Because education involves transformative and developmental processes, it affects the inclusion, equity and development of learners in the practices of global and national educational systems. Learning environments need to reflect the values human rights, shared responsibility, inclusion and the protection of human fulfillment (Kuter, Altinay Gazi and Altinay Aksal, 2012).

Access is a compulsory quality indicator of education systems in which all learners have access to education and learning environments anytime and anywhere. In transforming learning and teaching, educational processes need to encourage inclusion and equality for all learners through assuring access. By proposing meaningful learning and professional development opportunities in lifelong learning processes, open education commits to promoting universal access and participation. In ensuring motivation, equality, evaluation of learning progress and creativity, we must rethink learning and teaching environments to enhance the quality of education (Gazi, 2011). Educational quality includes both knowledge creation and creativity in terms of skill development within the processes by which educators plan and restructure learning environments to meet learners' expectations, including global and local standards in education. Significantly, higher education practices need to include equitable and increased access to quality education and research for the continuous improvement in the quality of their practices. Technology-supported learning environments, such as open education, acquire strength through knowledge dissemination, innovation and collaboration to meet global standards.

References

Aksal, A. F. (2011), Action Plan on Communication Practices: Roles of Tutors at EMU Distance Education Institute to Overcome Social Barriers in Constructing Knowledge, *The Turkish Online Journal of Educational Technology — TOJET*, 8(2), 33–47.

Barber, M., Donnelly, K. and Riezvy, S. (2013), *An Avalanche is Coming: Higher Education and the Revolution Ahead*, London: Institute for Public Policy Research.

Bonk, C. J., Lee, M. M., Reeves, T. C. and Reynolds, T. H. (Eds.) (2015), *MOOCs and Open Education Around the World*, London: Routledge, http://dx.doi.org/10.4324/9781315751108

Bucklow, C. and Clark, P. (2000), The Role of the Institute for Learning and Teaching in Higher Education in Supporting Professional Development in Learning and Teaching in Higher Education, *Teacher Development*, 4(1), pp. 7–13, 10.1080/13664530000200101

Butcher, N. and Moore, A. (2015), *Understanding Open Educational Resources*, in M. Sanjaya (Ed.), *Commonwealth of Learning*, http://oasis.col.org/bitstream/handle/11599/1013/2015_Butcher_Moore_Understanding-OER.pdf?sequence=1&isAllowed=y

Castaño Muñoz, J., Redecker, C. Vuorikari, R. and Punie, Y. (2013), Open Education 2030: Planning the Future of Adult Learning in Europe, *Open Learning: The Journal of Open, Distance and E-Learning*, 28(3), pp. 171–186, 10.1080/02680513.2013.871199

Chen, Y. C. and Tsai, C. C. (2009), An Educational Research Course Facilitated by Online Peer Assessment, *Innovations in Education and Teaching International*, 46(1), pp. 105–117, http://dx.doi.org/10.1080/14703290802646297

Courtney, M. and Wilhoite-Mathews, S. (2015), From Distance Education to Online Learning: Practical Approaches to Information Literacy Instruction and Collaborative Learning in Online Environments, *Journal of Library Administration*, 55(4), pp. 261–277, http://dx.doi.org/10.1080/01930826.2015.1038924

Creelman, A., Ehlers U. and Ossiannilsson, E. (2014), Perspectives on MOOC quality — An Account of the EFQUEL MOOC Quality Project, *International Journal for Innovation and Quality in Learning*, 3, pp. 79–87, http://lup.lub.lu.se/search/record/4648237

Cormier, D. (2015), *Re: A Practical Guide to Rhizo 2015*, http://davecormier.com/edblog/2015/04/10/a-practical-guide-to-rhizo15

Daniel, J. (2012), Making Sense of MOOCs: Musings in a Maze of Myth, Paradox and Possibility, *Journal of Interactive Media in Education*, 2012(3) (Article 18), http://doi.org/10.5334/2012-18

de los Arcos, B., Farrow, R., Perryman, L.-A., Pitt, R. and Weller. M. (2014), *OER Evidence Report 2013–2014*, OER Research Hub, http://oerresearchhub.org/about- 2/reports

Devlin, M. and Samarawickrema, G. (2010), The Criteria of Effective Teaching in a Changing Higher Education Context, *Higher Education Research and Development*, 29(2), pp. 111–124, 10.1080/07294360903244398

Du, J., Xu, J. and Fan, X. (2015), Help Seeking in Online Collaborative Group Work: A Multilevel Analysis, *Technology, Pedagogy and Education*, 24(3), pp. 1–17, 10.1080/1475939X.2014.897962

Dweck, C. (2006), *Mindset: The New Psychology of Success*, New York: Random House.

Downes, S. (2012), *A True History of the MOOC*, http://www.downes.ca/presentation/300

Downes, S. (2016), Personal and Personalized Learning, *EMMA Newsletter*, February 17, http://us8.campaign-archive2.com/?u=17ce08681f559814caf135 9d3&id=fa1770e58d&e=6fb1272e29

Edwards, R. (2015), Knowledge Infrastructures and the Inscrutability of Openness in Education, *Learning, Media and Technology*, 40(3), pp. 251–264, 10.1080/17439884.2015.1006131

European Commission (2013), *Opening up Education: Innovative teaching and learning for all through new Technologies and Open Educational Resources*, http://eur-lex.europa.eu/legal-content/EN/TXT/?uri=CELEX%3A52013DC0654

European Commission (2014), *High Level Group on Modernisation of Higher Education. Report to the European Commission on New Modes of Learning and Teaching in Higher Education*, http://ec.europa.eu/education/library/reports/modernisation-universities_en.pdf

Gaebel, M. (2014), *MOOCs: Massive Open Online Courses, An Update of EUA's First Paper* (2013), The European Association (EUA), http://www.eua.be/Libraries/publication/MOOCs_Update_January_2014.pdf?sfvrsn=2

Gaebel, M., Kupriyanova, V., Morais, R. and Colucci, W. (2014), *E-learning in European Higher Education Institutions: Results of a Mapping Survey Conducted in October–December 2013*, Brussels: European University Association.

Gazi, Z. A. (2011), A Step for Evaluating Constructivist Approach Integrated Online Courses, *Turkish Online Journal of Educational Technology — TOJET*, 10(3), pp. 13–20.

Gourley, B. and Lane, A. (2009), Re-invigorating Openness at The Open University: The Role of Open Educational Resources, *Open Learning: The Journal of Open, Distance and E-Learning*, 24(1), pp. 57–65, http://dx.doi.org/10.1080/02680510802627845

Haggard, S. *et al.* (2013), *The Maturing of the MOOCs: Literature Review of Massive Open Online Courses and Other Forms of Online Learning*, BIS Research Paper no. 10, Department for Business, Innovation and Skills.

Hewlett Foundation (2016), *The Open Educational Recourses Initiative*, http://www.hewlett.org/uploads/files/OER_overview.pdf

Inamorato dos Santos, A., Punie, P. and Castaño Muñoz, J. (2016), Opportunities and Challenges for the Future of MOOCs and Open Education in Europe, in E. de Corte, L. Engwall and U. Teichler (Eds.), *From Books to MOOCs? Emerging Models of Learning and Teaching in Higher Education*, Proceedings from a symposium held in Stockholm, 23 May 2015, 88, pp. 81–91, London: Portland Press, http://www.portlandpresspublishing.com/sites/default/files/Editorial/Wenner/PPL_Wenner_FM.pdf

Kanwar, A., Uvalić-Trumbić, S. and Butcher, N. (2011), *A Basic Guide to Open Educational Resources (OER)*, Vancouver: Commonwealth of Learning; Paris: UNESCO.

Keeling, R. P. (2009), Learning as Transformation: Resourcefulness and Renewal in Higher Education, *Journal of College and Character*, 10(3), pp. 1–4, 10.2202/1940-1639.1081

Kuter, S., Altinay Gazi, Z. and Altinay Aksal, F. (2012), Examination of Co-construction of Knowledge in Videotaped Simulated Instruction, *Educational Technology & Society*, 15(1), pp. 174–184.

Latchem, C., Özkul, A. E., Aydin, C. H. and Mutlu, M. E. (2006), The Open Education System, Anadolu University, Turkey: E-transformation in a Mega-university, *Open Learning: The Journal of Open, Distance and E-Learning*, 21(3), pp. 221–235, http://dx.doi.org/10.1080/02680510600953203

Mapstone, S. (Ed.), Buttendijk, S. and Wiberg, E. (2014), Online Learning at Research Intensive Universities, *LERU Advisory Paper no. 16* (2014), http://www.leru.org/files/publications/LERU_AP16__Online_Learning_at_RIUs_final.pdf

Open Education Consortium (OEC) (2016), *What is Open Education?*, http://www.oeconsortium.org/about-oec

Open Education Working Group (2014), *The Open Education Handbook*, http://education.okfn.org/handbook

Ossiannilsson, E. (2016), Challenges and Opportunities for Active and Hybrid Learning Related to UNESCO Post 2015, in J. Keengwe and G. Onchwari (Eds.), *Handbook of Research on Active Learning and the Flipped Classroom Model in the Digital Age*, pp. 333–351. Hershey: Information Science Reference, http://dx.doi.org/10.4018/978-1-4666-9680-8

Ossiannilsson, E. (2016), Let the Learners take the Lead for their Learning and Educational Lifelong Learning Journey, in J. Keengwe and G. Onchwari (Eds.), *Handbook of Research on Learning Centred Pedagogy in Teaching Education and Professional Development*, Hershey: IGI Global, http://dx.doi.org/10.4018/978-1-5225-0892-2.ch009

Ponti, M. (2014), Self-directed Learning and Guidance in Non-formal Open Courses, *Learning, Media and Technology*, 39(2), pp. 154–168, http://dx.doi.org /10.1080/17439884.2013.799073

Sangra, A. (2015), *Expanding Learning Opportunities for the Last 25 Years…and Beyond*, Keynote address, Expanding Learning Scenarios, EDEN Annual Conference 2015, 9–12 June, 2015, Barcelona, Spain.

Shan, D. (2015), MOOCs in 2015: Breaking Down the Numbers, *EdSurge*, https:// www.edsurge.com/news/2015-12-28-moocs-in-2015-breaking-down-the-numbers

Siemens, G. (2005), Connectivism: A Learning Theory for the Digital Age, *Instructional Technology and Distance Learning*, 2(1), http://www.itdl.org/ journal/jan_05/index.htm

UNESCO (2010), *High-level Meeting on the Millennium Development Goals*, http:// www.unesco.org/new/en/education/themes/leading-the-international-agenda/education-for-all/education-and-the-mdgs

UNESCO (2015), *Position Paper on Education Post-2015*, http://unesdoc.unesco. org/images/0022/002273/227336E.pdf

Weller, M. (2011), *The Digital Scholar: How Technology is Transforming Scholarly Practice*, London: Bloomsbury Academic, http://dx.doi. org/10.5040/9781849666275

Weller, M. (2014), *The Battle for Open: How Openness Won and Why it Doesn't Feel like Victory*, London: Ubiquity Press, http://dx.doi.org//10.5334/bam

Wheeler, S. (2015) *Learning with 'e's: Educational Theory and Practice in the Digital Age*, London: Crown House Publishing.

Wood, L. N., Vu, T., Bower, M., Brown, N., Skalicky, J., Donovan, D., Loch, B., Joshi, N., and Bloom, W. (2011), Professional Development for Teaching in Higher Education, *International Journal of Mathematical Education in Science and Technology*, 42(7), pp. 997–1009, 10.1080/0020739X.2011.608864

Yuan, L. and Powell, S. (2013), *MOOCs and Open Education: Implications for Higher Education*, JISC CETIS, http://publications.cetis.org.uk/wp-content/ uploads/2013/03/MOOCs-and-Open-Education.pdf

9. Three Approaches to Open Textbook Development

Rajiv S. Jhangiani, Arthur G. Green, and John D. Belshaw

In this contribution, three open textbook authors outline the motivations and mechanics of three successful yet different approaches to writing open textbooks. These approaches include textbook creation and adaptation projects, individual and collaborative efforts, and traditional timeline and compressed "sprint" models. Following these cases, the authors discuss similarities and differences across approaches, along with broader issues concerning how particular disciplines and philosophies of teaching influence writing open textbooks.

Three Approaches to Open Textbook Development

> We believe that we are entering a technological age in which we will be
> able to interact with the richness of living information — not merely in the
> passive way that we have become accustomed to using books and libraries,
> but as active participants in an ongoing process, bringing something to it
> through our interaction with it, and not simply receiving something from
> it by our connection to it (Licklider and Taylor, 1968, p. 21).

Introduction

In October 2012, the British Columbia (BC) Ministry of Advanced
Education launched the Open Textbook Project (OTP) (http://open.
bccampus.ca). The project's goal was to create sixty open textbooks in
the forty highest-enrolled subject areas in post-secondary education in
the province. As a provincial agency that supports teaching, learning
and educational technology, BCcampus was chosen to lead the project.
Four years later, BCcampus has surpassed their initial targets with over
150 open textbooks in the BC Open Textbook repository. These textbooks
have been adopted by nearly 200 faculty teaching 606 courses at thirty-
one (twenty-three public and eight private) post-secondary institutions.
The savings to BC students are estimated at $1,850,715-$2,298,878 USD
(BCcampus, 2016), a small fraction of the $174 million that students
worldwide have saved as a result of open textbooks from organizations
that include OpenStax College and MIT's OpenCourseWare (Creative
Commons, 2015).

These significant financial savings do not come at the expense of
educational outcomes. Indeed, students who have been assigned open
textbooks perform just as well as or better than those assigned traditional
textbooks (see Hilton, 2016, for a review). The story remains the same
for retention and program completion. These results — improved
access, significant cost savings and equivalent or improved educational
outcomes — have encouraged philanthropic organizations to support
the development of entire college programs without traditional
textbooks costs (Bliss, 2015).

Yet, the very success of open textbooks raises a series of questions,
not the least of which is how this beneficent system can be sustained
and why a faculty member would ever undertake the onerous work of

creating or adapting an open textbook. In the absence of royalty cheques, prestige, or institutional recognition, faculty have few professional incentives. For faculty with the will, little is understood about the different approaches available and even less about how these different approaches may align with disciplinary requirements. In other words, we know the elixir works, but we know far less about its methods of production.

The authors of this chapter have created five successful open textbooks as part of BC OTP.[1] In what follows we outline the motivations and mechanics of three different approaches to writing open textbooks. These approaches include textbook creation and adaptation projects, individual and collaborative efforts, and traditional timeline and compressed "sprint" models. Following these cases, we discuss similarities and differences across our approaches, along with broader issues concerning how our particular disciplines and philosophies of teaching influence our approaches to writing open textbooks.

History Making in Open Textbooks

John Douglas Belshaw

The open textbook project was, for me, an intersection of interests, obligations, and coincidence. My interests begin in my work as a teaching and research-active Canadian historian. With conventional texts, we are held hostage to the table of contents. A 13-week course is bound to follow fairly closely the chapter organization of the narrative textbook — which is typically and not surprisingly built around 12–15 chapters. This is one of several teaching-to-the-textbook traps that one encounters. Beyond that, I am concerned as a pedagogue that history textbooks tend to adhere to a core "master narrative" tradition (which can be very difficult to escape). Twenty years ago this was a more entrenched phenomenon: the arc of the pre-Confederation historical

---

1   *Canadian History: Pre-Confederation* (Belshaw), *Canadian History: Post-Confederation* (Belshaw), *British Columbia in a Global Context* (Green), *Research Methods in Psychology* (Jhangiani), and *Principles of Social Psychology* (Jhangiani). All these open textbooks are available at: https://open.bccampus.ca/find-open-textbooks

tale begins with European-Aboriginal contact and culminates in colonial union in 1867. No matter how much economic and social and demographic history was considered, and no matter how vigorously it was reiterated, it still came out as a story of power and the voice of what is called the "Nationalist School" echoed throughout. Now, it is true that the most critically sophisticated text might challenge the master narrative but it would still be a static object constrained by its own structure and materiality. Scholarly history is a fast-moving field, stereotypes of stodgy old academics wearing suede elbow patches notwithstanding. Technologically and theoretically it is very dynamic and the conclusions drawn by historians have repeatedly shifted public policy. Getting those ideas into a conventional textbook is enormously challenging if not impossible.

I felt, too, that I owed it to my students to advance the open textbook experiment. My classes are all delivered online through Thompson Rivers University — Open Learning (TRU-OL). Each new student receives in the mail what we call a "pizza box" — a cardboard container that includes the course outline, a hefty manual, some audio lectures, and textbooks. One of the textbooks is a narrative and is among the most widely used in the country. It is now into its 7th edition and the value-added proposition of each successive edition seems to me subject to the law of diminishing returns. The release of a new edition, however, necessitates a revision of the course materials, a process that is both time-consuming and costly. TRU-OL has to contract instructors (like me) to deal with content; the production side of the house has to be involved. Hours of institutional labor occur because Chapter Y has been split in two and the pagination has completely changed or there is a new set of suggested readings. A "minor revision" contract may be welcome but the roll-out is not. Our courses are continuous-entry, non-cohort, and asynchronous: any change in course material necessitates two iterations of the course until we have flushed out of the system the old materials (and students). The fact that TRU — along with Kwantlen Polytechnic University — is a member of the Open Educational Resource Universitas (the OERu) gave my colleagues and I an institutional context for addressing these issues.

Coincidence enters into the equation as regards our audio lectures. These were compiled in the late 1970s or early 1980s by academic historians mostly in Toronto. While some were timeless, the collection was really quite dated. Newer fields — such as gender history, Aboriginal history, and environmental history — were not represented at all. The best-before date on the audio resource had come and gone; we were ready to assemble new lecture material. The open textbook created an opportunity to build a multimedia instrument, one that included the written word but also video and sound — embedded right in the textbook (that is, in its HTML form). This seemed to me a delightfully Harry Potteresque possibility wherein an expert in the field speaks to the student right off the page.

Canadian History: Pre-Confederation was able to exploit some existing Open Educational Resources (OERs). European, American, and (remarkably) Aboriginal history of credible quality could be found in the Creative Commons in the form of other open textbooks. Beyond that, however, the material had to be created from scratch. This was a significant undertaking both intellectually and in terms of person-hours. Learning how to manipulate the Wordpress-based PressBooks platform on which the open textbook was fashioned constituted another challenge.[2] Looking beyond those issues, my principal concern was how the textbook would be received. Colleagues in several institutions in at least three provinces are already using it and report favorably, so I am pleased on that front.

Approaching the "sequel", *Canadian History: Post-Confederation*, I decided to engage a large number of historians in crafting small- to medium-sized sections of the text. Nearly three dozen historians from almost every province participated. This strategy had three advantages, the first of which was an opportunity to draw on expertise that I would otherwise struggle to approximate. Not everyone can jump nimbly from nineteenth century women's organizations to the role of Aboriginal soldiers in two world wars to the opportunities presented by oral and digital histories. I certainly can't. Much better to include the most up-to-date interpretations by the most up-to-date academics. Secondly, this was a chance to introduce students to experts in a huge range of special

---

2   The BCcampus open textbooks are usually compiled and delivered on a custom-built platform called "PressBooks". It is an adapted version of Wordpress that allows collaborative authoring and is capable of importing and exporting a variety of file formats.

fields, not by quoting them but by getting their voice and passion into the text. Finally, and perhaps most importantly, involving colleagues is a way to introduce them to the open textbook as a teaching resource. As someone put it, they've got skin in the game.

These projects have not advanced without objections. Giving up one's intellectual property to the Creative Commons runs contrary to some scholarly instincts. On the one hand, it's called intellectual *property* for a reason. We long ago commodified our output and there isn't a historian who doesn't dream of becoming the next Eric Hobsbawm or Fernand Braudel — the sort of national historian whose books sell and for whom traffic stops and the nation mourns at their passing. As a writing historian, I have produced a number of books on aspects of Canadian history and that is part of the gig: the road to tenure is paved with peer reviewed publications. Few monographs in the Humanities and Social Sciences, however, make much in the way of royalties because they generally do not make much in the way of sales (especially in a relatively small market like Canada). All that effort and within one year the "fresh" list on which your title appeared is lining the bottom of the budgie cage. That is the moment when most of us realize that what we wanted, really, was not royalties but *readers*. The commodification of intellectual property can be criticized, then, for erecting a monetized barrier between the "creator" and the "consumer", a singular reason for supporting OERs and shifting more intellectual product to the Creative Commons. But, as I said, this runs against the powerful current in our culture that privileges proprietorship of knowledge.

Furthermore, rule changes are involved. Among historians, the well-crafted footnote is a thing of beauty. Our sources are often so arcane and deeply buried in dusty archives that we devise citations as precise as coordinates for an airstrike. If intellectual property holds us back from releasing material into the commons, it is *intellectual integrity* that stops us from adapting OERs. One might blame the American historian, Stephen Ambrose (1936–2002), who was to historical writing what Lance Armstrong is to the Tour de France: undeniably amazing but the stain of dishonesty won't wash away (Harris, 2010). So, borrowing whole tracts from other open textbooks — effectively a cut-and-paste operation — flies in the face of everything we have been taught about integrity; and one feels compelled to model good behavior for students by *not* copying lengthy passages verbatim. The CC-BY-SA seal is, however, permission from the creator of material to use at will.[3] At the same time, the onus remains on the scholar to ensure that one does not use inaccurate material. And that is where the tradition of intellectual integrity continues to matter. This strikes a nice balance, one that younger scholars seem able to reach sooner than those of us who are closer to retirement seminars than to tenure committees.

When the Ministry of Advanced Education in British Columbia announced that it was committed to the creation of open textbooks, these concerns came home to me. I have written several intellectual property policies and integrity policies as well. I know first-hand how strongly some scholars feel about ownership of everything from a patent through innovation and journal article to an instructional manual. I know, as well, plenty of textbook writers whose efforts brought revenue to publishing houses, bookstores, and their own pockets and I have respect for their contribution to the learning community. Embracing the open textbook project required serious second thought about a paradigm with which I had grown up.

It is worth the candle, as they say. I have come to believe that the old paradigm has become a barrier to intellectual vitality. Academics wringing their hands about the high costs of education can seize upon open textbooks as a viable solution. As well, historians ought to be seen to be doing history, not depending on someone else to provide the all-inclusive, palatable to the greatest number interpretation in three or four editions. In a world of Wikipedias, we need to show students how intellectual integrity actually functions, not by cracking down on plagiarism but by working collaboratively to improve livestock grazing across the Creative Commons. While it may be true that some folks will no longer get rich off conventional textbooks in an OER world, it is worth recalling that the monumental works in our field are not and have never been *textbooks*. Writing two open textbooks has shown me where the scholarly historian can simultaneously become a public scholar, an activist for greater educational access, a directly-engaged member of a community of pedagogues and a champion for integrity in this very important field.

---

3   The Creative Commons licensing system provides an alphabet soup of designations. In the development of OERs like open textbooks the "CC-BY-SA" designation is the trifecta of openness. It signals: Creative Commons material with a responsibility to attribute the material's origin (whom it is "BY") and Share-Alike.

Sprinting Towards an Open Geography

Arthur "Gill" Green

Three moments led me to co-author an open textbook. The first moment was when my undergraduate university roommate loaned me his copy of Freire's *Pedagogy of the Oppressed*. Freire advocates that a change to a liberated society requires liberating education — that is, we must rethink the basic modalities of education. He writes, "Education must begin with the solution of the teacher-student contradiction, by reconciling the poles of the contradiction so that both are simultaneously teachers *and* students [...]" (Freire, 2000, p. 79). This reconciliation encourages learners to participate in the creation of knowledge rather than simply focus on consumption of knowledge. Freire's ideas influenced my pedagogical approach and, eventually, my belief in the game-changing importance of OER.

The second moment came in my first year teaching geography. One day after an introductory human geography class, I saw some students lingering in the back of the classroom taking pictures with their phones. Curious, I approached to see what they were doing. These were not selfies. Apparently the most photogenic item in the room was our textbook. The students explained that they were sharing a textbook because it cost too much. Each week, one of them would take the textbook home and the two others would take pictures of the textbook pages in order to read them on their phones. Perhaps most disturbing was that they were apologetic, as if they were doing something wrong. This was the canary in the coal mine for me. It was time to get out. It was time to get off of the conventional merry-go-round of corporate textbooks, where the "new edition is better [...] now with more colorful insets, an exam question bank, slides, and online videos and quizzes". This approach profits at the expense of students, and caters to the weaknesses of the modern, harried educator.

I have come to believe that the conventional textbook issue is not someone's fault, but it *is* everyone's problem. This merry-go-round is a logical result of the current educational labor system and the growing tendency to see the education sector as an unmined profit source (students as consumers) rather than a source of a public good (learners as productive citizens). Faculty keep pace with the textbook merry-go-round because they are accustomed to it and sometimes reliant on it as a crutch to help balance all the other demands on their time. Even so, most faculty that I know have complaints about the textbooks they adopt and subsequently require students to buy (missing coverage on key areas, the sequencing of chapters, out of date facts, etc.). Yet complaints are no longer enough. To truly care for students and ourselves, we as faculty have to make a full stop. We must change the system within which we teach, learn, and work.

I would argue that the most important contribution of open textbooks is not the commonly cited cost savings, but that they relieve the pedagogic burden that conventional textbooks impose on students and faculty. Conventional textbooks are for transferring information to consumers — what Freire calls the banking approach to education. The teacher or textbook has the knowledge. The knowledge is purchased (at great expense), deposited in the student (account), and the student regurgitates it on demand with little to no interest (pun intended). Open textbooks are an alternative that allow flexible adaptation of the book to pedagogies that suit the learning relationship.

Despite my ambition, I was unable to locate any geography open textbooks that addressed Canadian or British Columbian perspectives. So, I decided to write an open textbook. The hurdles were significant. First, the time required — I was teaching full-time, designing courses and finishing a PhD. Second, colleagues advised me against writing a textbook, let alone an open textbook. The common logic was that an academic should focus on feeding the publication mill. Writing a textbook is just one publication, when several articles could be produced in the same time. Third, no professional credit for open textbooks. I was told they were seen as "self-publishing" ebooks compared to writing niche books (with exorbitant price tags) within publishing corporations. Fourth, why work for free when confronted with the potential and well-known employment hazards of sessional work in academia? Fifth, the unfamiliar language of esoteric terms, abbreviations, and overlapping licenses seemed to be an additional hurdle in simply trying to understand open education. Despite Freire and the canary, the disincentives caged me in.

In 2014, BCcampus gave me my third moment as they recruited a team to write a BC regional geography open textbook. This textbook would be unlike any of the previous textbooks supported by BCcampus as it would be written through a book sprint — a collaborative, rapid (less than a week) writing method. The book sprint required bringing a team together for four days to collaboratively outline and produce a textbook. The authors would be supported by a librarian, a graphic artist, facilitators and BCcampus staff. Each author would receive a stipend. The methodological innovation, support staff, stipend and fact that I already had four years of content developed from teaching BC regional geography broke down the disincentives for me to get to work. I was the first of five authors to sign up.

We worked over four days to complete the first draft. The first day we met each other, learned how to use the online writing platform, learned the book sprint method and collectively outlined the book. We identified service learning and community based research as important pedagogical aims and decided to provide example activities for each textbook section. Some content sections that we identified as critical had never before been included in a BC regional geography textbook (e.g. food systems). The following days involved a frenzy of writing and editing. Book sprint participants are encouraged to not prepare materials before meeting as a team. We soon found that as a geography textbook there were a number of images and maps that we needed to obtain permissions to use or to create from scratch. We soon realized that the time pressure would force us to rely on some background materials for both these images and for content. So, I opened up the materials that I created during four years of teaching BC regional geography. Giving access to my course content to all my colleagues was at first a bit intimidating. Then, I realized that this was part of the process of being open. I had just created OERs by sharing my course materials. Through daily 12–14 hour cycles of text creation and editing, the textbook evolved into a coherent draft and I came to understand that all open textbooks are simply drafts that should be further adapted. After four days, we emerged with a nearly 200-page open textbook. BCcampus spent the following months conducting a peer review process and converting the book to their online open textbook repository. This institutional support was critical in garnering colleagues' respect for the work.

Most of the challenges we encountered were specific to the book sprint method and our team composition. One of the first things we learned is that while the official book sprint method emphasizes making everything on site, this is a challenge for a textbook — especially for a geography course that combines insights from numerous sub-disciplinary areas in human and physical geography. In retrospect, the unique requirements of a textbook might require changes to the book sprint method. For example, a preliminary meeting of authors for establishing the content of the book would allow them time to find resources that they could bring to the book sprint. This would have allowed us to contribute better materials, identify our weak content areas and spend more book sprint time on creatively crafting the text and our pedagogical approach. In our book sprint, we found our team was weak in the area of physical geography. As well, division of labor issues negatively impacted workflows and brought up concerns about free riders. This might also be addressed by a preliminary meeting that allows a better division of labor and accountability as it would allow content experts to create quality first drafts or lists of core concepts within their area of expertise that could then be introduced to the collaborative writing process.

There were additional challenges, but these are truly opportunities. For example, we did not have time to develop ancillary resources — now commonly expected with conventional textbooks. Yet, the presence of ancillary resources influences teacher-student interactions and assessment choices when educators are pressed for time. Perhaps a more sustainable approach is to crowdsource, inviting others to share the ancillary resources that they develop in an associated OER repository. This could provide many different approaches to the same open textbook material and opens up pedagogical discussion.

To recap, there are unique challenges to sprinting through an open textbook. Yet this sprint format can create a first draft and open us to potential, because all open textbooks really are first drafts waiting for improvement. The sprint format is a point of departure for the reconciliation of the student and teacher relation. This format can be adopted for course projects to improve textbooks. Open education resources reveal possibilities for liberating geographic education from the pedagogic burdens that conventional textbooks place on how we think about geography as a discipline, our students as people, ourselves as educators and the foundations of a truly democratic society.

Review, Revise, Adopt. Rinse and Repeat

Rajiv S. Jhangiani

My red pill moment was when I first heard the term "OER" uttered by David Wiley in May 2013 at an annual workshop held at Thompson Rivers University for faculty in their Open Learning division. This is when I began to see the Matrix for what it was — an artificial, parasitic, publisher-driven system in which faculty are unwitting carriers. I am ashamed to say that it never occurred to me to look beyond the unsolicited glossy hardcovers that appeared in my mailbox every week. Or to reach out to my university librarians, instead of relying solely on the affable representatives who periodically knocked on my office door asking if I had a spare moment, offering greater automation and promising better outcomes (and when that would not work, inquiring about sponsorship opportunities). The complicity of higher education with the interests of for-profit publishing houses is truly staggering. It is a partnership that successfully preys on heavy faculty workloads while peddling the false notion that higher education is about delivering scarce (and therefore valuable) content. A textbook case of a principal-agent problem.

A summer break from teaching allowed David's message to incubate. So when the open textbook team at BCcampus put out a call for faculty to review the open textbooks they had harvested from other repositories, I expressed an interest in reviewing two open textbooks, one of which (*Principles of Social Psychology* by Charles Stangor) was in their repository, and another (*Research Methods in Psychology* by Paul C. Price) that was not, but which I brought to their attention.

Over that summer I evaluated both open textbooks using a rubric from College Open Textbooks that (perhaps fittingly) had itself been twice adapted, initially by Saylor Academy and subsequently by BCcampus (see https://open.bccampus.ca/bc-open-textbooks-review-criteria). Happily, both textbooks passed muster and fell well within what I considered to be one standard deviation from a traditional publisher's offering (my internal threshold for adoption).

Emboldened by my generally positive evaluation, I took the leap and formally adopted the open textbook for the one section of the Research Methods in Psychology course that I was scheduled to teach during the

Fall semester. However, a number of deficiencies remained related to context (e.g., US vs. Canadian research ethics policies), currency and the absence of navigational tools such as a table of contents or glossary. Which meant work. Moreover, there was no available suite of ancillary resources (a question bank paramount among these). Which required an ongoing commitment.

With three weeks remaining before the first day of class, I performed a little triage to determine the most urgently required revisions, using my own review and those of other faculty to guide this process. The availability of the open textbook as a Microsoft Word file meant that I would be able to make the necessary edits within a familiar platform. And so I did, using every one of those twenty-one days to make only the most critical additions and changes to the content. Along the way, I taught myself about Creative Commons licensing and added a cover and a table of contents to make the 377-page document more presentable, before uploading the newly revised textbook (in two digital formats) to the University's learning management system and my personal website.

And so the adoption proceeded, with the 35 students in my Research Methods course that Fall making for rather happy guinea pigs, having saved $135 USD apiece (the cost of the incumbent textbook). Although some had to be taught how to use the navigational features of a digital textbook, the students overwhelmingly reported positive experiences with the book, ranging from the ability to print pages as necessary to being able to read the book on all of their digital devices. One unexpected collateral benefit of this was the stronger rapport that resulted from my choice to save my students' money and improve their access, something which paid dividends throughout the semester and even in my end-of-semester evaluations.

One student wrote to me in an email at the end of the semester:

> Being a mature student on a tight budget, not having to pay $120 for a textbook is a big deal. That's one of the many reasons I really enjoyed the free textbook for Research Methods. Having many years of school left it would be nice that more teachers and schools could use these kinds of books to help take off some of the financial strain that students like me face.

Funnily enough, I did not think to inform the folks at the BC OTP about my adaptation and adoption or to share the modified files until the end of the semester. Awareness of my efforts at BCcampus led to a press release from the Ministry of Advanced Education and a post on the university blog, attention that served as quite a contrast to my twenty-one-day salute to social justice. But while concerns about student access provided me with the motivation, several factors enabled my work:

1. The benefit of a non-teaching semester and no institutional requirement to perform research provided the necessary time.

2. The small size of my then-institution meant that mine was *the only section* of Research Methods offered that semester. This in turn meant that that the choice of textbook was mine alone and did not belong to a committee that might have raised questions about textbook standardization or prattled on about their preference of the smell and touch of a physical book.

3. First reviewing the open textbook served as a foot-in-the-door to the revision process, providing me with the necessary familiarity with the book's strengths and weaknesses.

4. My experience teaching this course at other institutions provided familiarity with different institutional expectations and allowed me to evaluate whether any critical material was missing or required revision.

5. I was able to modify the textbook using familiar technology (Microsoft Word), even if this technology imposed its own technical constraints.

6. My competency-based approach to teaching Research Methods made it easier for me to adopt the book in the absence of any ancillary resources, an outlying position within a discipline for which reliance on publisher-supplied question banks and test generation software is the norm.

In the two years since this minor revision was completed, my commitment to open textbooks has deepened. In the Summer of 2014, I organized and facilitated the "Great Psychology Testbank Sprint" in which twenty psychology faculty members from seven BC institutions and with complementary areas of expertise came together for two days and created an 870-question test bank to accompany an open textbook for Introductory Psychology (See http://thatpsychprof.com/the-great-psychology-testbank-sprint)

I have since also completed major adaptations of the *Principles of Social Psychology* (2014) and *Research Methods in Psychology* (2015) open textbooks. Unlike my earlier experience, both of these adaptations were completed under the auspices of the OTP using the PressBooks platform and with the assistance of a collaborator (Hammond Tarry from Capilano University and I-Chant Chiang from Quest University). Importantly, both Hammond and I-Chant were partners who complemented my content expertise and shared my commitment to good pedagogy and the principles of open.

I am particularly proud of these recent revisions as they take fuller advantage of the open licenses. In the case of the Social Psychology textbook we addressed the reusability paradox by producing the first international edition, deliberately using examples and statistics from a wide variety of cultural contexts. And in the case of the Research Methods textbook we embedded audiovisual media (video clips, QR codes, hyperlinks to interactive tutorials) and wove throughout the text discussions of recent and emerging developments within the field, including discussions of Psychology's "reproducibility crisis" and the resultant shift towards open science practices that are gradually transforming psychological science into a more transparent, rigorous, collaborative and cumulative enterprise. Rather like an open textbook.

Discussion

Several common themes emerge across our experiences creating open textbooks. Foremost is our shared interest in creating and adapting course materials that reflect the dynamic nature of our disciplines. Traditional textbooks are, at best, pedagogically impoverished, context-neutral content in an age where internet connectivity affords access to rich multimedia and dynamic, contextualized knowledge. Consider then the typical introductory course textbook chosen by a committee, the one that no one loved but, crucially, that no one despised. The one whose imperfections the faculty have learned to live with. Then imagine instead being able to omit, augment or revise sections as desired. Or embed and scaffold course assignments within and across chapters. Imagine being able to update it immediately in response to breaking developments in your field, embedding video clips, interactive simulations and other rich media. To bring in local examples, current public debates or references to immediate cultural touchstones. In short, imagine having the freedom to modify the instructional materials to suit your course and your context and your students rather than having it be the other way around. All of these imaginary frontiers have been underexplored — worse, surrendered — territory in discussions of professional and social responsibility.

A second common theme is our recognition of the importance of access, broadly construed. Textbook costs continue to rise, having increased 1041% since 1977 and 82% since 2002 (US PIRG, 2014). These increases have been greeted by relatively little change in the amount that students actually spend on textbooks, on average about $600 USD (Caulfield, 2015). How is that possible? Nearly 65% of students opt out of buying a required course textbook (even though 94% of these recognize doing so hurts their performance), 49% take fewer courses, 45% do not register for a course, and 27% drop a course, all due to concerns over cost (Florida Virtual Campus, 2012). Those who do obtain a copy of the required textbook often do so by buying used copies, renting, sharing with classmates, using a reserve copy, photocopying and illegally downloading. These student choices are forced and stressful, yet largely invisible to faculty.

Of course issues of access go well beyond affordability. Open textbooks grant access that is immediate (no student loan delay), permanent (no need to resell), flexible (across formats and devices), and compatible with assistive learning technologies. Conventional textbooks dictate pedagogical decisions that limit opportunities for people with different learning preferences. In creating and adopting open textbooks, educators and learners have an ability to tailor the text to their own unique needs and pedagogical concerns. The open textbook approach offers a means to tackle issues of academic honesty. The growth of essay-writing services has generated policies on and the policing of plagiarism. This absorbs time, effort and money which in turn has led professors to either drop or substantially change the writing components of courses. The open textbook presents an alternative paradigm in that it can be *added to*. Getting students to consider and articulate contrasting approaches can generate original thinking that can contribute to textbooks and to their own learning community. It is one thing to say that students learn how to write by writing essays; it is another to be able to demonstrate the quality of writing and analysis that a course generates by pointing to student-created textbook content.

A third theme is finding a counterbalance to the lack of academic incentives to create an open textbook. The authors of this chapter each note challenges regarding workload, time and lack of disciplinary recognition of open textbooks — which impact obtaining employment and tenure. The role of external factors in overcoming these challenges cannot be underestimated. In one way or another, all of the open textbooks described here have benefitted from governmental, institutional and foundational support. Without agencies like BCcampus and the OERu, without a political mandate and funding allocation, and without foundations like the Hewlett Foundation, the external factors mentioned by the authors are often enough to stymie creation, adaptation and distribution of OERs.

A fourth common theme is the importance of collaboration. The basis of participating in OER is understanding your work is part of a chain of collaborations. Indeed, an open textbook may be best conceptualized as an invitation to co-create rather than an object to consume. The importance of collaboration was emphasized in the case of Arthur Green's book sprint with a diversity of geographers, the case of John Belshaw's approach to collaboratively building a history textbook and the cases of Rajiv Jhangiani's psychology test bank sprint and approach to choosing collaborators for revising open textbooks. Beyond the benefits collaboration has for creation, having many collaborators leads to more adoptions and more positive impacts for students. If we as authors do not collaborate, our contributions — already weakened by the limits of individual expertise — will likely be lost.

Conclusion

The separate and distinct trajectories each of us followed in this contribution reflect our respective teaching philosophies. Comparing these approaches to the creation of open textbooks reveals the many layers at which creation occurs and the multitude of purposes served by these educational tools. Yet, despite our different approaches to writing an open textbook, we found many common components of success. For example, we found that making OER allowed us to fulfil our need for course materials that can be dynamically adapted to our unique teaching contexts and pedagogies. We found that, while textbook cost is a common and formidable barrier, working on open textbooks unleashes a creativity that exposes many less-evident but critical barriers to teaching and learning with conventional textbooks. We each encountered challenges to getting professional recognition for our work on OER, as our disciplines have similar limitations to recognizing open textbooks. Strategies for overcoming biases against these innovations had to be devised. We identified that at the heart of each of our open textbook processes is collaboration and an understanding that academic freedom is not enclosing our knowledge in proprietary packages but opening our work to the commons. Indeed, part of the commons and of showing people that OER is subject to quality control is the peer review of other open education materials. Finally, we recognized that public and private funding that supports OER was a key trigger for solving logistical constraints for our own production of OER. These investments continue to be critical and are direct paths to making education more accessible. We arrived, then, at the same conclusions. The promise of the open textbook model, even when focused solely on improving access, is enormous. But when the approach to open textbook development reflects dynamism, respects agency and relishes collaboration it becomes a truly liberating form of pedagogy.

References

BCcampus (2016), *Open Textbook Stats*, https://open.bccampus.ca/open-textbook-stats

Caulfield, C. (2015), *Asking What Students Spend on Textbooks is the Wrong Question*, Hapgood, http://hapgood.us/2015/11/09/asking-what-students-spend-on-textbooks-is-the-wrong-question

Bliss, TJ (2015), *Z as in Zero: Increasing College Access and Success Through Zero-textbook-cost Degrees*, Work in Progress: The Hewlett Foundation Blog, http://www.hewlett.org/blog/posts/z-zero-increasing-college-access-and-success-through-zero-textbook-cost-degrees

Creative Commons (2015), *State of the Commons*, https://stateof.creativecommons.org/2015/sotc2015.pdf

Florida Virtual Campus (2012), *2012 Florida Student Textbook Survey*, Tallahassee: Author, http://www.openaccesstextbooks.org/pdf/2012_Florida_Student_Textbook_Survey.pdf

Freire, P. (2000), *Pedagogy of the Oppressed*, New York: Bloomsbury Academic.

Harris, P. (2010), Band of Brothers Author Accused of Fabrication for Eisenhower Biography, *The Guardian*, https://www.theguardian.com/world/2010/apr/25/stephen-ambrose-eisenhower-biography-scandal

Hilton III, J. (2016), Open Educational Resources and College Textbook Choices: A Review of Research on Efficacy and Perceptions, *Educational Technology Research and Development*, 64(573), http://dx.doi.org/10.1007/s11423-016-9434-9

Licklider, J. C. R. and Taylor, R. W. (1968), *The Computer as a Communication Device*, http://www.utexas.edu/lbj/archive/news/images/file/20_20_03_licklider-taylor-1.pdf

US PIRG (2014), *Survey Shows Students Opting out of Buying High-cost Textbooks*, http://www.uspirg.org/news/usp/survey-shows-students-opting-out-buying-high-cost-textbooks

10. What Does It Mean to Open Education? Perspectives on Using Open Educational Resources at a US Public University[1]

Linda Vanasupa, Amy Wiley, Lizabeth Schlemer,
Dana Ospina, Peter Schwartz, Deborah Wilhelm,
Catherine Waitinas and Kellie Hall

The proliferation of Open Educational Resources (OER) is a disruptive innovation. At first glance, using OER simply consists in replacing a traditional text with an alternative. Often, little attention is paid to the process of adopting and adapting OER materials. In the course of creating a learning community for faculty who intended to use OER, we experienced that this seemingly minor shift of instructional resources opened onto an entire landscape of questions around the meaning of education, the nature of social and political power in education systems, the meaning of authority and credibility, the risks associated with change and our own identities as participants in higher education. We present here the themes that emerged from our learning community, which consisted of an OER librarian and seven faculty members. These themes related to the process and methods of teaching, the goals of using OER and our fundamental goals as educators. This modest case study reveals that a peer-to-peer research and learning community that is designed to support transformative learning enables a faculty member to derive the full benefit of using OER. Such a learning community not only builds personal capacities for making conscious choices beyond one's conditioned tendencies, it also revitalizes the spirit of scholarship.

1   This work was supported in part by a grant from the National Science Foundation (DUE1044430). All views represented are those of the authors and do not necessarily represent those of the National Science Foundation. We gratefully acknowledge the helpful insights provided to us by John Belshaw, Rajiv Jhangiani, Ken Udas and Patrick Blessinger.

http://dx.doi.org/10.11647/OBP.0103.10

Introduction

The proliferation of Open Educational Resources (OER) is a disruptive innovation that many instructors embrace for ethical, practical and financial reasons, with the financial reasons often spearheading such experiments. Between 2003 and 2013, college textbook prices in the United States rose 82%, approximately triple the rate of US inflation in overall consumer prices during the same time period (28%) (Government Accountability Office, 2013). Given these increasing textbook costs as well as the increasing availability of OER, at first glance using OER can appear to be a logical, simple replacement of the traditional text with alternative, low-cost options.

Despite today's greater availability of OER, often little attention is placed on the faculty process of adapting and adopting OER materials. To explore this process, a group of eight educators at an institution that grants both Bachelors and Masters degrees convened as a learning community for a quarter-long participatory experiment in the use of OER. Our learning community consisted of an OER librarian and faculty: three from English, two from engineering, one from physics, and one from kinesiology. From our first meeting, participants expressed a range of reasons for their participation, discussed below.

By our second meeting, the decision to "open" our classrooms with OER quickly took on a more philosophical character. Much as in improvisational theatre, the simple act of saying "yes" to OER opened our participants to an unforeseen sense of disorientation and confusion. We realized not only the existential absurdities at work in the current system of selecting and assigning textbooks, but also the occasional conflict of interest for educator-authors.

As depicted in Figure 1 below, we realized that in asking a relatively straightforward question about using different learning materials — "What does it mean to use Open Educational Resources?" — we were, in fact, looking at the foundations of higher education itself. We were not just asking about credible educational resources; we were asking, "What does it mean to *open* education?" In so doing, we also began to question how much the systems of higher education are themselves *closed* and self-replicating. We questioned how these systems prioritize conserving the educational institution itself over actual mastery of content and developing intellectual habits of mind. Through our discussions, "opening education" grew to mean encouraging a revival within our students and ourselves of the essence of scholarship: to experiment and discover rather than to assert and repeat, and to engage in a practice of openness as part of a community of teacher-learners — both inside *and* outside of the classroom.

In this modest case study, we describe the research context, the methods that we used in capturing our understanding, the themes that arose and our conclusions.

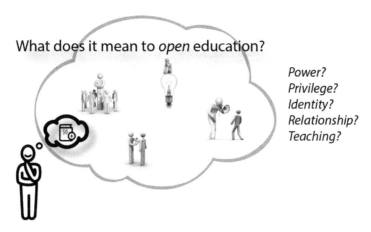

Figure 1. Conceptual depiction of questions that arose in our process. The grey characters and smaller yellow characters represent people who are called "students". We initially imagined that using OER was a simple replacement of high-cost with low-cost texts (bold thought bubble). However, the collaborative exploration of using OER caused us to consider a whole set of questions related to power, privilege, identity and our relationship to learning (the range of concepts in the larger thought bubble).

The Learning Community as the Research Context

Our exploration took place at an institution classified as Masters-Large (*About Carnegie*, 2015), with the undergraduate instructional program being Professional plus Arts and Sciences with some graduate program coexistence. The mission of our institution is primarily undergraduate, with "scholarship" an unfunded mandate. As is common with undergraduate-focused institutions (Wright *et al.*, 2004), there is an expectation of scholarship that the workload formulas rarely accommodate. Our typical full-time teaching loads range from

12–23 in-class contact hours per week plus five weekly office hours. Opportunities to explore new ways of teaching and learning are difficult to find amongst teaching, scholarly and administrative obligations.

The learning community members responded to an open invitation from Schlemer and Vanasupa. All were offered stipends of $1,000USD for the eleven-week project. Some were seeking to learn from others who already were in the process of using OER; some were looking to understand more about how to make OER more available; some were interested in large questions about social equity in education. What these participants shared was a commitment to teaching and learning, and these diverse interests grew into the participants' individual experiments (Table 1). Table 1 below provides details on the participants and their roles in the university.

Table 1. The learning community participants and their OER interests.

Participant/ discipline	Institutional relationship	OER Practices/ Experiments	Role in learning community
Kelly Hall Kinesiology	tenured faculty member	OER texts	participant
Dana Ospina OER Librarian	Open Education librarian	OER	resource specialist/ participant
Lizabeth Schlemer Engineering	tenured faculty member	badging system with self-authored OER videos	researcher/ participant
Peter Schwartz Physics	tenured faculty member	OER texts, self-authored OER video curricula	participant
Linda Vanasupa Engineering	tenured faculty member	badging system with self-authored OER	researcher/ participant
Catherine Waitinas English	tenured faculty member	self-authored OER text, self- and student-edited OER materials, student-created OER videos	participant
Amy Wiley English	adjunct faculty member	OER course supplements, self-authored texts, student-authored texts	participant
Deborah Wilhelm English	adjunct faculty member	OER course supplements, self- and student-created OER	participant

Method

We used participatory action research (PAR) as the research method. PAR has all the qualities of action science (Reason and Torbert, 2001) and takes place in the social setting of a learning community of research practice. In PAR, participants often collaboratively design and reflect on experiments, which includes inquiring into motivations and assumptions. This method involves practitioners as both researchers and subjects of their own research (Mills *et al.*, 2006). The rigour in action research comes in the recursive praxis of individual experiments that take the form of positing theories, testing them in one's life and reflecting on the results (Argyris and Schön, 1989).

Action research differs from traditional laboratory (or "reductionist science") in many ways. The aim of conventional reductionist science is to posit and validate causal relationships that can be generalized to other settings; thus, controlling variables and reducing variation during the experiment is essential in conventional reductionist science. Unlike these traditional laboratory experiments, in action science one instead observes the situational factors, attempts to make sense of how the factors contribute to the result and adjusts variables *throughout* the experiment to achieve the desired result — a process that may vary from person to person and may change over time. With respect to our process, participants enacted the participatory, reflective praxis of PAR by conducting individual experiments and collaboratively reflecting on these experiences. We chose PAR because of its relevance to complex social systems, particularly the education setting (Torbert, 1981; Reason and Torbert, 2001).

We began the eleven-week experiment with a three-hour "kick-off" workshop. We then met every other week for one hour to share thoughts and experiences. The *way* we ran our meetings was integral to building community and facilitating the learning process and therefore a critical part of this case study. The meetings were structured to accommodate participants' emotional states, since features of cognition that are essential to learning are "both profoundly affected by emotion and in fact subsumed within the process of emotion" (Immordino-Yang, 2015, p. 37). Each meeting involved a practice of managing our attention through an initial "check-in", in which participants were invited to speak without restrictions, to free their attention in order to be present. The discipline in this practice is for listeners to simply hear the speaker, rather than to respond to what is being said. For the person speaking, consciously choosing to set down what is taking one's attention frees that same attention for new learning. For the persons listening, the discipline of listening without engaging the content shifts the neurobiological state to a resting state that promotes deeper learning (Northoff, Duncan and Hayes, 2010; Spreng *et al.*, 2010).

Meetings were openly structured in the tradition of Bohm (1996), which prioritizes attention to what emerges, with the intent of discovery. The challenges or insights that people were encountering in their OER experiments created a "live" case study that we contemplated together. This method of reflection involved deep listening which requires the listener to suspend immediate judgment.

In addition to the collective face-to-face dialogues, participants periodically responded to online prompts and wrote about their experiences in blog posts. Examples of prompts were:

- What has motivated us to commit to this time together?
- What do you find most challenging about OER in this moment?
- What does success look like?
- What role does the "meaningfulness of the learning situation" play in sustaining the engagement of both faculty and students?

At the end of the experience, we revisited the themes of our individual and communal narratives. Using the qualitative research known as "coding" (Rossman *et al.*, 1998; Hesse-Biber and Leavy, 2010; Lincoln and Guba, 1985, Saldana, 2009) we uncovered and culled common themes. Coding involved individually reading through the narratives to discover and name the emergent ideas; we then discussed and adjusted these themes as a whole in a consensus-building process. After deciding on the themes, we reviewed the narratives again to re-code them against the common themes. This coding process is a way to glean themes from the rich narrative; the iterations in coding establish face validity as well as intercoder reliability. The final, resulting themes are grounded in our own experiences. Of course, there are many interpretations of the same data set; the process of collaboratively negotiating the themes corroborates their shared nature. The intent with this process is not to objectively validate a single, "accurate" result, as one might seek to do in positivist scientific traditions but instead to crystallize insight for the action research. In the following section, we introduce our themes, provide excerpts from our narratives and offer additional reflections on each.

Themes

The meaning of education

> I'd originally thought that opening education meant reflecting on what "open" is, but what I really find myself pondering is what "education" is. — Deborah

> [...] in terms of the planetary conditions, social and environment, I see that there is a need to transition to ways of being that honour all sentient beings. This is a lofty aspiration, I realize, but it's one that originally inspired me to get involved in the current research around open education resources. So, I see that there is a need in higher education to adapt to complexity in which we are living. As I see it, we [engineering educators] don't know how to do this. — Linda

Our effort to use OER catalyzed questions about the activity that we call "education". In a lament about the global path of environmental and economic inequity, Linda (an engineer) asked how educators would design education if not just humans, but also animals were equally invested and vocal stakeholders in higher education. Many disciplines treat such universalism as a given value. However, engineering curricula in the US tend to prioritize technical skills and to treat as politically neutral the *lack* of consideration of the political questions of engineering (Cech, 2014).

We realized that we do not often scrutinize our daily contributions to this system of higher education and that our deeply-held values are often displaced by what seem to be the "necessities" of our employment. For example, our institution, like many in the US, includes in its mission references to values such as life-long learning and ethical development, and yet markets the neo-liberal value of the college degree as a means to future employment. For what are called "professional degree programs" (Brint *et al.*, 2005; *About Carnegie*, 2015), such as in engineering or architecture, the curricula are often substantially informed by external advisory boards that are populated by industry representatives. Many faculty, administrators and students assume that educators' roles are to "equip" the "students" with the necessary skills and knowledge for their future employment. These assumptions then drive course design. Courses are organized around inherited learning objectives, historically fashioned by what someone, somewhere has deemed useful to students' future employment. Moreover, "useful" is often defined very narrowly within the course content, such as numerical problem-solving of basic mechanics. With limited focus and industry-driven content coverage, textbooks often overlook universally useful content and practices, leaving course builders without support or resources for integrating such practices as group work, student-led problem-solving or metacognitive skills. While our institution espouses values of critical thinking, ethical reasoning, discovery and making positive contributions to society, its structure and practices often prioritize the interests of stakeholders who have social and economic power; the interests of those who lack power are not considered. Throughout the course of our meetings, our PAR became increasingly aware of our habitual participation in the value of education as a means to the end of employment. (For some of us participants representing the liberal arts, this was noted as, perhaps, an unconscious but nonetheless real survival technique in an environment that questions the value and sometimes the very presence of our disciplines — thus, the "end of employment" here is a challenge that applied to both students and faculty).

To be clear, it is not that we desire unemployment: rather we noted that in the triage that is teaching, any development that supports humanistic goals is often displaced by any development that seems "necessary". We, therefore, began to ask questions such as

- Who is being served by this education?
- Who is not being served?
- What does it mean to educate?
- Is this education missing something of critical importance?

While these philosophical questions may be without an answer, we recognized that they are questions that often go unasked — yet these are the very questions upon which the meaning of education rests. The education philosopher Krishnamurti emphasizes that we can find the beginning of such meaning in a scholar's ability to confront and recognize the extent to which her scholarship creates not "a subtle form of escape" from uncertainty but rather a means by which to *embrace* uncertainty about both self and subject matter (Krishnamurti, [n.d.]). We, in part because of our work with OER, see teaching as an experimental scholarly discipline (McKeachie, 2006), a laboratory for discovery — self-discovery as well as student-discovery — through critical listening and "teaching with your mouth shut" (Finkel, 2000).

Indeed, teaching openly calls to pedagogy as political action, such as Paolo Fiere's seminal *Pedagogy of the Oppressed* (1970) argues, with the dynamics of education greatly determining the effectiveness of education. As Fiere makes explicit, "banking" models that emphasize transmission over critical thinking and knowledge ownership are mirrored by the educational dynamics implicit within the physical artefact of the authoritative classroom text: an artefact that professors select, assign and parrot through assignments, lectures and activities; an artefact that students purchase, absorb and reproduce by demand.

The assigned authorized textbook divests students and teachers of their own critical and creative thinking capacity, of the sense of community discovery, inquisitiveness and collaboration. Instead, the textbook provides a fixed, repetitive model that carries the feeling of safety and authority without the necessary challenges to organization that true learning and knowledge ownership requires. Embracing an alternate dynamic embodied through not a singular, static artefact but rather through the organizational challenges presented by a customizable course of study — perhaps via OER — invites a certain degree of disruptive, creative chaos. This chaos is an opportunity for both the instructor and the student to delve more deeply into subject-knowledge and self-knowledge in a manner that has tremendous implications for educational efficacy.

As we began to work through our individual experiments and to reflect on their progress with one another, each of our seven instructors employed "a text" in various ways (Table I). Six created self-authored texts and five instructors engaged students in a variety of authoring activities. For instance, Deborah had students produce OER texts for state school students' use. Catherine had current students create video materials for future students' learning. And Amy used student-authored texts within the classroom.

This variety of approaches began immediately to enlarge our understanding of what is involved in using OER. The extent to which our small sample of instructors (and their students) authored novel material while using OER suggests that there may be something about OER or shedding the notion of "purchased text" that encourages an active, audience-driven voice to emerge, and that encourages some instructors to include their students in the generative, creative process. In embracing "authorship", these instructors also confront the struggles that deep understanding of knowledge — and the production of knowledge itself — entail, placing them either directly or sympathetically on the plane of learning *with* their students, rather than the plane of transmission *above and apart from* their students.

The textbook enhances power differentials in education

> As the instructor I can act as a guide with the great and less-great — and [OER have increased] my own willingness at last to relinquish some of the control that I felt I needed to have when I first started teaching. — Deborah

> I didn't want to write micro-managing, authoritarian tests or endless margin and end comments all quarter [...] I wanted my students to feel empowered and powerful, to walk out of the class not just knowing new things but feeling the impact these things *were already having* in their lives. [...] I wanted to feel that way, too: empowered, not mired down. Strong and free — not strong in spite of having been beaten down. Bigger and lighter and more dynamic than the systems that attempt to contain me. — Amy

The replacement of traditional textbooks with open or low-cost options opens onto the trust and power dynamics at play in the relationship between faculty members and students. James Koch (2014) claims that, historically, the textbook market has been considered a "trust market": students purchase textbooks because a trusted authority tells them to do so. A problem with trust markets is that "the person who tells you to buy something is not the person who has to pay for it" (Koch, 2014) — and the person who tells you to buy something is sometimes the person who benefits financially from its sale, as is sometimes the case with faculty-authored textbooks. The selection of a textbook thus has broader implications than the determination of appropriate course content; it factors into the relationship that students enter into with faculty. These financial, emotional and relational considerations make the decision to move to open resources particularly significant.

All the participants in this learning community are committed to creating trustworthy environments and to actively contemplating the power differentials at play in higher education. As faculty we are attempting to establish relationships with our students that make transparent not only course expectations but also self-reflections on processes and intentions. That first point of contact in building trust is often through the "required textbook".

Teachers typically encounter the textbook through a combination of channels. Some university instructors write their own textbooks, but that model is far less common. In the more usual scenario, an instructor chooses a text because it is one traditionally employed within the discipline, one that is familiar, or one that has been recommended by a publisher's representative. In the case of self-authored textbooks, the authority and credibility of the instructor becomes both augmented by the existence of this evidence of expertise, and problematized in light of the instructor's profit from its required purchase.

We believe that an OER model promotes critical thinking, community interest and self-knowledge more effectively than the traditional ways in which faculty select textbooks. When faculty select or create OER, consultation with the publisher's representative is often replaced by consultation with a university librarian (or some other specialist) who can assist in identifying and locating openly licensed materials and who prioritizes the interests of the students, instructors and university. This person is knowledgeable about OER and motivated by efficacy, inclusivity and support. By working closely with faculty across multiple disciplines and courses, the librarian becomes a hub of institutional memory, a point of contact and dissemination not only of resources but also of educational practices, concerns and culture based on community and educational goals — the very premise upon which the institution is predicated.

Students, for their part, must form their own ideas of the institution's goals. Students typically encounter the textbook through a campus bookstore and the initial, meaningful signifier the book offers as to its significance, potential or burden, is that of price. According to a 2014 study conducted by Ethan Senack and the Student Public Interest

Research Groups (Student PIRGS), 65% of students surveyed reported opting not to purchase a textbook because it was too expensive (Senack, 2014). The current generation of entry-level students, born and raised with a wealth of freely available resources via the internet, has less and less reason to perceive the "required textbook" as anything other than a costly imposition. While this impression is sometimes perceived as an empty complaint made by some, the fact is that for many under-privileged students, especially first-generation and financially disadvantaged students, the cost of textbooks can be a deterrent to enrolling or remaining in a course — or in higher education at all.

Meanwhile, publishers' educational products are becoming more complex and multi-media driven in an attempt to cater to every aspect of every student's educational needs. Materials are far more than "texts" — they are more comprehensive, interactive and visually stimulating. Instructors receive materials for integrated presentation, testing and learning-exercise systems. All of these *already determined features* drive up textbook and course costs while increasing distance between teachers, students and content — their value for improving student learning is still to be researched. Indeed, recent experiments in fully online education indicate that the personal relationship that develops between a teacher and a student is critical to both student success, as well as student retention among underrepresented learners (Jaegers and Smith 2010; Means, B. *et al.* 2010). It is our experience that OER, in contrast, invites students to feel they are part of the educational process because of the value their instructors place on OER choices. By replacing the publisher's representative with the librarian, the closed-access text with an open education resource, and pre-packaged technological systems with tailored, personally designed points for student-teacher interaction, the OER educator closes the educational gap and opens possibilities for the university to function more as a community and less according to corporate models of educational banking.

The meaning of authority and credibility

I've had to really consider whether I am the sole credible author of education in the classroom [...] challenging my identity as a teacher.
— Linda

Opening education resource[s] eventually meant, for me, an opening up to myriad conflicting issues of credibility. — Amy

Being "open" in this way has made me think about who authorized a point of view. In my mind it is the existing power structure (which is most of the time White [sic] male). — Liz

Such fundamental questioning of expertise can be, for individuals certified as "experts" and produced by the same system, disconcerting. For example, Liz became increasingly aware that authorized points of view in the field of engineering in the US predominantly derive from the field's white-male demographic. What are alternative "credible authorities"? If we do not consider the questions of who has credible authority in education, are we at risk of unconsciously reinforcing existing inequitable power structures? And how does one become a credible authority?

As academics, we have systems in place for assessing and evaluating the strength of the materials we use in our classrooms — systems that help to cut down on the time-consuming process of researching new materials. We rely on tradition and on efficient short-cuts to assessing credibility via famous names, institutions, publishers and the recommendations of colleagues or publishing representatives. All of these lean more toward conservation and repetition than toward our group's aims of education: exploration and development of new approaches, ideas and insights into content. Furthermore, all of these defer the question of credibility and authority, putting off "the moment of crisis". Indeed, to paraphrase T. S. Eliot's Prufrock, those habits of text selection can become such unquestioned, conventional habits that they rob us of the strength required to roll the moment towards its crisis and ask, "Do I dare? Do I dare? Do I dare disturb the universe?" (1920).

Collaboratively reflecting on our OER experiments caused us to see and question our use of and deference to authority. Many of us experienced crisis and exhilaration in equal measures as we sought to develop not only materials but the means of distributing, engaging and organizing those materials. During our meetings and in blog posts, instructors voiced their unanticipated encounters with questions such as "Do I get to say this without reference to a text or something that represents the traditional perspective?" "How much of this do I myself know empirically, and how much am I reporting?" or "At what point did this thing I think I know and hold to be true, unconventional or original, become my own?"

Of course, such crises of self-knowledge, subject-knowledge and self-reflection should form the basis of most academic inquiry. They are, to be sure, questions we explicitly or implicitly challenge our students to confront almost daily. Placing ourselves in an attitude and position to ask them of ourselves makes students of us too, and serves to help us identify with our students at the same time that we strengthen our intellectual authority and credibility. Just as we constantly ask our students to change themselves, so do we need to engage ourselves to model this change process. The tradition of scholarship itself demands no less than constant, rigorous, intellectual and personal development — and *that* requires the confidence to place one's credibility and authority at risk.

The Risks Associated with Change

It is the case for me that I feel myself "failing" to accomplish what I desired to accomplish. [...] When I am thinking about my own failures (and this is all too frequent), I find myself afraid, filled with fear and sad. Sometimes I even seem to "create" the very thing that I DON'T want. I think there is a lesson to learn in this. — Linda

It strikes me that fear, of failure or of other things, is exactly what we're trying to help our students get comfortable with. [...] I'm trying to be a little bit gentle with myself about the time frame [...] trying to anticipate and build in the delays that heretofore have certainly felt like failure. — Catherine

I've been thinking more deeply about [failure] lately because of the discussion at our last meeting, in which I was saying that I felt tired and somewhat burdened by all of the ground work that I was doing for my students to help get this new project launched, and Linda asked me why I felt like I had to do all that. Well, I felt like I had to do all that because I want the project to work, because I want the students to be in the best position to learn, blah, blah, blah [...] or maybe I just need to be in control of every single thing and I'm not willing to let the students fail a bit. After all, their worry or frustration may reflect badly on me! (Cue wicked grin.) So I've pulled back a bit, trying to ask the right questions and help them ask the right questions, waiting to see what happens. — Deborah

I am fearful — of too many things to list here at the moment. But reading about my colleagues' fears, their reminders of the value of fear and failure, and their refusal to despair, is a kind of joyous reminder of what we, too are here for — and not just our students. We are here for the ongoing project of "wow", for the learning we couldn't anticipate, the epiphanies that come with the struggles. In that sense, I think that the support of a group like this, even when it's at a distance, is precisely the kind of support I have needed here at Cal Poly. — Amy

The risk of using a different type of educational resource can bring about the fear of failure. At the level of classroom, we start to ask questions such as, "Might the students miss out on learning if I choose the wrong text, or if I let them create OER?" We felt this fear as we let go of the safe structures of publishers and traditional textbooks. We also felt fear as we self-authored videos, not only viewing our image on camera but also realizing how often we make errors in lectures and how "goofy" we look. All of this is quite visible when we step into the role of an OER co-learner. In fact, we no longer appear as an expert to ourselves. All our failures, desire to control outcomes and insecurities are available for view — and re-view.

There is also fear stemming from the institution of higher education that is charged with conserving the status quo. Textbook publishers, bookstores and authors all may challenge us and ask questions such as, "What is the basis for your choice in educational resources?" These valid questions fuel a sense of uncertainty as we traverse this OER landscape.

There have also been tragic examples of institutional backlash. The case of Alain Bourget, a math professor at California State University — Fullerton, provides a very recent example of the risks involved in selecting course materials that may not be embraced by departmental authorities. Bourget selected what he believed to be a better set of materials for his "Introduction to Linear Algebra and Differential Equations" course than those mandated by his department and authored by the department's chair and vice chair; they also were less expensive (one text was free). His decision resulted in an official reprimand and the threat of dismissal, with the university contending that he "violated policy and went against orders from the provost and former dean of the math and sciences college" (Leung, 2015). Bourget contests this claim, but was aware that his decision could raise issues:

"I knew it would cause me trouble in the department (but) I feel completely dishonest trying to sell a book I don't believe in" (Leung, 2015). Setting aside the questions of protocol and the sacred pillar of academic freedom raised in this particular case, the issue of risk associated with change is powerfully exposed by Bourget's experience. While our learning community participants were not constrained by departmental mandates, the risk of departmental disapproval and/or disciplinary action is one of which we were all aware. It is clear that the fear of running afoul of even an unspoken departmental preference for certain materials can contribute to a faculty member's decision about whether or not to adopt or create an open resource.

Questions about our Own Identity as Participants in Higher Education

I wanted to bring those practices, community, and critical reflection to my classes here! Part of that journey has meant a need to be willing to set aside my own biases about education (I have this special knowledge which I will impart to you, and I will assess how well I impart that knowledge by grading YOU!) and open my classes to an approach that is more about formation (I have been at this a while, and I can and want to help you, and I, too, am learning and growing and looking for transformation from all sources, including you.) — Deborah

By opening up the protocols to learn, and then even the goals, I have learned profoundly from my students. I have looked at myself as the subject that I was learning about, and used my students as the teachers and the data to see myself. — Pete

[...] this experience placed me squarely in the same sort of territory I was asking my students to stand: to be unfinished, exploratory, open to new ideas and discoveries, and to finding a path toward new knowledge or understanding of their subject instead of grasping frantically at what they already thought they knew or believed. It required me to bring my espoused values into line with my practices, and my perspective into line with my students' own. — Amy

As educators, our identity includes the label "expert". We have spent years building our reputations. We found that using OER actually causes a deep questioning about our positions in society. Krishnamurti (1953) sums up the depth of the shift:

What is the true function of an educator? What is education? Why are we educated? Are we educated at all? Because you pass a few examinations, have a job, competing, struggling, brutalizing ambition, is that education? What is an educator? Is he one who prepares the student for a job, merely for a job, for technical achievement in order to earn a livelihood? That is all we know at present. There are vast schools, universities where you prepare the youth, boy or girl, to have a job, to have technical knowledge so that he or she can have a livelihood. Is that alone the function of a true educator? There must be something more than that...

We were confronted with the reality that our students sometimes know more about how to be publicly learning: students model the grace of voicing uncertainty and curiosity for us. Even as "experts", we too need to learn much not only about our subjects but also about our relationship to our subjects. These questions of identity were made more approachable by the open and accepting nature of the OER faculty learning community.

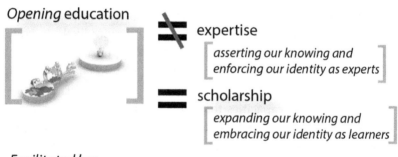

Opening education ≠ expertise
[*asserting our knowing and enforcing our identity as experts*]

= scholarship
[*expanding our knowing and embracing our identity as learners*]

Facilitated by:

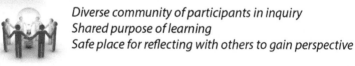

Diverse community of participants in inquiry
Shared purpose of learning
Safe place for reflecting with others to gain perspective

Figure 2. A pictographic representation of the insights gained through opening education in community. Opening education through the use of OER revived the essence of scholarship through a shift in individuals' identity as learners and an expansion in our knowing. This *opening* was facilitated by a diverse community with a shared purpose that created a safe place, offering normally-hidden perspectives and allowing deep self-reflection.

Conclusions

Through the process of collaboratively engaging with OER we encountered some of the ways that we embody and perpetuate dominant power in our education system. We found ourselves, through our process of community dialogue and exploration, contemplating normally unexamined assumptions: the meaning of education; the nature of power differentials in education; the meaning of authority and credibility; the risks associated with change; and our own identity as participants in higher education. Choosing to use Open Educational Resources revives the premises, practices, and socio-political implications of scholarship in its ideal form. That makes adopting OER a radical move in a system that needs more radical movement. Such adoption placed our expert educators in a position that more closely resembles that of learners and positioned us more empathetically in relation to our students, turning us into not just a faculty learning community exploring OER but a much broader community of co-learners that included our students as experts on their own learning processes and requirements. A strong support system for such radical moves can make these experiences both easier to navigate for students and faculty and more likely to endure in the institutional memory — especially if support staff including librarians can become impartial custodians. In summary, this modest case study has revealed that educators must build personal capacities in implementing OER, capacities that are facilitated through community support — a community that in its essence *opens* itself to the diversity of values, interests and being that individuals embody, that *opens* itself to sharing the experience of elation and failure that accompanies classroom experimentation and that *opens* itself to being *educated* in the process of being supportive *resources* to one another.

References

About Carnegie Classification (2015), The Carnegie Classification of Institutions of Higher Education, http://carnegieclassifications.iu.edu

Argyris, C. and Schön, D. A. (1989), Participatory Action Research and Action Science Compared, *American Behavioral Scientist*, 32(5), pp. 612–623, http://dx.doi.org/10.1177/0002764289032005008

Böhm, D. (1996), *On Dialogue*, London and New York: Routledge.

Brint, S., Riddle M., Turk-Bicakci, L. and Levy, C. S. (2005), From the Liberal to the Practical Arts in American Colleges and Universities: Organizational Analysis and Curricular Change, *Journal of Higher Education*, 76, pp. 151–180, http://dx.doi.org/10.1353/jhe.2005.0011

Cech, E. A. (2014), Culture of Disengagement in Engineering Education?, *Science, Technology & Human Values*, 39(1), pp. 42–72, http://dx.doi.org/10.1177/0162243913504305

Eliot, T. S. (1920), The Love Song of J. Alfred Prufrock, *Prufrock and Other Observations*, New York: Routledge.

Fiere, P. (1970), *Pedagogy of the Oppressed* (trans. by M. B. Ramos), New York: Continuum.

Finkel, D. L. (2000), *Teaching with Your Mouth Shut*, Portsmouth, NH: Heinemann.

Government Accountability Office (2013), *College Textbooks: Students Have Greater Access to Textbook Information*, http://www.gao.gov/assets/660/655066.pdf

Hesse-Biber, S. N. and Leavy, P. (Eds.) (2010), *Handbook of Emergent Methods*, New York: Guilford Press.

Immordino-Yang, M. H. (2015), *Emotions, Learning, and the Brain: Exploring the Educational Implications of Affective Neuroscience (The Norton Series on the Social Neuroscience of Education)*, New York: W. W. Norton & Co.

Jaegers, S. S. and Baily, T. (2010), *Effectiveness of Fully Online Courses for College Students: Response to a Department of Education Meta-analysis*, Community College Research Center, Columbia University, http://ccrc.tc.columbia.edu/publications/effectiveness-fully-online-courses.html

Koch, J. (2014), *An Economic Analysis of the Market for Textbooks: Current Conditions, New Developments and Policy Options* [Online Conference Proceedings], http://www.jamesvkoch.com/uploads/Turning_the_Page_Lumina_Foundation_0713.pdf

Krishnamurti [n.d.], *Education and the Significance of Life, Chapter 2: The Right Kind of Education*, http://www.jkrishnamurti.org/krishnamurti-teachings/view-text.php?tid=51&chid=66907

Krishnamurti (1953), *Second Talk in Madras*, Krishnamurti's Talks 1953 (Verbatim Report), Madras. J. Krishnamurti online, http://www.jkrishnamurti.org

Lincoln, Y. S. and Guba. E. G. (1985), *Naturalistic Inquiry*, Newbury Park: Sage Publications.

Leung, L. (2015), *Should a Cal State Fullerton Math Professor be Forced to Have His Students Use $180 Textbook, Written by his Boss?*, Orange County Register, http://www.ocregister.com/articles/bourget-688288-math-book.html

McKeachie, W. J. and Svinicki, M. (Eds.) (2006), The College or University Culture, *McKeachie's Teaching Tips: Strategies, Research and Theory for College and University Teachers*. New York: Houghton Mifflin.

Means, B., Toyama, Y., Murphy, R., Bakia, M. and Jones, K. (2010), *Evaluation of Evidence-Based Practices in Online Learning: A Meta-analysis and Review of Online Learning Studies*, U.S. Department of Education: Office of Planning, Evaluation, and Policy Development Policy and Program Studies Service, http://www2.ed.gov/rschstat/eval/tech/evidence-based-practices/finalreport.pdf

Mills, J., Bonner, A. and K. Francis (2006), The Development of Constructivist Grounded Theory, *International Journal of Qualitative Methods*, 5, pp. 1–10.

Northoff, G., Duncan, N. W. and Hayes, D. J. (2010), The Brain and its Resting State Activity — Experimental and Methodological Implications, *Progress in Neurobiology*, 92(4), pp. 593–600, http://dx.doi.org/10.1016/j.pneurobio.2010.09.002

Reason, P. and Torbert, W. (2001), The Action Turn: Toward a Transformational Social Science, *Concepts and Transformation*, 6(1), pp. 1–37, http://dx.doi.org/10.1075/cat.6.1.02rea

Saldana, J. (2012), *The Coding Manual for Qualitative Researchers*, London: Sage Publications Ltd., http://doi.org/10.1007/978-1-84800-273-9

Schwartz, P. (2016), Full Curricula for Two Classes: (1) Calculus Based Introductory Mechanics, and (2) Energy, Society, and the Environment, http://sharedcurriculum.wikispaces.com

Senack, E. and Student Public Interest Research Groups (2014), *Fixing the Broken Textbook Market: How Students Respond to High Textbook Costs and Demand Alternatives*, http://www.studentpirgs.org/sites/student/files/reports/NATIONAL Fixing Broken Textbooks Report1.pdf

Spreng, R. N., Stevens, W. D., Chamberlain, J. P., Gilmore, A. W. and Schacter, D. L. (2010), Default Network Activity, Coupled with the Frontoparietal Control Network, Supports Goal-directed Cognition, *Neuroimage*, 53(1), pp. 303–317, http://dx.doi.org/10.1016/j.neuroimage.2010.06.016

Torbert, W. R. (1981), Why Educational Research has Been so Uneducational: The Case for a New Model of Social Science Based on Collaborative Inquiry, in P. Reason and J. Rowan (Eds.), *Human Inquiry: A Sourcebook of New Paradigm Research*, pp. 141–151, Chichester: Wiley and Sons, Ltd.

Wright, M. C., Assar, N., Kain, E. L., Kramer, L., Howery, C. B., McKinney, K., *et al.* (2004), Greedy Institutions: The Importance of Institutional Context for Teaching in Higher Education, *Teaching Sociology*, 32(2), pp. 144–159, http://dx.doi.org/10.1177/0092055x0403200201

Rossman, G. B. and Rallis, S. F. (1998), *Learning in the Field: An Introduction to Qualitative Research*, Thousand Oaks: Sage.

11. Expanding Access to Science Field-Based Research Techniques for Students at a Distance through Open Educational Resources[1]

Audeliz Matias, Kevin Woo, and Nathan Whitley-Grassi

Adoption of Open Educational Resources (OERs) by the science, technology, engineering and mathematics (STEM) community has yet to become an integral part of higher education classrooms. Many STEM faculty have been reluctant to develop and use OERs because the process of developing these resources is time-consuming and finding appropriate resources for higher education remains overwhelming. We developed a process to help generate OERs for topics that are generally associated with laboratory equipment or field research techniques in ecology and earth sciences, as well as general science. This project draws on the need to develop resources and expand access to scientific field-based research techniques through OERs for students learning at a distance. Engaging in undergraduate scientific virtual field experiences is an educational opportunity for students with a desire for an enriched learning experience in the sciences, particularly in ecology and earth sciences, but that cannot participate in a traditional field-based curriculum. In this chapter, we discuss the current status of the use of OERs for STEM education and our approach to developing three OERs in the areas of microscopy, geologic history interpretation and biodiversity. We conclude by sharing some of the challenges and lessons learned in the process.

1   This work has been funded by an Innovative Instructional Technology Grant (IITG) awarded through the State University of New York (SUNY) Provost's office (Tier One, 2014). Part of the equipment was acquired through funding from the Research Foundation for SUNY program to Enhancing STEM Research Experiences for SUNY Undergraduates. The work could not have been completed without our talented instructional designer Mark Lewis. We also thank Lorrie Anthony (SUNY Empire State College) for her guidance and encouragement in carrying out this project. Finally, we would like to thank the reviewers for their insightful comments on the chapter.

Introduction

Research shows that incorporating hands-on, field experiences with lectures has the potential to create a problem-based learning environment that engages learners in authentic scientific inquiry (Orion, 1993; Simmons *et al.*, 2008). However, due to the distributed environment and online-enriched educational model that many institutions are now facing, opportunities for students to engage in scientific field experiences are often minimal in the curriculum. Engaging in undergraduate scientific virtual field experiences is an educational opportunity for students with a desire for an enriched learning experience in the sciences, particularly in ecology and earth sciences, but who cannot participate in a traditional field-based curriculum.

We firmly believe that motivated students in science, technology, engineering and mathematics (STEM) concentrations with demanding schedules or other barriers to access should have the opportunity to learn about scientific field research while they acquire professional development. Thus, we developed three OERs and a process to help generate them for topics generally associated with laboratory equipment or field techniques. Phase 1 of the project included OERs that aim to teach students about: the basic functionality of microscopes (Introduction to Microscopy); the geologic history interpretation of rocks exposed at the surface (Geologic Outcrop Analysis and Relative Dating of Rocks); and the identification of invertebrates (Biodiversity Sampling of Invertebrates). The project draws on the need to develop resources and expand access to scientific field-based research techniques for students learning at a distance or with other barriers to access.

The value of this project lies in increasing access and portability to scientific techniques while supporting an instructional model that allows for further refinement, development, growth and use across and beyond our institution. In this chapter, we discuss the current status of the use of OERs for STEM education and our approach to developing OERs as well as the challenges and lessons learned in the process.

Status of OERs in STEM

The concept of OERs is nothing new to the science, technology, engineering and mathematics (STEM) community. If you have searched for educational resources online, you have probably noticed that there is no shortage of STEM resources for teaching. Major government funded institutions in the US such as the National Aeronautics and Space Agency (NASA), for instance, provide powerful free to use teaching tools. Additionally, as recent research has demonstrated, the OER movement continues to gain traction across campuses globally (Johnson *et al.*, 2015). Why, then, do educators at colleges and universities not embrace the plethora of open digital educational libraries and repositories in STEM?

Unfortunately, the vast majority of openly available resources are targeted towards primary and secondary education rather than higher education. In recent years, more and more professional associations and institutions have embraced the OER movement by encouraging faculty and researchers to share educational materials (e.g. lesson plans) openly in their sites. Table 1 shows some examples of sites that adhere to the openly available principle of OER access for STEM subject areas as well as sites that serve as search engines to a wide range of resources.

Perhaps, one of the most important issues affecting creation and adoption of STEM OERs is the culture of STEM education itself. Departmental and institutional cultures often do not adequately value, support and reward effective pedagogy. Teaching excellence is rarely a deciding factor for tenure in many STEM departments, particularly at research-oriented institutions. Consequently, many STEM faculty are left with the decision to prioritize scholarship over teaching effectiveness. Furthermore, even when educators know about the existence of OERs, most of the repertories remain disconnected from each other and one must invest a lot of time and energy searching for materials adequate for the different subjects and academic levels. STEM educators are not the only ones suffering from this difficulty. In 2014, an in-depth exploration of OERs in higher education by the Babson Research Group revealed that half of the over 2,000 member strong faculty surveyed were deterred from using OERs due to the lack of a comprehensive catalog of materials (Allen and Seaman, 2014). According to their report, faculty perception of the time and effort required to find and evaluate OERs remains a significant barrier for their adoption.

Table 1. Examples of repertoires specifically for STEM OERs (higher education included) and websites that search across platforms.

	STEM Area	**URL**
American Association for Physics Teachers (AAPT) comPADRE Network	Physics and astronomy.	www.compadre.org
Digital Library for Earth System Education (DLESE)	Earth science, geology and environmental science.	www.dlese.org
Chemical Education Digital Library (ChemEd DL)	Chemistry.	www.chemeddl.org
Applied Math and Science Education Repository (AMSER)	Wide range of STEM fields, built specifically for use by those in community and technical colleges.	amser.org
Science Education Research Center (SERC) of Carleton College	Geosciences.	serc.carleton.edu
The National Science Digital Library (NSDL)	All STEM fields, both formal and informal educational resources.	nsdl.oercommons.org
OER Commons	Wide range of areas including science and mathematics.	www.oercommons.org
Multimedia Educational Resource for Learning and Online Teaching (MERLOT)	Wide range of areas including STEM.	www.merlot.org
temoa	Wide range of resources, including for STEM fields compiled by the Tecnológio de Monterrey, Mexico.	www.temoa.info
European Union Open Science Research Project	Wide range of STEM areas.	www.openscience resources.eu

Another important issue is the lack of standards and quality control between repertories. A standard categorization or curating method might help faculty, especially faculty in STEM fields, in their adoption of OERs. Porcello and Hsi (2013) discuss the use of crowdsourcing as an option to improve the quality of STEM OERs. They also talk about four components essential to the success of OERs, emphasizing application to STEM: convergence toward common metadata; balancing expert and community definitions of quality; community input; and interoperability. Efforts by programs like the Multimedia Educational Resource for Learning and Online Teaching (MERLOT) of the California State University System (US), where communities engage in building OERs based on evaluation standards, leverage the STEM OER community to develop quality content that is easy to use and have the potential to be effective teaching tools.

Our Approach

The development of OERs is growing in popularity as more faculty and administrators realize the collective power they can attain by sharing resources in higher education (Cannell *et al.*, 2015; Clements *et al.*, 2015; Johnson *et al.*, 2015; Porcelle and Hsi, 2013). But the process of developing these resources can be time consuming and often requires the use of additional assets. Thus, many faculty continue to be reluctant to develop OERs. This is particularly noticeable in STEM areas where field work is essential for learners' training, such as ecology and geology, where most of the available OERs are for pre-college education or do not have the rigour expected by many higher education instructors. For instance, the field setting provides the ability to see the interconnections among different components of the Earth system. In nature, students have the opportunity to learn from nature and about science. This important learning experience is difficult to replicate in the online environment, hence the learning environment could be enhanced with field-based OERs. Based on the necessity to infuse our online and blended courses with hands-on field experience, we developed a process to help generate stand-alone OERs for topics that are generally associated with laboratory equipment or field techniques in the areas of ecology and earth sciences, as well as general science. Drawing on that process, we designed a series of OERs that will soon be available to the larger community.

The Project

The OER project builds on our established, blended summer course with a three-day face-to-face meeting at the State University of New York (SUNY) Oneonta's Biological Field Station and Upland Interpretive Center in Cooperstown, New York. Our project leverages resources utilized during the summer course to create a series of OERs. For example, both facilities visited during the face-to-face component are adjacent to Ostego Lake, which provided us with the opportunity to showcase general ecology, earth science and scientific inquiry activities. We developed dynamic OERs based on field experiences at these facilities incorporating scientific equipment as well as mobile devices, which could be adapted for a broad audience and/or science subject.

The goal of the project is to provide students with the research skills they need to increase their competency in scientific research after graduation by engaging them in common field-based research techniques and methods for data collection and analysis through a series of interactive online activities. Field-based learning helps students strengthen their ability to reason spatially, to integrate information and to critique the quality of data. As educators, we can help students make these connections by fostering pathways from observation to interpretation. Through the application of current technological tools, we engaged in an innovative approach to STEM learning and the application of the scientific method by developing OERs on: Introduction to Microscopy (basic principles of using a microscope), Geologic Outcrop Analysis and Relative Dating of Rocks (geologic history interpretation of rocks exposed at the surface) and Biodiversity Sampling of Invertebrates (identification of invertebrates). With the creation of these OER, we would like to engage students virtually in activities that typically involve a field trip. At the time of the preparation of this manuscript, these OERs were on their final stages and will be shared with the community in the near future through the Multimedia Educational Resource for Learning and Online Teaching (MERLOT) and any appropriate OER repository.

The Process

The process of developing the OER fell to two people, the "Content Developer" and the "Instructional Designer" (Figure 1). Each of these individuals worked both collaboratively and independently. Figure 1 shows both roles and their respective tasks during the development process. The two primary responsibilities of the content developer were to envision the incorporation of the field- or laboratory-based experience within the OER and to provide the subject matter content. The instructional designer's main responsibilities included creating the digital objects and keeping the project moving. As such, the team worked actively together at the beginning and end of the process (tasks shown as dark grey in Figure 1), and independently during the rest of the development period (tasks shown as light grey in Figure 1).

Figure 1. Visual of roles in the OER design process. The content developer and instructional designer worked collaboratively during tasks shown in dark grey, and independently (but simultaneously) during tasks shown in light grey

The collaboration with the instructional designer at the beginning enabled the content developer to better frame the OER in what could, and should be done technically and pedagogically. Selecting the appropriate approach to convey the subject matter and to provide experiential learning that normally occurs outdoors proved to be an overwhelming task in both scope and complexity. Thus, progress was often halted by the amount of time required from the content developer and the unrealistic expectations of the available resources. During the initial stages, the instructional designer also completed a content inventory on the particular subject of the OER. The content inventory included a list of all materials needed in order to create the OER as envisioned by the developer, such as multimedia elements, images, video clips and written content.

Our process thus came to evolve into a parallel but extensive consultative process from the curriculum developer with an instructional designer used to frame the goals and outcomes of the specific OER. This was done through the use of a lesson plan template we developed (see Figure 2). The template allows the content developer to conceptualize the learning objectives, identify the necessary resources, background information and the learning that should happen for the learner to meet the objectives. At the same time, the instructional designer collected the necessary resources to achieve the objectives and decided on different interactive approaches to present the content. For example, the microscopy OER uses a simple approach using pop-ups to show the basic functionality of the microscope. On the other hand, the Geologic Outcrop OER utilizes videos and animations to convey how geologists interpret rock formations in the field.

Time Frame:	Description of Activity:
Levels 100/200/300/400:	
Learning Objectives (3-5 objectives):	
Required Background Information:	
Materials Needed (including equipment to be purchased):	
Procedure / Flow of Lesson:	
Assessment Plans and Documents: (Attach: e.g. tests, checklists, observation protocols, and rubrics)	
Context for Content:	
Resources to be Developed:	
Representative Courses:	

Figure 2. Template form used by content developers to provide the pedagogical goals of the OER to the instructional designer

An important aspect of utilizing the OER pre-development form (Figure 2) is that it focuses on the pedagogical aspects rather than the technology. It was imperative to have clear learning objectives and outcomes before developing any content and/or pieces of the OER. After the lesson plan was completed and resources (e.g. photographs and/or videos in the field) collected, the developer focused on the production of content materials and the instructional designer began to map the content for the OER. We quickly learned the usefulness of concept maps when mapping the different content aspects of the OER. Figure 3 shows an example of the organizational concept map for the Microscopy OER. In this example, two main types of microscopes and their components are presented in the OER through the use of images, text and audio.

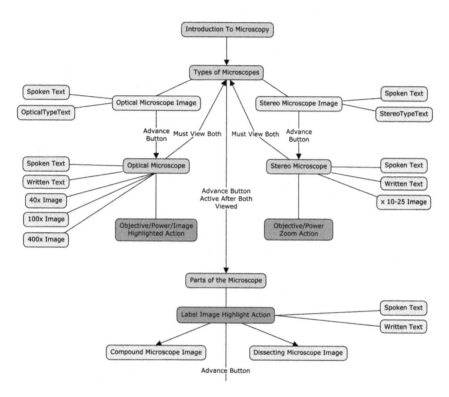

Figure 3. Example of a concept map drawn by the instructional designer based on the consultation with the content developer previous to the development of the storyboard

The next step in the process involved the use of a storyboard approach by the instructional designer to create a mock-up of the components of OER. The storyboard document specified the visual elements, text elements, audio elements, interactions and branching of every screen in the OER. After both team members agree on the design presented in the storyboard, the content developer role is to provide with the content material for the demonstration and/or activity that meet the objectives originally proposed. Probably the most time consuming and arguably difficult part of the process was the content development. It was essential to share tasks in order to create content in a timely manner. Photographs and videos were taken in the field in parallel to the content development.

As the pieces of content came together, the instructional designer began to develop a mock up or sample of all of or parts of the OER (see Figure 4). The storyboard and eLearning content for the OERs was created in HTML 5 using the authoring tool Adobe Captivate ®. This tool help us create interactive that area accessible through multiple devices (e.g. computer and mobile). An important advantage to using this particular tool over others currently available (e.g. Articulate Storyline) is the ability to move seamlessly from the storyboarding step into a mock-up and final learning object. After the team reviewed each mock-up, revisions and corrections to the design and layout were made. For instance, the mock-up for the Geologic Outcrop Analysis and Relative Dating of Rocks OER revealed the need for more contextual information for the activity where students are asked to identify rocks for a specific section from a photograph. Completing the lesson plan document (Figure 2) at the beginning of the development process was of great help when trying to figure out what was missing from the activity. Hence, we were able to isolate the skills needed to simulate the field experience virtually into the OER Inevitable, sometimes drastic changes were needed based on impute from one or both the instructional designer and curriculum developer.

The process does not end with the final production of the interactive learning object. Each final object was checked for American with Disabilities Act (ADA) compliance and attributions using the Creative Commons added. In the United States of America, and as a public institution of the New York State, we are required to adhere to the Federal Section 508 Accessibility Program (http://section508/gov). In order to ensure that our OERs were in compliance, we followed the guidelines provided by the US Board Standard for Electronic and Information Technology (EIT). We particularly focused on providing the following: textual alternatives to non-text context such as photographs; appropriate document structure, such as headings, to allow for clear meaning and facilitate navigation; and, captions and/or transcripts for videos and narrations (see Figure 5). Additionally, OERs were created using HTML 5 output as opposed to Flash to allow for access through multiple platforms, including mobile devices.

At the end, we aim to create OERs that are both technologically functional and pedagogically sound to meet the needs of our learners. In the near future, we would like to expand the process to also include the revision and redesign of the OERs based on feedback from our students. As mentioned at the beginning of the chapter, at the time of the preparation of this manuscript, the OERs developed during the first phase of our project are on the final stages of production and will be shared with the community in the near future through the Multimedia Educational Resource for Learning and Online Teaching (MERLOT) and any appropriate OER repository.

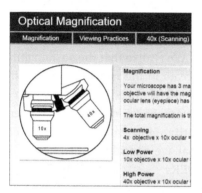

Figure 4. Screenshot of a storyboard slide used in the Introduction to Microscopy OER

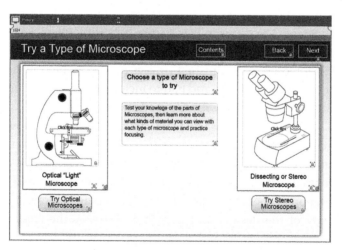

Figure 5. Screenshot of part of the Introduction to Microscopy OER showing the ADA compliant, high contrast responsive design approach used in this project. The storyboard and eLearning content for the OERs was created in HTML 5 using the authoring tool Adobe Captivate ®

Challenges and Lessons Learned

In the long-term, our OERs will likely experience the same kinds of challenges that many virtual learning environments may encounter, such as the sustainability of the project (e.g., typically through funding availability or maintenance of material and interface), evaluation and feedback, computing infrastructure, and inequity of access to the materials depending on country or socioeconomic status (Atkins *et al.*, 2007). It seems clear that sustainability is likely the most salient issue, as it encompasses the interaction of all large-scale challenges that enable the success, failure, or longevity of Open Educational Resources, such as the virtual (e.g., software, computer-based platforms, advancement in disciplines) to the realistic (e.g., funding, staffing, maintenance, evolution of technology) (Downes, 2007). We realize that the sustainability of our OERs, and those we wish to create in the near future, may inherently confront the same challenges, and we need to take steps to meet the individual obstacles as they surface. Some longitudinal challenges may be difficult to proximally identify. However, in the short-term, there were some clear challenges that we considered necessary to address before we could produce our OERs.

In building our OERs, one of the major decisions that we needed to make was to choose a specific software program in which to design our virtual content. The decision was particularly difficult as we needed to identify a platform on which it was easy to design, edit, and modify our content. Moreover, each finished project needed to be universal to all popular operating systems, and had to include the ability to function on all popular web browsers with appropriate plug-ins.

The failure of many virtual laboratories, OERs, or online supplementary materials is the inability to work on cross-platforms, and therefore selectively biases the students who may have access to the formatted software, operating system, or browser and plug-ins. The incorporation of these software and programming layers increases the complexity of the design, and therefore decreases the ability for our OERs to operate on more universal or cross-platform systems. Indeed, if the OERs were inaccessible to the target population of traditional students, and as in the case with our students at SUNY Empire State College who were non-traditional, then it clearly created an additional bias for populations that were already challenged by the norms of accessible technology.

Another major challenges that we faced was to create OERs that were truly accessible for all kinds of disabilities. Our OERs were designed on visual platforms with images, videos, text, and voiceovers to accommodate individuals with disabilities that made hearing and seeing difficult. However, the challenges also extended beyond sight and sound, and may include the inability to manually move through each exercise because of the inability to use hands or fingers. These challenges meant that we needed to create a version of each OER that accommodated all possible likely disabilities, or create multiple versions of our virtual learning environments in which students could select the best mode of delivery.

Furthermore, we considered the implementation of various types of assistive technology that may enable students to access material more efficiently. For our field component, we employed the use of more sophisticated technology, such as tablets and handheld GPS units, which were visual, but were specifically operated by touch. It is likely that we may need to consider other kinds of assistive technology, such as text-to-speech, speech recognition software, augmentative communications software, mobility or positioning equipment, instructional formats created in different modes, or various input/output devices. Clearly, the available options for assistive technology are extensive, and we may need to consider individual student needs as they enroll for our course.

Finally, in terms of resources and the field-based aspect of the OERs, finding time to engage in the necessary field activities and weather conditions certainly prove to be a limiting factor. Without clear commitment to the collaboration from the institutions, faculty acting as content developers and instructional designers may find it hard to dedicate the required amount of time.

Future Work and Final Remarks

The rationale and process for designing OERs creates an innovative tool for more readily open access to an otherwise underutilized aspects of sciences. Laboratory studies are often assumed as exclusively physical and hands-on, yet this bias clearly limits access to various students, particularly those who exemplify underserved or underrepresented populations. Thus, our OERs will allow all students to experience virtually common field techniques in ecology and earth systems without undermining the integrity of the disciplines.

In the near future, we would like to extend our current work to include other common field techniques, such as mapping using Global Positioning System (GPS). As methods may adopt the use of more technology, it also seems practical to include the use of emerging technologies in our virtual content. Consequently, we need to continue to update and improve upon our current versions of OERs to include the latest advances in methodology, technique, and technology. In addition to the three virtual field experiences created during the first phase of our project, we intend to create OERs in areas such as: species identification (e.g. invertebrates and flora), mapping of species using a GPS (e.g. invasive species), and animal behavior.

Clearly, there are other kinds of experimental field techniques that we could also incorporate in virtual exercises. However, our intent is to continue to create easily replicable methods that can be adapted to a variety of science and non-science areas. For instance, the use of GPS technology for mapping enables real-time data collection applicable to geosciences, agriculture, conservation biology, social sciences, business, and emergency management.

The creation of our OERs also extends beyond mere implementation. We hope that the models serve as an initial blueprint in which others can base their OERs in terms of the platform, software, content, and organization. Ideally, the OERs can be utilized to suit the likely needs of individual educators and their targets population of students regardless of their subject matter area. The flexibility in our design is a critical feature of our OERs, such that it can serve multiple applications and that it may enable others to use the programming framework and only need to modify the content.

Furthermore, the model can be expanded beyond our focus of ecology and earth systems. There is no limitation on content, and hence we believe that likely adaptors may wish to utilize the OERs in other STEM areas (e.g. Introduction to Microscopy could also be used in genetics or cell biology courses) or to replicate the approach in other disciplines within the within the physical sciences of chemistry and physics. Moreover, we can look across the STEM curriculum to identify courses that may benefit from the addition of OERs, either to supplement current physical or virtual components, or to increase the level of accessibility for students with disabilities. Additionally, other non-STEM areas, such as the humanities and the arts, may also be able to emulate the general platform design and approach using field-based activities to create their own learning virtual environments with content from their respective disciplines. We hope that the process of integrating hands-on, field work into the OERs to recreate the experience needed to develop important research skills is transferred and replicated in non-STEM areas that have a clear applied learning component, such as performance (e.g., theatre, dance, music) and visual arts (e.g., photography, drawing, painting, ceramics). There is already an inherent interdisciplinary interaction across disciplines, as the visual designs of the virtual interface may employ artistic aptitude, and the craft of the text may be influenced by writing and literature.

The ultimate purpose of the OERs was to be able to disseminate instructional content to audiences who seek alternative means for education or require access to learning content because of accessibility issues. At the present we have a repository for OERs and other STEM resources within the State University of New York (http://navigator. suny.edu). However, our intention is to make them available beyond our educational system. There is the potential for global dissemination of by placing them in the Multimedia Educational Resource for Learning and Online Teaching (MERLOT) and any appropriate OER repository. Advocacy by many international government and non-profit groups to promote STEM education further suggests that this approach could potentially provide students around the globe with another opportunity for engagement in the sciences.

References

Allen, I. E. and Seaman, J. (2014), *Opening the Curriculum: Open Educational Resources in U.S. Higher Education*, Needham: Babson Survey Research Group, http://www.onlinelearningsurvey.com/reports/openingthecurriculum2014. pdf

Atkins, D. E., Brown, J. S. and Hammond, A. L. (2007), *A Review of the Open Educational Resources (OER) Movement: Achievements, Challenges, and New Opportunities*, http://www.hewlett.org/uploads/files/ReviewoftheOER Movement.pdf

Cannell, P., Macintyre, R. and Hewitt, L. (2015), Widening Access and OER: Developing New Practice, *Widening Participation and Lifelong Learning*, 17(1), pp. 64–72, http://dx.doi.org/10.5456/wpll.17.1.64

Clements, K., Pawloeski, J. and Manouselis, N. (2015), Open Educational Resources Repositories Literature Review — Towards a Comprehensive Quality Approaches Framework, *Computers in Human Behavior*, 51, pp. 1098–1106, http://dx.doi.org/10.1016/j.chb.2015.03.026

Downes, S. (2007), *Models for Sustainable Open Educational Resources*, National Research Council Canada, http://www.hewlett.org/library/grantee-publication/models-sustainable-open-educational-resources

Johnson, L., Adams Becker, S., Estrada, V. and Freeman, A. (2015), *NMC Horizon Report: 2015 Higher Education Edition*, Austin: The New Media Consortium, http://www.nmc.org/publication/nmc-horizon-report-2015-higher-education-edition

Orion, N. (1993), A Model for the Development and Implementation of Field Trips as an Integral Part of the Science Curriculum, *School Science and Mathematics*, 93(6), pp. 325–331, http://dx.doi.org/10.1111/j.1949-8594.1993. tb12254.x

Porcello, D. and Hsi, S. (2013), Crowdsourcing and Curating Online Educational Resources, *Science*, 341, pp. 240–241, http://dx.doi.org/10.1126/science.1234722

Simmons, M. E., Wu, X. B., Knight, S. L. and Lopez, R. R. (2008), Assessing the Influence of Field- and GIS-based Inquiry on Student Attitude and Conceptual Knowledge in an Undergraduate Ecology Lab, *CBE Life Sciences Education*, 7(3), pp. 338–345, http://dx.doi.org/10.1187/cbe.07-07-0050

12. A Practitioner's Guide to Open Educational Resources: A Case Study

Howard Miller

Entering into the world of Open Educational Resources (OERs) is not simply a matter of embracing a social justice-oriented stance about cutting ties to expensive textbooks and providing greater access to higher education. There is a practical side to making the transition from textbook-dependent courses to OER and, especially, for an individual professor or group of faculty members working without an existing OER-supportive institutional infrastructure (i.e. experienced OER users to serve as models and mentors, librarians well-versed in identifying and accessing OER, and instructional designers able to provide assistance), there are a number of very real challenges. This contribution examines one college professor's journey to OER, along with challenges and lessons learned along the way, as he strove to gain an understanding of how to implement an OER-supported curriculum. The chapter provides a model of a an OER-based course module, discusses the impact of the "Four R's" of OER (Reuse, Revise, Remix, and Redistribute) on decisions regarding how best to employ OER within a new or existing college course and ends with a series of questions to consider when preparing to engage with the transition to OER.

http://dx.doi.org/10.11647/OBP.0103.12

Introduction[1]

In June of 2012, the United Nations Educational, Scientific and Cultural Organization (UNESCO) set forth a list of ten recommendations in support of Article 26 of the *Universal Declaration of Human Rights*, which had been adopted by the United Nations General Assembly in 1948 on the heels of World War II. The *Universal Declaration of Human Rights* is a soaring document that envisions a world where freedom and dignity, safety and security, are viewed as the norm. Among the 30 articles that comprise the Declaration, the one that is most germane to the context of this book and chapter is that of Article 26, which states that "everyone has the right to education" (United Nations, 1948). Of course, back in 1948, no one was thinking about the application of this principle to higher education beyond the notion that it must be "equally accessible to all on the basis of merit" (United Nations, 1948). While accessibility to higher education remains a significant issue globally, a vast majority of institutions serving the educational needs and interests of post-secondary students at present are less bastions of meritocracy then they are pathways to knowledge and skills necessary for the workplace and for the possibility of upward mobility that is linked to the kinds of employment that require a college education. By the time of the 2012 UNESCO World Open Educational Resources Congress in Paris, the concept of "access" had become less narrowly focused on the delivery of instruction to the "best and brightest" and more on meeting the needs of the "interested and willing".

Conceptually, that is exactly what the OER movement has been about, the free access to educational tools, resources and content to the widest possible audience, with a general call for the democratization of higher education. Specifically, the World OER Congress called for:

1. A universal fostering of awareness and use of OER.
2. Enabling the use of information and communications technologies.

---

1 The opening two paragraphs of the Introduction appeared previously as part of an editorial, co-written by the chapter author and Jordan Jay, Professor of Education, Lincoln University, Missouri, published in *Global Education Review* (Volume 2, Number 3) an open access journal, in September 2015. The writers served as co-editors for a special issue of the journal on the theme: "Open Education Resources and MOOCs", http://ger.mercy.edu/index.php/ger/issue/view/21

3. Developing and reinforcing strategies and policies on the use of OER.

4. Promoting the understanding and use of open licensing frameworks.

5. Supporting capacity building for the development of quality learning materials.

6. Fostering strategic alliances for the widespread use of OER.

7. Encouraging the development and adaptation of OER across languages and cultures.

8. Encouraging research on OER.

9. Facilitating finding, retrieving, and sharing of OER.

10. Encouraging the open licensing of educational materials produced with public funds.

These are lofty goals, indeed. But what do these mean to the typical college faculty member? How do we translate these goals into everyday practice? The purpose of this contribution is to address these questions from the perspective of one faculty member, who began making the transition from textbook-based to OER course content in the same year as the aforementioned 2012 UNESCO World Open Educational Resources Congress was meeting in Paris.

First Contact

I first became aware of OER as an option for replacing textbooks when I was invited to participate in a grant project funded by the Bill and Melinda Gates Foundation and the Hewlett Foundation.[2] Its purpose, as it was initially explained to me, was to develop course materials in support of learning outcomes that would be made available to multiple participating institutions. My initial reaction was one of skepticism, concerned that I might be asked to participate in a project that would get me involved in a tug-of-war between competing industries (technology and book publishing). Nevertheless, I agreed to attend a preliminary meeting in Cerritos, California under the aegis of Lumen Learning, which had obtained the New Generation Learning Challenges grant under

---

2   For more information about the project, see "Adopting OER: A case study of cross-institutional collaboration and innovation", co-authored with Nancy Pawlyshyn, Dr. Braddlee, and Linda Casper, http://er.educause.edu/articles/2013/11/adopting-oer-a-case-study-of-crossinstitutional-collaboration-and-innovation

which we would be working. There we met with faculty from a number of partnering colleges from across the country gathered to discuss the proposed project. It was at that meeting and, subsequently, at the Open Education Conference in Park City, Utah that I began to understand the distinct advantages of making the transition to OER — advantages that convinced me to set aside my initial reticence.

To begin with, OER frees students from the expense of textbooks, amounting to a saving of millions of dollars (University of Minnesota, 2015; Lumen Learning, 2016). Efforts to increase the use of OER as a means of reducing costs include a bill known as the Affordable College Textbook Act (2015) that was introduced in both the US Senate and the US House of Representatives in October of 2015.[3] While the bill never made it beyond the point of being referred to a committee, it is notable for calling for the expansion of the production of open textbooks at colleges and universities, and for disseminating these under a "nonexclusive, permanent license to the public". That bill referenced a report by the College Board identifying the cost of textbooks and supplies at four-year public institutions of higher education during the 2014–15 academic year to be $1,225, a figure that is more meaningful to an individual college student than the millions of dollars cited as an overall savings.

Beyond the cost factor, however, there are other benefits to adopting OER. The use of such resources provides students with access to learning materials from the very first day of class. This is no small consideration. In a survey of more than 2,000 college students from 150 institutions across the country, 65% of respondents reported they had decided against purchasing their textbooks due to the cost (Center for Public Interest Research, 2014). A majority of these (94%) said they made the decision despite their concerns that failure to buy the textbooks might negatively impact their grades. In addition, half of those surveyed said the cost of textbooks influenced their decisions on how many courses to take per semester. And while it was not part of this survey, many students who do buy their textbooks postpone doing so, pending release of financial aid funds. Certainly, the availability of course materials from the start of the semester puts all students on an equal footing, at least in terms of access.

---

3   The Affordable College Textbook Act was co-sponsored in the Senate by Dick Durbin (D-IL), Al Franken (D-MN) and Angus King (I-ME), and in the House of Representatives by Rubén Hinojosa (D-TX) and Jared Polis (D-CO).

OER can be delivered in ways that are supportive of students' schedules and learning styles. Short videos and narrations (e.g. voice-over PowerPoint presentations) available online at any hour of the day can enhance the comprehension of visual and auditory learners in ways that textbooks cannot begin to duplicate. Using the "flipped classroom" model, students can be directed to these materials prior to class so they can be better prepared for in-class activities. For courses that are taught exclusively online, such delivery models also provide a sense of "presence" of faculty members, especially when they incorporate videos of themselves explaining the content or use recorded narratives presentations that incorporate their own voice.

From the perspective of faculty members, OER allows classes to get off to a "running start", with the full expectation that all students have access to the course materials and can start using them immediately. The OER model allows faculty to draw on many different sources and adopt or adapt them in ways that make sense for the course scope and sequence, and for the students. It encourages faculty to be creative in the delivery of course materials, to reshape existing materials, design new ones, collaborate with colleagues who are teaching the same course at their home institution or at other colleges or universities or to "bring the world" to their students through connections with outside agencies or speakers. Faculty are limited only by their imaginations and the availability of supportive technologies that allow them to incorporate virtual museum tours, guest lectures, lab experiments and other experiences to enhance the students' learning. Finally, using OER provides opportunities for doing research on the effectiveness of various teaching approaches and course delivery systems. The OER "movement" is still relatively young and evidence of its impact on student learning, engagement and retention is very much open for research.

Adopting/Adapting Open Educational Resources

A number of those who attended these initial sessions with me decided not to continue with the project. One issue of concern that several expressed was the potential loss of autonomy and academic freedom regarding their courses. Some, too, were loath to abandon their textbooks, while others hesitated at freely distributing their "intellectual property". Nevertheless,

I was sufficiently convinced that there would be a definite advantage to our faculty and students, and I agreed to table my own concerns and become a participant in the grant. In my capacity as an experienced literacy educator, I began working with my cross-institutional colleagues to focus on developing a common set of student learning outcomes that were broad enough to encompass our collective goals, yet with sufficient room for meeting local needs. What we had in common was a target body of college freshmen and a goal of identifying OER materials that would support their reading skills in ways that would improve their ability to understand the wide range of texts they would come across during their first two years as college students within the general education curriculum. What we failed to anticipate, however, was what we did not have in common — the specific students with whom we were working. Each of us worked with students with varying learning needs and degrees of "college readiness" and while we could agree to the learning outcomes, we determined that the best approach for us would be to set about applying them to our local purposes.

Challenges and a Plan

In my case, the target students were college freshmen enrolled in our institution's "Freshman Seminar" course (now reconceptualized as "Critical Inquiry"). My introduction to OER had consisted largely of an immersion into the beliefs, values, and potential benefits of using freely accessible, openly licensed content and instructional media in lieu of the traditional textbook. But coming face-to-face with the task of converting a conceptual framework into practical reality was daunting. There is a certain sense of assurance in using a familiar textbook and supplementing it with lectures, models and practice materials; it is quite another thing to eschew the textbook altogether. Hence, the most challenging question for me was this: To what extent, and how quickly, would I be able to turn the course around? This challenge was exacerbated by the fact that I did not "own" the Freshman Seminar course, which was a key component of the general education curriculum, with a well-established set of competencies to be met. Fortunately, I benefited from having a very positive relationship with those who did have that responsibility. I had conducted numerous workshops for the instructors and had laid out the groundwork for their understanding of critical literacy, an important focus they were very much interested in. They were eager for specific materials they could use with their students; now all I had to do was to come up with them.

In the end, I decided to tackle the task by creating a series of self-contained modules. The benefit for using modules is that these can be brought into the course at any point, allowing instructors the academic freedom to use one or more of them at any given time, dependent on the needs of their particular group of students. I decided to apply the skills to academic texts in math, science, and history, since most freshmen take courses in these areas in their first or second semester. The initial set of skills is identified here:

Table 1. Skills Addressed in Critical Literacy Course Modules

Module	Outcome(s) Addressed	Brief Description	Exercises
MODULE 1 Reading Math 1	Understanding core vocabulary	Strategy lessons on comprehending vocabulary (using math text)	Exercise 1: Using the Context Exercise 2: Using external sources
MODULE 2 Reading Math 2	Comprehending text	Identifying main ideas and key concepts (using math text)	Exercise 1: Identifying main ideas (explicitly presented in text)
MODULE 3 Reading Math 3	Comprehending, analyzing, and drawing conclusions from text	Comprehending, analyzing, and drawing conclusions from text (using math text)	Exercise 1: Applying skills to "unpacking" math word problems
MODULE 4 Reading Science	Drawing inferences from text	Identifying main ideas and key concepts where these are implicit rather than explicit	Exercise 1: Inferring main ideas
MODULE 5 Reading History	Analyzing, synthesizing, drawing inferences, and evaluating text	Critical analysis of text (using history text)	Exercise: Questions 1–4 (drawing on textual content)

The Search for Resources

Once the skill set was identified, the next step was to begin the search for OER materials that would appropriately address the desired outcomes. As a veteran educator with a long history of using search engines and a knack for coming up with the right combination of key words to find the elusive perfect materials, I was optimistic about quickly obtaining what I would need. Unfortunately, however, as I was embarking on this project, the broader focus of the education community with respect to OER was on MOOCs, those "massive open online courses" being developed simultaneously at that time by Coursera, Udacity, edX and many others, aimed at drawing in many thousands of students and opening up the possibilities of higher education to all comers. The creation of repositories of well-vetted OER materials that could be easily accessed by individual faculty members was not yet a high priority and the quality of existing repositories was not at all certain (Atenas and Havemann, 2014). In brief, I hit a snag, albeit a fortuitous one that led me to gaining a fuller and more authentic understanding of what is meant by the "Four R's" of OER: Reuse, Revise, Remix, and Redistribute — all of which came into play as I embarked on the creation of these course modules.

The Four R's in Practice

The target audience for these modules was college freshmen who, as readers, tend to struggle (or decline to struggle) with content literacy, especially where the content and topics are unfamiliar. Even familiar words may cause confusion when they acquire new meanings that are content-specific (Module 1). Well-written texts provide support, but students need to know how to recognize and avail themselves of the support (Module 2). Unfortunately, not all texts are helpful; rather, they may assume a degree of knowledge and experience that may or may not exist, and students need to learn to draw inferences when there is little other support available to them (Module 3 and Module 4). Finally, students need to learn to read with a critical eye, recognizing that what they are reading represents a number of decisions on the writer's part: what to include, what to leave out, how to sequence the information, what support to provide and what words to choose. There is always a bias — something that college students should learn to understand so that they can evolve as engaged learners rather than passive note-takers and memorizers of information (Module 5).

The modules, along with their attendant exercises, were created so that they could be used in accordance with the needs of the students and the purposes of the instructor. They can be used individually or collectively; sequentially or reordered during a short, focused time period or spread throughout a course or portion of a course. They can be presented to students to do independently by way of introducing or practicing a set of skills, or under the direct guidance of the instructor. The modules, however, were not, designed with the intent of serving as substitutions for direct instruction. Thus, it is expected that the instructor will introduce the skill set addressed in any given module, and will follow-up with an analytic discussion and/or additional work — preferably applying the skills to other types of course-related reading.

Each module consists of an instructional component and a set of exercises. The tone of the instructional component is intentionally friendly and inviting, in the manner of a supportive teacher, with the expectation that the students will be engaging with the material independently and will perhaps be more responsive to a "guiding voice". One sample module is laid out below: Reading A Math Textbook — Main Ideas and Key Concepts. In creating the module, I reused, revised and remixed existing OER text (in this case, drawn from an open source math textbook) by combining it with instructional content that I developed. I subsequently redistributed the newly minted module via this chapter and by uploading it (and all of the other modules) into the OER Commons website[4] for others to reuse, revise, remix and redistribute.

---

4   All of the modules have been uploaded to the OER Commons website (https://www.oercommons.org) and can be readily accessed there and used under a CC By Creative Commons license.

SAMPLE MODULE: INSTRUCTIONAL CONTENT

Reading A Math Textbook — Main Ideas and Key Concepts

Introduction

There are books available that you may elect to read to find out more about the history of mathematics or to gain insights into the mind of a particular mathematician. But the typical math textbook you will encounter will be packed with information, examples and problems to solve. Think of it as a guide for "doing math".

Through this set of short lessons and exercises, you will learn and practice using the kinds of skills that will help you to read and understand a mathematics textbook.

Reading for Main Purpose

Read this excerpt from a college algebra textbook.* Read it the way you normally would.

Objective: Evaluate expressions using the order of operations, including the use of absolute value.

When simplifying expressions it is important that we simplify them in the correct order. Consider the following problem done two different ways:

$2+5\cdot3$	Add First		$2+5\cdot3$	Multiply
$7\cdot3$	Multiply		$2+15$	Add
21	Solution		17	Solution

The previous example illustrates that if the same problem is done two different ways we will arrive at two different solutions. However, only one method can be correct. It turns out the second method, 17, is the correct method. The order of operations ends with the most basic of operations, addition (or subtraction). Before addition is completed we must do repeated addition or multiplication (or division). Before multiplication is completed we must do repeated multiplication or exponents. When we want to do something out of order and make it come first we will put it in parenthesis (or grouping symbols). This list then is our order of operations we will use to simplify expressions.

> <u>Order of Operations:</u>
> **Parenthesis (Grouping)**
> **Exponents**
> **Multiply and Divide (Left to Right)**
> **Add and Subtract (Left to Right)**
>
> Multiply and Divide are on the same level because they are the same operation (division is just multiplying by the reciprocal). This means they must be done left to right, so some problems we will divide first, others we will multiply first. The same is true for adding and subtracting (subtracting is just adding the opposite).

Now go to **Exercise 1**. [Note: Exercises can be found following this instructional component of the module.]

[*This and all other textbook samples used as part of the learning module on reading math are excerpted from Beginning and Intermediate Algebra by Tyler Wallace, an open source (CC-BY) textbook available for free download at http://wallace.ccfaculty.org/book/book.html]

Rule 4: Slow down, but first speed up.

OK. Let's take another look together.

Here is the excerpt again:

> **Objective: Evaluate expressions using the order of operations, including the use of absolute value.**
>
> When simplifying expressions it is important that we simplify them in the correct order. Consider the following problem done two different ways:
>
> | | | | | |
> |---|---|---|---|---|
> | $2+5\cdot3$ | Add First | | $2+5\cdot3$ | Multiply |
> | $7\cdot3$ | Multiply | | $2+15$ | Add |
> | 21 | Solution | | 17 | Solution |
>
> The previous example illustrates that if the same problem is done two different ways we will arrive at two different solutions. However, only one method can be correct. It turns out the second method, 17, is the correct method.

The order of operations ends with the most basic of operations, addition (or subtraction). Before addition is completed we must do repeated addition or multiplication (or division). Before multiplication is completed we must do repeated multiplication or exponents. When we want to do something out of order and make it come first we will put it in parenthesis (or grouping symbols). This list then is our order of operations we will use to simplify expressions.

<u>Order of Operations:</u>
Parenthesis (Grouping)
Exponents
Multiply and Divide (Left to Right)
Add and Subtract (Left to Right)

Multiply and Divide are on the same level because they are the same operation (division is just multiplying by the reciprocal). This means they must be done left to right, so some problems we will divide first, others we will multiply first. The same is true for adding and subtracting (subtracting is just adding the opposite).

I asked you to read the excerpt and then answer two questions.

    1. What would you say the author has in mind as the main purpose of this section of the textbook?

        a. To show you different ways to work through a math problem.

        b. To introduce the mathematics concept of "order of operations"

        c. To introduce new mathematics vocabulary words

        d. To show how adding, subtracting, multiplying and dividing can be done in any order

    2. What has the author done to help you to see the main purpose of this section?

        a. Put things in a logical order than can only lead to one conclusion

        b. Underline key points

        c. Tell you up front what the purpose is

        d. Summarize the main purpose at the end of the selection

The correct answers are **b** and **c**, respectively.

How do I know?

Good question.

You will often be asked to summarize what you have read, or to identify the main purpose or to find the main idea or the key points. This is not an easy task. The truth is, you are not really being asked to make your own judgment about these things. Instead, you are being asked to get inside the mind of the author and determine what that person considers to be the main idea.

It really is the writer's (and the editor's) responsibility to give you some guidance. Good readers know how to appreciate and take heed of that support.

In the case of this textbook excerpt, you have been given guidance. The author has identified the purpose right up front:

Objective: Evaluate expressions using the order of operations, including the use of absolute value.

You could quibble (and I would agree) that the phrase "including the use of absolute value" throws things off a bit, but the author has done you a real service by providing the objective and by **using bold face** to draw your attention to it. You may not know a hill of beans about "order of operation" going into the chapter, but at least you understand that this is what the chapter will be about. Every little bit helps!

The writer also has given you additional visual clues to help you stay focused on the main points of the excerpt. Notice the use of indentation, underlining and additional bold face to focus your eye on what is important.

Remember, the purpose at the point is to determine and stay focused on the main idea of a selection. That does not mean you can afford to ignore everything else on the page. Still, it is a start.

Rule 4: Slow Down, But First Speed Up

Poor readers don't concern themselves with the kinds of clues that we have been talking about. The goal is to get from the top left-hand corner of the page down to the bottom right-hand corner as quickly as possible. But it's not a race. The purpose of reading the textbook is to actually learn something.

You will need to do some careful reading. But it pays to begin by trying to grasp the main ideas(s) that will be covered in the selection. Look for words that are highlighted in some fashion, or words like **"objective"**, **"purpose"**, **"introduction"**, or **"summary"**. Most textbooks will offer these supports, with the specific intention of guiding you toward understanding the main idea.

With a little bit of practice, you will learn to do this quickly and efficiently. You can either make a mental note of these key points, or — even better—write them down so that you get into the habit of creating chapter-by-chapter summaries.

Now go to **Exercise 2** [Note: Exercises can be found following this instructional component of the module.]

END SAMPLE MODULE — INSTRUCTIONAL CONTENT

SAMPLE MODULE EXERCISES WITH
INSTRUCTOR'S ANSWER KEY

Questions and Instructor's Answer Key for Module 2: Reading Math — Main Ideas and Key Concepts

Exercise 1 (For correct answers and discussion, go to Content Module)

1. What would you say the author has in mind as the main purpose of this section of the textbook?

    a. To show you different ways to work through a math problem.

    b. To introduce the mathematics concept of "order of operations"

    c. To introduce new mathematics vocabulary words

    d. To show how adding, subtracting, multiplying, and dividing can be done in any order

2. What has the author done to help you to see the main purpose of this section?

    a. Put things in a logical order than can only lead to one conclusion

    b. Underline key points

    c. Tell you up front what the purpose is

    d. Summarize the main purpose at the end of the selection

Exercise 2 (Intended to be done independently)

Read the following excerpt from the same college algebra textbook. Make note of the clues you are provided.

Objective: Add, Subtract, Multiply and Divide Positive and Negative Numbers.

The ability to work comfortably with negative numbers is essential to success in algebra. For this reason we will do a quick review of adding, subtracting, multiplying and dividing of integers. **Integers** are all the positive whole numbers, zero, and their opposites (negatives). As this is intended to be a review of integers, the descriptions and examples will not be as detailed as a normal lesson.

When adding integers we have two cases to consider. The first is if the signs match, both positive or both negative. If the signs match we will add the numbers together and keep the sign. This is illustrated in the following examples

Example 1.

$$-5+(-3) \qquad \text{Same sign add 5+3 keep the negative}$$
$$-8 \qquad \text{Our Solution}$$

Example 2.

$$-7+(-5) \qquad \text{Same sign add 7+5 keep the negative}$$
$$-12 \qquad \text{Our Solution}$$

Question 1: In one sentence, explain the main or key purpose of this excerpt.

> FOR INSTRUCTOR: *The purpose of this excerpt is to give some basic understanding, with examples, of how to add, subtract, multiply, and divide positive and negative numbers.*

Question 2: How do you know?

> FOR INSTRUCTOR: *The purpose is stated directly at the beginning of the excerpt, and the author has boldfaced the heading in order to alert the reader as to the purpose.*

END SAMPLE MODULE — EXERCISES WITH INSTRUCTOR'S ANSWER KEY

Conclusion and Lessons Learned

The above represents one model of how OER can be adapted without incorporating costly textbooks that may or may not provide the content that meets the needs of a particular course taught by a particular faculty member to a particular group of students. That is the real strength of OER — its malleability to serve many different purposes, whether it is used to supplement or to supplant existing materials within a course. This chapter has focused on the pragmatic questions encountered by one faculty member in a journey towards making the use of OER a common practice in the college classroom.

The lessons learned are these: anyone considering transitioning a course from a textbook-reliant style to an OER-based one needs to go in with both eyes open wide to the challenges that exist. Faculty should also carefully consider all of their options, including the possibilities of retaining the textbook, seeking a new textbook, using OER to supplement an existing textbook or making the transition to OER a gradual one, allowing for time to try out various components and/or methods of delivery. Faculty should consider these questions as a means of guiding their decisions regarding the use of OER:

- Do you "own" the course you are thinking of developing or switching over to OER? Are there approvals required for courses changes, curriculum committees to consult? Are there components of the course that must be retained?

- Will changes impact previously identified student learning outcomes?

- Will changes impact course assessments?

- If you wish to (or are required to) collaborate with others teaching the same course, would this be a barrier?

- How do you want to deliver course content? Do you need the assistance of an instructional designer to work out how to incorporate videos, voice-over PowerPoint presentations, podcasts or other technology?

- Do you want to switch to a "flipped classroom" model that incorporates more pre-class experiences for your students and that opens up live classroom time for other kinds of activities? If so, what changes would you want to make in the face-to-face classroom time?

- Similarly, if you want to use a model that is strictly online, how will you organize the course materials so there is a logical sequence for the students to follow?

- Is there someone to turn to for help if unanticipated technological problems arise that interfere with students' access to the course materials?

- Are you prepared to preview all of the course elements prior to the start of each semester, knowing that websites or links to them sometimes change or disappear altogether? Do you have a "Plan B" in mind, just in case?

- Are you prepared to update content on a regular basis in order to take advantage of changes or innovations in your field?

- Are you willing to share your materials in the true spirit of OER?

There is still a need for further research into the impact of OER on student learning, and there is a need to continue the development of the tools and resources to support the transition to OER. Much of the work in doing that has been funded by various foundations — Hewlett, Gates and others — and much of the funding has been absorbed by the top tier colleges and universities that have the infrastructure and the additional financial means to support it. But attention spans are short and pockets are not infinitely deep. It will take local efforts by individuals and groups of faculty, along with cross-institutional collaborations, in order to make the use of OER the norm rather than the "pilot project" at our institutions of higher education.

References

Atenas J. and Havemann, L. (2014), Questions of Quality in Repositories of Open Education Resources: A Literature Review, *Research in Learning Technology*, 22, pp. 1–13, http://dx.doi.org/10.3402/rlt.v22.20889

Center for Public Interest Research (2014), *Fixing the Broken Textbook Market: How Students Respond to High Textbook Costs and Demand Alternatives*, http://uspirg.org/sites/pirg/files/reports/NATIONAL Fixing Broken Textbooks Report1.pdf

Congress. Gov. (2015), *Affordable College Textbook Act*, https://www.congress.gov/bill/114th-congress/senate-bill/2176/text

Lumen Learning (2016), *Open Outcomes: Cost Savings*, http://lumenlearning.com/cost-savings

United Nations (1948), *Declaration of Human Rights*, http://www.un.org/en/documents/udhr/index.shtml

United Nations Educational, Scientific and Cultural Organization (2012), *2012 Paris OER Declaration*, http://www.unesco.org/new/fileadmin/MULTIMEDIA/HQ/CI/CI/pdf/Events/English_Paris_OER_Declaration.pdf

University of Minnesota (2015), *U of M's Open Textbook Network Reports Student Savings of $1.5 Million from Open Textbooks*, https://twin-cities.umn.edu/news-events/u-m's-open-textbook-network-reports-student-savings-15-million-open-textbooks-0

13. Open Assessment Resources for Deeper Learning

David Gibson, Dirk Ifenthaler, and Davor Orlic

This chapter outlines the design concepts for the creation of a global Open Assessment Resources (OAR) item bank with integrated automated feedback and scoring tools for Open Educational Resources (OER) that will support a wide range of assessment applications, from quizzes and tests to virtual performance assessments and game-based learning, focused on promoting deeper learning. The concept of "promoting deeper learning" captures the idea that authentic assessment is fundamental to educative activity and the concept of "item bank" captures the idea of reusability, modularity and automated assembly and presentation of assessment items. We discuss the different assessment structures, processes and quality measurements across various types of assessments and outline how a globally distributed technology infrastructure aligned with and linked to OER could help advance education worldwide. Six core operational services of higher education service delivery — content, interaction, assessment, credentialing, support and technology — are used as a foil for the discussion and analysis of the changes in brand differentiators in these services, which are emerging due to OER and can be enhanced with OAR.

Introduction

Imagine a tutor or sessional instructor anywhere in the world who wishes to know something about what students know and can do. With knowledge about Open Assessment Resources (OAR), a repository is visited that is linked to many sites frequented by instructors and instructional designers. The website links existing OER activities with open assessment resource activity-prompts for online student responses. Within the assessment component of a selected OER, the instructor finds a searchable data bank of concepts linked to core content and activities related to what is being taught. The assessment activity-prompt packages can be made, modified or found and used for the instructor and students cross-linked with the OER. Or one can start by searching for any OER to find an assessment of a transferable skill (e.g. leadership, collaboration, problem-solving) to be assessed. As instructors in new contexts modify the OER over time, the associated open assessment resources developed in that context remain linked to and responsive to those changes.

Some of the assessment activity-prompts require short answers; others require the student to construct something. A few require several steps of a process and collaborative processes over a period of time. At the end of the search and curriculum construction process, a link is received which can be shared with students (e.g. on twitter, social media or embedded in their online course or unit homepage). Students visit the link and interact with their tutor's creation, which may take from a few minutes to several days. Their individualized interactions are automatically stored, analyzed and visualized, and narrated in reports. Automated interventions and help suggestions guide students to explore, think, create, interact, solve and respond, and based on what they do, the products they create and the resources they use, ongoing and final reports are emailed or channeled to them and their tutor. The visualizations and text of the report diagnose current status compared to a variety of cohorts selected by the instructor and make recommendations for "next steps" and "additional activities" concerning the concepts selected by the tutors. This is our vision of a globally networked formative open assessment resource network that can mine the social and intellectual creativity of the world's front line of teaching, and can learn from instructors as well as their students.

Formative assessment purposes such as these are typically low stakes (e.g. ungraded, advisory in nature) and are focused on helping the learner to perform and achieve (e.g. to aide in acquiring knowledge and skills). Summative assessment purposes, in contrast, are high stakes (e.g. success or failure of a unit or course by an individual, obtaining a credential or license) and focused on making a decision that classifies the learner (e.g. as a "B" student, as a licensed practitioner). The Open Assessment Resources (OAR) framework proposed here delivers these new capabilities to the instructor for formative, low stakes, rapid feedback while also providing a new global infrastructure for improving summative assessment.

Open Educational Resources according to the William and Flora Hewlett Foundation are:

> [...] teaching, learning, and research resources that reside in the public domain or have been released under an intellectual property license that permits their free use and re-purposing by others. Open educational resources include full courses, course materials, modules, textbooks, streaming videos, tests, software, and any other tools, materials, or techniques used to support access to knowledge.[1]

With an emphasis on free access, OER has taken "content" off the table as a brand differentiator for higher education institutions (Atkins, Brown, and Hammond, 2007; Conrad, Mackintosh, McGreal, Murphy and Witthaus, 2013). What does a typical higher education institution have to offer in the way of paid content that cannot be freely accessed from the top universities in the world or directly from the primary source of the information? While there might be some areas of unique content that are not yet in OER, increasing quantities of the general curriculum and a great many advanced courses are in the public domain in OER repositories (Robertson, 2010; Wilson, Schuwer, and McAndrew, 2010). The rush into and hype concerning Massive Open Online Courses (MOOCs) has helped to bring this fact to life and has shrunk the pool of differentiators further by including the learning interactions including assessment (Pappano, 2012). Are the remaining core operational services of higher education (credentialing, support, and technology according to Anderson and McGreal, 2012) reconfigurable into a new business model, if content, interactions and assessment cease to be primary services?

Perhaps the answer to this question is one of the barriers to OER uptake in higher education, which has been slowed in no small measure

---

1   http://www.hewlett.org/programs/education-program/open-educational-resources

by a lack of clarity concerning formative versus summative assessment, certification and accreditation.

> Institutional participation in the development and use of OER has been low, with few institutions indicating that they either produce or use OER. Even fewer institutions have implemented open courses for assessment and accreditation. (Conrad *et al.*, 2013)

Perhaps institutions are resisting OER because they focus on the problems of summative assessment, which prevents them from embracing their formative assessment possibilities.

In response to this context, this chapter focuses on formative feedback, which can play a critical role in formal assessment systems. Wagner and Wagner (1985) consider feedback to be any type of information provided to learners and Schimmel (1983) found that feedback is most effective under conditions that encourage the learner's conscious reception and engages the learner in reflecting on the response. Such feedback focuses on improvement information and usually implies multiple attempts at performance because without a second chance to perform, feedback cannot be formative for improvement. Formative feedback is "low stakes" and remains at a distance from certification and accreditation, which rely almost exclusively on "high stakes" summative judgements of academic achievements that result in a determination of status (Harlen and James, 1997). The core idea proposed here is that an open assessment resources (OAR) approach has the potential to increase trust in and use of OER in formal educational systems by adding clarity about assessment purposes and targets in the open resources world. The OAR framework outlined here makes use of the full range from human-scored and human-produced feedback to semi- and fully-automated forms of feedback. Semi-automated feedback approaches include humans and machines working together to make complex judgments, systems that remain open to human shaping and correction after initial machine learning training and gamification techniques where assessment feedback is embedded within the learning experience.

> OAR-supported generalized formative feedback is also distinguished from the highly personalized feedback approaches of adaptive assessments and adaptive curriculum, both of which are increasingly playing a role in institutional practices. Personalized adaptive curriculum and assessment approaches require a tight alignment and control of content to provide personal recommendations based on a learner profile and computational

matching algorithms that trigger appropriately tagged alternative learning experiences and interactions (Ifenthaler, 2015). The personalized adaptive approaches are hard to federate across varied institutions (e.g. in the sense of a group of providers agreeing upon standards of operation in a collective fashion, as in information science), especially as they are integrated into locally unique educative experiences as part of the value propositions of the higher education institution. In addition, personalization involves several challenging ethical dimensions such as privacy of information, security of data and validation of achievement of individual students (Ifenthaler and Widanapathirana, 2014).

In contrast, OAR assessments with generalized formative feedback are aligned with a specific educative purpose expressed by some user of a specific OER towards the utility and expectations for using that OER to achieve an educational outcome. The generalization of feedback can follow anonymous crowd behavior (e.g. common misconceptions, common pathways of performance) in the OER rather than individualized behavior. The OAR framework does not add the complexity of a particular student and the availability of a bank of appropriately meta-tagged alternative learning experience options, leaving this challenge for other developers to use the OAR application programming interface (API) for those purposes. Rather, the OAR approach is focused on a few high-level assessable outcomes (e.g. collaboration, problem-solving, communication, creativity) and the feedback (e.g. recommendations for improved performance, prompts for further elaboration of ideas, suggestions for alternatives) that pertain to supporting and achieving these outcomes within a specific OER with fewer ethical challenges. The higher-level deeper learning outcomes are valued by many, are broadly agreed upon as worthy aims of education and, if appropriately supported and scaffolded by the proposed OAR technology, can be shared and federated. The mechanics of the OAR evidence model is comprised of federated algorithms that capture expert domain knowledge as well as crowd behavior and are then used to make automated feedback, recommendations and decisions within the learning object world of the specific OER. See Architecture of OAR below for a detailed description of the instantiation of alignment, focus and agreement in the assessment outcomes.

We do not address here all of the challenges of assessing deep learning processes (e.g. collaborative problem-solving, creativity, analysis, self-regulation, metacognition), as distinguished from lower level objectives such as remembering, understanding and applying knowledge in some specific field (Anderson, Krathwohl, and Bloom, 2001). The stance taken here is that any area of authentic academic or professional performance can be appropriately documented and measured when there is professional agreement about what someone knows and can do when a level of performance is in evidence. We further assert that "the machine", by which we mean the globally cloud-sourced distributed intelligence of humankind facilitated by network technologies and computational resources, can play an appropriate and increasingly sophisticated role in network-based educational assessment. These challenges are not insurmountable, but here we are focusing on the broad objective of the framework to create a globally relevant, emergent and continuously improving assessment activity item bank linked to specific OERs with integrated automated feedback and scoring tools.

The OAR system will support a wide range of assessment applications, from quizzes and tests to virtual performance assessments and game-based learning, focused on promoting deeper learning. The concept of "assessment activity" expresses the idea that authentic assessment is fundamental to educative activity, and the concept of "item bank" implies reusability, modularity and automated assembly and presentation of assessment items.

Background

Assessment in the context of Open Educational Resources has been discussed primarily as a matter of summative accreditation and credentials (Conrad *et al.*, 2013). Here, we use that discussion as a context to introduce the social and cognitive benefits of rapid, scalable, formative feedback at a global level.

Of the six core services provided by higher education, that is, content, interaction, assessment, credentialing, support and technology (Anderson and McGreal, 2012) future trends in global education predict a migration of services into new configurations within as well as outside of higher education. Some services will divide into free offerings, some into globally shared resource spaces and some into sharper focus as specialized core competencies in basic research, the application of knowledge and excellence in teaching and learning, following the global trend toward unbundling the corporation's three primary functions of finding customers, serving them with content and operating the organization (Hagel and Singer, 1999). We envision these migrations of service delivery options occurring in two complementary trends as higher education institutions strive for global reach and to differentiate themselves from others: one aimed at scale supported by lower interaction costs and the other aimed at uniqueness and brand differentiation driven by a complex system of history, reputation, outcomes and impacts (Table 1).

The trends of scale and uniqueness are not antithetical, but are instead integral to the role of higher education in society as one of the pillars of the advancement of knowledge and the economy. Developing higher educational experiences that are unique to one institution and yet can scale to the world implies a broad conception of quality because a higher education institution's reputation rests on the quality of its offerings, interactions, and products, and includes the quality of its research productivity, excellence of teaching, the perceptions and ratings that impact world ranking, employer satisfaction ratings and the institution's impacts on societal and cultural advancement (Sheehan and Stabell, 2013). An institution's contributions to the world include advancing knowledge and helping to meet the global demand for accessible education, which ultimately demonstrates its considerable influence and power to improve living conditions and its social and economic impacts through sustainable development activities in all fields of knowledge (van Vught, 2008).

Within the six-services context, we propose the Open Assessment Resources (OAR) model of free automated formative assessments (and free support for semi-automated and fully human formative assessments) to advance the trend toward scale. To advance the trend toward uniqueness by creating a new common ground of deeper learning, which allows universities to focus on higher levels in terms of their specialities, we propose to focus the OAR on transferrable deep learning processes (e.g. collaborative problem-solving, creativity, self-regulation, metacognition) from specialized fields into broader contexts, which are to be distinguished from other objectives of assessment such as acquiring knowledge and applying it in a specific field of knowledge. Several organizations — Hewlett Foundation, Educause, Education Week, Alliance for Excellent Education and others have used the term "deeper learning" — as a way to highlight higher order learning skills. The Hewlett Foundation (2010) identifies deeper learning with five groups of abilities:

- Mastering core academic content;
- Critical thinking and problem solving;
- Working collaboratively;
- Communicating effectively; and
- Learning how to learn independently.

In the next section, we discuss new mechanisms and leverage points for embedding these deeper learning abilities across the six-services model, while pointing out major strategies for utilizing the OAR technology to simultaneously achieve scale and uniqueness.

OAR and the Core Services of Higher Education

The intersection of the six core services of higher education with the two trends scale and uniqueness provides a structure for OAR interactions that will be elaborated in this section. The costs to learners in the OAR model varies from free, low and medium to high-cost across the six core services depending on options within the trends of scale (an institution's need to achieve sustainable scale) and uniqueness (an institution's need to build and maintain brand differentiation).

In the next sections we present details of this broad outline. We will work backwards with "the end in mind" by starting with the concepts of automated and semi-automated formative assessments and the architecture of OAR. Then we will discuss each of the six core services and include the contexts of the trends toward scalability and uniqueness. Finally, we will conclude by bringing the OAR model back into the larger context of higher education worldwide, with implications for various next steps in research and development.

Table 1. Six dimensions of higher education services with two trends: scale and uniqueness

Services	Description	Toward Scale	Toward Uniqueness
Dimension 1: Content	Lectures, online learning materials, printed study guides produced by the institution or licensed third-party copyright materials	FREE: MOOCs, OER courses and units	HIGH COST: Content producers of unique, locally validated research knowledge, some of which is made into OER for both internal and external consumption.

Dimension 2: Interaction	Learner-experts (Tutors, discussions, feedback on assignments)	FREE and LOW COST: Video experts from anywhere, semi-automated expert interactions with masses. LOW COST: Adaptive curriculum automating some decision points of curriculum and instruction path planning and preparation	HIGH COST: Traditional Hands-on Interactions (e.g. laboratories, scholarly apprenticeships, face-to-face communications) MEDIUM COST: Semi-automated personalized guidance and instruction from teaching focused scholars
	Learner-content (Class activities, Labs, Internships)	FREE: Google and Wiki MOOC-like content, media and interactions	FREE and LOW COST: Highly interactive content (e.g. Game-based, Transmedia Engagement)
	Learner-learner (Study and discussion groups)	FREE: Self-organizing study groups	FREE: Social media market economy (eBay of Learning)
Dimension 3: Assessment	Formative — Feedback on assignments and performance	FREE: Automated and adaptive personalized formative assessment	MEDIUM COST: Adaptive curriculum
	Summative — grades, exams, challenge exams	MEDIUM to HIGH COST: Adaptive high-stakes assessment, Fee-for-service	MEDIUM to HIGH COST: Adaptive high-stakes assessment, Fee-for-service
Dimension 4: Credentialing	Transcripts, articulation agreements, credit-transfer processes among institutions and awarding of accredited credentials	LOW COST: Fee-for-service semi-automated recognition of prior learning for diagnostics, study plans and badges	MEDIUM COST: Fee-for-service recognition of prior learning and semi-automated challenge exams for micro-certifications HIGH COST: Semi-automated assessment-based credentials, traditional study plans and graduation
Dimension 5: Support	Learning support, career guidance and counselling, library services and academic study skills support	FREE: Shared service models (e.g. licensed service groups, globally shared services)	Personalized and semi-automated personalized service (FREE and LOW COST Fee-for-services)
Dimension 6: Technology	Infrastructure and support for blended and technology enabled learning including online course delivery	LOW COST: Distributed and open	LOW COST: Private cloud

ƒ

Automated and Semi-automated Formative Assessment

Automation and semi-automation (e.g. humans and machines working together) to provide feedback, observations, classifications and scoring are increasingly being used to serve both formative and summative purposes. For example, in teaching and testing writing skills, results from a comparison of automated essay scoring applications (Shermis and Hamner, 2012) demonstrated that "scoring was capable of producing scores similar to human scores for extended-response writing items with equal performance for both source-based and traditional writing genre" (p. 2). The report concluded that, "As a general scoring approach, automated essay scoring appears to have developed to the point where it can be reliably applied in both low-stake assessment (e.g. instructional evaluation of essays) and perhaps as a second scorer for high-stakes testing" (p. 27). The scalability of OER provides a great opportunity for large numbers of training samples and human judgment to be combined at a global level.

Extending beyond writing and other basic issues of human learning and performance, an international group of researchers has been developing the technology and tools for a highly integrated model-based assessment platform for assessing the acquisition and development of complex cognitive skills (Al-Diban and Ifenthaler, 2011; Ifenthaler, 2010, 2014; Pirnay-Dummer, Ifenthaler, and Spector, 2010). In addition, a global workgroup co-founded by UNESCO and a collaboration of national technology in education entities — EDUsummIT — has devoted its biannual summits 2006 to a range of topics connected to assessment, deeper learning, and the use of emerging technologies to improve education throughout the world. One of the summit's discussion groups has published analyses and evidence-based position papers on the role of technology in assessment (Gibson and Webb, 2013, 2015; Webb and Gibson, 2015; Webb and Gibson, 2011; Webb, 2011).

Architecture of OAR

In this section, we outline model architecture for the OAR framework. The architecture supports the inclusion of assessment materials linked to specific OER learning materials and provides a high level completed road map to instantiate, pilot and validate the system with large-scale providers of OER resources and services (Figure 1).

The overall concept of such a solution is based on the bottom-up approach of applying simple scripts and snippets to the OER sites that would be linked to the strong server analytics side. This is how such a system will provide cross-site functionalities to every site using scripts and snippets, thus creating a network of interconnected OER sites.

Figure 1 shows the high-level architecture for such a solution. In the middle are various OER sites that would install a few simple line scripts to provide the server side analytics platform with the data for the analytics. The two streams of analytics services will be implemented there:

- Server side off-line content analytics (colored red in the figure); and
- Server side real-time user modelling (colored green in the figure).

Both services will provide back to the OER sites information about (i) the user and their learning model that will be used for learning personalization across the sites, (ii) cross-recommended content that is related to users' current learning statuses and predicted learning paths, (iii) semantically structured information from automated and semi-automated processes that meta-tag the content that will be used by OER repositories for additional content preparation and (iv) a validation feedback of the OAR assessment.

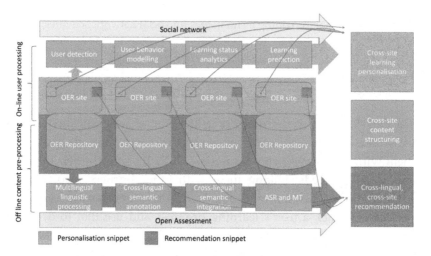

Figure 1. Model Architecture for Open Assessment Resources
Integration with Open Educational Resources. ASR = automatic speech
recognition; MT = machine translation

Below is the example of the simple script on a site for learning analytics:

```
$.ajax({
url: "http://log2.quintelligence.com/qlog.js", type: 'get', dataType: 'script', cache: true,
success: function() { setTimeout(function() {quintTracker(3);},100); }
});
```

The OAR offers innovative technology elements that will integrate the currently scattered use of many OER sites across the globe and make those sites act as an innovative learning environment. Current OER repositories have objects that utilize various kinds of interoperable frameworks.

The OAR solutions that will be offered to OER sites and their elements are:

- Cross-site: providing technologies to transparently accompany and analyze users across sites;
- Cross-domain: providing technologies for cross domain content analytics;
- Cross-modal: providing technologies for multimodal content understanding;
- Cross-language: providing technologies for cross lingual content recommendation;
- Cross-cultural: providing technologies for cross cultural learning personalization;
- Cross-social: providing technologies for social network activities; and
- Cross-assessment: technologies for cross-site assessment of the impact of OER materials on learning (e.g. population performance metrics).

The development of the network will follow a waterfall model with early versions concentrating on engaging users through providing them with information about different OERs that match their interests and learning needs, linking them with other learners who may be suitable discussants, either as equals, as advisors or as advisees. The project will track a user's learning progress and use that to drive an analytics engine driven by state-of-the-art machine learning that can improve recommendations through better understanding of users, their progress and goals, and hence their match with knowledge resources of all types. The project will run a series of pilot case studies that enable the measurement of the broader goals of delivering a useful and enjoyable educational experience to learners in different domains, at different levels and from different cultures.

Six Dimensions of OAR Impacts on Higher Education Services

With the rationale and architecture of OAR in mind, the next section discusses the major impacts on the six core operational services of higher education institutions.

Dimension 1: Content

A major impact of OER is that content is free and widely available. Content therefore does not in and of itself constitute a point of differentiation among higher education institutions for a great many discipline areas. For example, one can study accounting anywhere in the world from any institution and be fairly well assured of acquiring a common foundation of knowledge with transferable skills and certifications. OER ideally extends that accessibility to many more fields of knowledge. The end point of the global accessibility of OER content when fully implemented is that a person can study and interact with learning materials on any subject in any field of knowledge from anywhere at anytime.

OAR adds value to OER's openness and accessibility by assuring that the learner has acquired or can demonstrate capability with new knowledge. What OER does for content, OAR does for the assurance of what a student knows and can do. OER includes learning resources such as lecture notes and videos of lectures, online learning materials, printed study guides produced by the institution or licensed third-party copyright materials. OAR creates an assessment context for a specific purpose of those specific OER learning resources — an OER-OAR pairing — by adding a prompt to the learner, a specific assessment task to use during or after interacting with the resources, and feedback based on the performance of the assessment task. The assessment purpose, task and feedback package is a specific kind of content uniquely tied to the OER resource for a specific context of use. Multiple OARs for any particular OER (many pairings) make it possible for the OER to serve different learning purposes and provide evidence to the student as well as instructor that the intended learning objectives of an OER-OAR pair were met to some standard of observable performance.

The trend of scalable content is supported by the use of OER in courses and units; for example by lowering the cost of production of content for online courses (Conrad *et al.*, 2013). The OAR framework supports scalability of assessment as instructors re-use the OER-OAR package with or without modifications. Allowing local remixing and relicensing of OER-OAR by content producers of unique, locally validated research knowledge supports the trend of unique content.

Dimension 2: Interaction

Content is inert until a learner comes into contact with it, so interaction is key to engagement and learning, as implied by psychological theory (Carson, 1969; Chamorro-Premuzic and Furnham, 2004). In addition to learner-content interaction, experts such as instructors, mentors, researchers and tutors are typically part of a higher education class experience. Peer based and social group learning can also play a role. From the viewpoint of the OAR framework, all of these approaches can be maintained and scaffolded but perhaps most important, due to the unique affordances of eLearning, learner-content interactions can be highly interactive, providing choice and responsive content at higher levels than non-technological delivery in face-to-face contexts (see Benitez-Guerrero, 2013; Manninen, 2001). This is perhaps one of the reasons research has shown the superiority of blended learning over either all online or all face-to-face (Bonk and Graham, 2006; Tayebinik and Puteh, 2012). Three examples of interactions supported by the OAR design follow: learner-expert, learner-content, and learner-peer.

Learner-experts (e.g. Tutors, instructor-led discussions, feedback on assignments)

Supporting the trend of scalability, the availability of free and low cost video experts accessible anywhere at anytime is an example of providing semi-automated expert interactions with masses. Leaner-expert interactions have been typified along a continuum of one-to-many, and when combined with individual or small group exercises, then extending into one-to-one support, when peers act as experts. Using a peer crowd to source experts in small discussion groups is supported by many-to-many interaction designs in a MOOC. Finally, when advice from a group is channeled toward the individual, it can be characterized as a many-to-one design. An example discussion of this continuum can be found in a reflective blog about the MITx U.Lab course (Scharmer, 2015). Typically, this expanding range of learner-expert interactions has thus far been designed for human-to-human communication, but the possibility with OAR and its capability for globally crowd-sourced semi-automated feedback is to envision where and how the machine can play a role in initiating, promoting, supporting and interacting with learners within this continuum.

For example, in an adaptive curriculum, the machine can automate some of the decision points of a curriculum or an instructional path, helping to support planning and preparation for learning, or skills practice as seen in digital games, group experiences as in serious games as well as reflective thinking and writing.

At a medium cost level, experts are trained and supported to provide semi-automated personalized guidance and instruction, for example, from teaching focused scholars, sessional and adjunct faculty members who use the OAR infrastructure as one of the tools of teaching. At the highest cost level are traditional hands-on interactions in real physical laboratories, scholarly apprenticeships that evolve over long periods of time and all forms of face-to-face communications, which might make minimal use of the OAR for exercises, quizzes and tests in a blended course.

Learner-content (e.g. Class activities, Labs, Internships)

The Internet provides learners with direct access to and interaction with content in a range, from read-only to highly interactive engagement. For example, Google and Wiki MOOC-like content, media and interactions provide massive access to read-only content. Some OER content designed for user actions (e.g. widgets, simulations, interactive visualizations) inhabit the medium level of production costs with distribution costs approaching zero. At the unique end of the continuum, and with the highest cost of production and data maintenance, is highly interactive content with embedded analytics. The leading edges supporting uniqueness include learning experiences that utilize Game-based (Gibson and Jakl, 2015; Ifenthaler, Eseryel and Ge, 2012) and Transmedia Engagement methods (Jenkins, Purushotma, Clinton, Weigel and Robison, 2006). The OAR design, with its capability for immediate feedback supported by crowd-sourced intelligence, supports the evolution of digital game-based and shared story-telling approaches to learning integrated with data analytics and allows learner-to-content interactions to become embedded with appropriate assessments as well as reusable at scale.

Learner-peer (e.g. Study and discussion groups)

There is considerable potential for self-organizing study groups to be supported by a globally distributed network of peers. OAR's role in peer-based communication can support a social media market economy for education (e.g. an "eBay" of learning) where anyone with value to add to anyone else will be facilitated into and out of appropriate relationships as an expert, a learner and a peer when appropriate. Similar to how OER has taken some of the friction out of content development and access, OAR will be part of a system to take the friction out of educative relationships by facilitating feedback and allowing the machine to play an appropriate role supporting decentralized and distributed intelligence and communication concerning performance (formative) as well as comparative classification (summative) assessment.

Dimension 3: Assessment

Authentic assessment is fundamental to providing formative feedback and determining the extent of what someone knows and can do in terms of appropriate, meaningful, significant and worthwhile forms of human accomplishment (Newmann and Archibald, 1992). In the context of someone learning with an OER, central to OAR is a globally distributed and crowd-sourced common ground of understanding among teachers and mentors about what kinds of formative feedback are useful for developing the authentic expertise of a novice in a relevant field of knowledge and practice. The common ground does not have to be created *a priori* for every OER by pre-arranged agreements; the OAR layer can be grown and developed naturally and automatically by observing and recording the actual feedback given to novices in similar digital performance circumstances, which requires the OAR to support evolving ontologies. With appropriate feedback from all users, the evolving distributed ontologies can range from a folksonomy to an expert-validated ontology for the OER (Angeletou, 2008; Gruber, 2007; Sturtz, 2004; Xie *et al.*, 2014).

The saved feedback can then be mined for automated formative assessment at scale. The infrastructure can also support the uniqueness of feedback needed to enable an adaptive curriculum by allowing for both private and public information layers to overlap and interact. For example, a new piece of private feedback could be compared to existing public feedback and then a decision could be made to edit the feedback, utilize the public resource, or continue with the new feedback as a new source for future machine learning training in either or both the private and public spheres.

Assessment also includes classification of a learner's performance, also known as summative assessment (Bennett, 2010; M. Webb, Gibson and Forkosh-Baruch, 2013; Wiliam and Black, 1996), which has been traditionally associated with grades, course exams and challenge exams for awarding recognition and credit. The OAR can serve as a foundational layer for fee-for-services from higher education institutions that wish to support scalable adaptive assessment (Almond and Mislevy, 1999) through a publicly available API and appropriate Creative Commons licensing (Hietanen, 2008).

Dimension 4: Credentialing

One of the important products of a higher education program is the degree or credential supported by a transcript of grades or performance quality in the program's courses. Recently, micro-credentialing and unbundling practices have also begun to appear due to evolving practices involving digital badges (Gibson, Ostashewski, Flintoff, Grant, and Knight, 2013; Grant, 2014). Credentialing is also involved in articulation agreements, which support credit-transfer processes among institutions, as well as in recognition of prior learning (RPL). We envision that OAR will support semi-automated RPL for diagnostics, study plans and microcredentials or badges because the infrastructure for credentialing maps closely to what is needed for summative assessment, where a current state of classification is the outcome sought from interactions with a learner. The infrastructure will also support semi-automated challenge exams for micro-certifications and assessment-based credentials, traditional study plans and graduation examinations.

Dimension 5: Support

Learning support services in higher education include, among other things, career guidance and counselling, library services and academic study skills support. Freely available shared service models utilizing OAR might include APIs for licensed service groups and globally shared student services. Utilizing the strategy of interacting private and public layers, uniqueness will be supported for personalized and semi-automated personalized services.

Dimension 6: Technology

The OAR design provides infrastructure and support for blended and technology-enabled learning including online course delivery through low cost distributed and open resources integrated with private cloud-based services for supporting unique added value technology developed and delivered by higher education institutions.

OAR in Global Higher Education

The proposed OAR structure will require global collaboration and investment over time by a number of primary actors in educational technology. In addition, a number of research topics need to be investigated and can be supported by the data of the emerging system. Once data begins to flow, highly detailed event-level records of student performance will be available for data mining and a number of questions become immediately feasible to address and elaborate, including:

- Assessment construct validity.
- Predictive analytics for construct level feedback based on earlier test items.
- Intervention strategies triggered during a formative assessment.

- Algorithms of data discovery and evidence rule generation.
- Human-computer interactions in an assessment ecosystem.
- Ethics and effective processes of saving and sharing learner profile histories.
- Exploration and validation of virtual performance assessment psychometric challenges.
- Modification and adaptation of assessment modules.
- Effects of teaching to authentic tests.
- Equity of treatment for subgroups.

These questions are now addressable primarily with small, single-study research designs by a handful of researchers who have built systems with sufficient teams of experts to enable inquiry into the wide range of related topics. As OAR becomes a reality, then these questions can begin to be addressed by a global community of like-minded educational researchers and access can be given freely to all higher educational institutions forming a new floor for student performance that raises standards of practice, doing for assessment what OER and MOOCs have begun to do for content and learning interactions.

References

Al-Diban, S. and Ifenthaler, D. (2011), Comparison of Two Analysis Approaches for Measuring Externalized Mental Models, *Educational Technology & Society*, 14(2), pp. 16–30.

Almond, R. and Mislevy, R. (1999), Graphical Models and Computerized Adaptive Testing, *Applied Psychological Measurement*, 23(3), pp. 223–237, http://dx.doi.org/10.1177/01466219922031347

Anderson, L., Krathwohl, D. and Bloom, B. (2001), *A Taxonomy for Learning, Teaching, and Assessing: A Revision of Bloom's Taxonomy of Educational Objectives*, New York: Longman.

Anderson, T. and McGreal, R. (2012), *Disruptive Pedagogies and Technologies in Universities: Unbundling of Educational Services*, 15, pp. 380–389.

Angeletou, S. (2008), Semantic Enrichment of Folksonomy Tagspaces. *Lecture Notes in Computer Science (including subseries Lecture Notes in Artificial Intelligence and Lecture Notes in Bioinformatics)*, 5318 LNCS, pp. 889–894, 10.1007/978-3-540-88564-1-58

Atkins, D. E., Brown, J. S. and Hammond, A. L. (2007), *A Review of the Open Educational Resources (OER) Movement: Achievements, Challenges, and New Opportunities*, William and Flora Hewlett Foundation, http://www.oerderves.org

Benitez-Guerrero, E. I. (2013), Mining Data from Interactions with a Motivational-aware Tutoring System Using Data Visualization, *Journal of Educational Data Mining*, 5(1), pp. 72–103.

Bennett, R. (2010), Cognitively Based Assessment of, for, and as Learning (CBAL): A Preliminary Theory of Action for Summative and Formative Assessment, *Measurement: Interdisciplinary Research and Perspective*, 8(2–3), pp. 70–91, http://www.tandfonline.com/doi/abs/10.1080/15366367.2010.508686

Bonk, C. J. and Graham, C. R. (2006), The Handbook of Blended Learning, *Global Perspectives, Local Designs*, 1, http://www.lavoisier.fr/livre/notice.asp?ouvrage=1584996

Carson, R. C. (1969), *Interaction Concepts of Personality*, Chicago: Aldine.

Chamorro-Premuzic, T. and Furnham, A. (2004), A Possible Model for Understanding the Personality-intelligence Interface, *British Journal of Psychology*, 95, pp. 249–264, http://dx.doi.org/10.1348/000712604773952458

Conrad, D., Mackintosh, W., McGreal, R., Murphy, A. and Witthaus, G. (2013), *Report on the Assessment and Accreditation of Learners Using OER*. Commonwealth of Learning, http://hdl.handle.net/11599/232

Gibson, D. C. and Jakl, P. (2015), Theoretical Considerations for Game-Based e-Learning Analytics, in T. Reiners and L. Wood (Eds.), *Gamification in Education and Business*, pp. 403–416, New York: Springer.

Gibson, D. C., Ostashewski, N., Flintoff, K., Grant, S. and Knight, E. (2013), Digital Badges in Education, *Education and Information Technologies*, 20(2), 403–410, http://dx.doi.org/10.1007/s10639-013-9291-7

Gibson, D. C. and Webb, M. (2013), *Assessment as, for and of 21st Century Learning*, International Summit on ICT in Education, Torun: EDUsummIT 2013, p. 17, http://www.edusummit.nl/fileadmin/contentelementen/kennisnet/EDU SummIT/Documenten/2013/6_WCCE_2013-_Educational_Assessment_ supported_by_IT_1_.pdf

Gibson, D. C. and Webb, M. E. (2015), Data Science in Educational Assessment, *Education and Information Technologies*, June(4), pp. 697–713, 10.1007/s10639-015-9411-7

Grant, S. (2014), *What Counts as Learning: Open Digital Badges for New Opportunities*, Irvine, CA: Digital Media and Learning Research Hub https://www.academia.edu/8022569/What_Counts_As_Learning_Open_Digital_ Badges_for_New_Opportunities

Gruber, T. (2007), Ontology of Folksonomy: A Mash-up of Apples and Oranges, *International Journal on Semantic Web & Information Systems*, 3(2), pp. 1–11, http://dx.doi.org/0.4018/jswis.2007010101

Hagel, J. and Singer, M. (1999), Unbundling the Corporation, *Harvard Business Review*, 77(March-April), pp. 133–141.

Harlen, W. and James, M. (1997), Assessment and Learning: Differences and Relationships between Formative and Summative Assessment, *Assessment in Education: Principles, Policy & Practice*, 4(3), pp. 365–379, http://dx.doi. org/10.1080/0969594970040304

Hietanen, H. A. (2008), Creative Commons' Approach to Open Content, Intellectual Property, pp. 1–88, http://dx.doi.org/10.2139/ssrn.1162219

Ifenthaler, D. (2015), Learning Analytics, in J. M. Spector (Ed.), *The SAGE Encyclopedia of Educational Technology*, 2, pp. 447–451, Thousand Oaks: Sage.

Ifenthaler, D. (2014), AKOVIA: Automated Knowledge Visualization and Assessment, *Technology, Knowledge and Learning*, 19(1–2), pp. 241–248, http://dx.doi.org/10.1007/s10758-014-9224-6

Ifenthaler, D. (2010), Relational, Structural, and Semantic Analysis of Graphical Representations and Concept Maps, *Educational Technology Research and Development*, 58(1), pp. 81–97, http://dx.doi.org/10.1007/s11423-008-9087-4

Ifenthaler, D. and Widanapathirana, C. (2014), Development and Validation of a Learning Analytics Framework: Two Case Studies Using Support Vector Machines, *Technology, Knowledge and Learning*, 19(1–2), pp. 221–240, http://dx.doi.org/10.1007/s10758-014-9226-4

Ifenthaler, D., Eseryel, D. and Ge, X. (2012), Assessment for Game-Based Learning, D. Ifenthaler, D. Eseryel and X. Ge (Eds.), *Assessment in Game-Based Learning, Foundations, Innovations, and Perspectives*, pp. 3–10, New York: Springer, http://dx.doi.org/10.1007/978-1-4614-3546-4

Jenkins, H., Purushotma, R., Clinton, K., Weigel, M. and Robison, A. (2006), *Confronting the Challenges of Participatory Culture: Media Education for the 21st Century, New Media Literacies Project*, Cambridge, MA: MIT, http://mitpress.mit.edu/sites/default/files/titles/free_download/9780262513623_Confronting_the_Challenges.pdf

Manninen, T. (2001), Rich Interaction in the Context of Networked Virtual Environments: Experiences Gained from the Multi-player Games Domain, in A. Blanford, J. Vanderdonckt and P. Gray (Eds.), *Joint Proceedings of HCI 2001 and IHM 2001 Conference*, pp. 383–398, London: Springer.

Newmann, F. and Archibald, D. (1992), The Nature of Authentic Academic Achievement, in H. Berlak, F. Newmann, E. Adams, D. Archbald, T. Burgess, J. Raven and T. Romberg (Eds.), *Toward a New Science of Educational Testing and Assessment*, Albany: SUNY Press.

Pappano, L. (2012), The Year of the MOOC, *New York Times*, http://www.nytimes.com/2012/11/04/education/edlife/massive-open-online-courses-are-multiplying-at-a-rapid-pace.html?pagewanted=all&_r=0

Pirnay-Dummer, P., Ifenthaler, D. and Spector, M. (2009), Highly Integrated Model Assessment Technology and Tools, *Educational Technology Research and Development*, 58(1), pp. 3–18, http://dx.doi.org/10.1007/s11423-009-9119-8

Robertson, R. J. (2010), Repositories for OER. *JISC CETIS*, http://www.slideshare.net/RJohnRobertson/repositoriesforoer

Scharmer, O. (2015), MITx u.lab: Education As Activating Social Fields, *Huffington Post*, http://www.huffingtonpost.com/otto-scharmer/mitx-ulab-education-as-ac_b_8863806.html?ir=Australia

Schimmel, B. J. (1983), *A Meta-Analysis of Feedback to Learners in Computerized and Programmed Instruction*, Paper presented at the AREA 1983, Montreal.

Sheehan, N. T. and Stabell, C. B. (2013), Reputation as a Driver in Activity Level Analysis: Reputation and Competitive Advantage in Knowledge Intensive Firms, *Corporate Reputation Review*, 13(3), pp. 198–208, http://dx.doi.org/10.1057/crr.2010.19

Shermis, M. D. and Hamner, B. (2012), Contrasting State-of-the-art Automated Scoring of Essays, in M. D. Shermis and J. Burstein, *Handbook of Automated Essay Evaluation: Current Applications and New Directions*, Routledge Handbooks Online, http://dx.doi.org/10.4324/9780203122761.ch19

Sturtz, D. N. (2004), *Communal Categorization: The Folksonomy*, INFO622 Content Representation, 16(29.03.2007), http://davidsturtz.com/drexel/622/communal-categorization-the-folksonomy.html

Tayebinik, M. and Puteh, M. (2012), Blended Learning or E-learning?, *IMACST*, 3(1), pp. 103–110.

van Vught, F. (2008), Mission Diversity and Reputation in Higher Education, *Higher Education Policy*, 21(2), pp. 151–174, http://dx.doi.org/10.1057/hep.2008.5

Wagner, W. and Wagner, S. U. (1985), Presenting Questions, Processing Responses, and Providing Feedback in CAI, *Journal of Instructional Development*, 8(4), pp. 2–8, http://dx.doi.org/10.1007/bf02906047

Webb, M. (2011), Feedback Enabled by New Technologies as a Key Component of Pedagogy, in M. Koehler & P. Mishra (Eds.), *Proceedings of the Society for Information Technology & Teacher Education International Conference 2011*, pp. 3382–3389, Chesapeake, VA: Association for the Advancement of Computing in Education (AACE)

Webb, M. and Gibson, D. C. (2015), Technology Enhanced Assessment in Complex Collaborative Settings, *Education and Information Technologies*, 4 (June), pp. 675–695, 10.1007/s10639-015-9413-5

Webb, M. and Gibson, D. C. (2011), Assessment to Move Education into the Digital Age: Brief Report from Thematic Working Group TWG 5 on Assessment, *EDUsummIT 2011: Building a Global Community of Policy-Makers, Educators and Researchers to Move Education into the Digital Age*, Paris: UNESCO.

Webb, M., Gibson, D. C. and Forkosh-Baruch, A. (2013), Challenges for Information Technology Supporting Educational Assessment, *Journal of Computer Assisted Learning*, 29(5), pp. 451–462, http://dx.doi.org/10.1111/jcal.12033

Wiliam, D. and Black, P. (1996), Meanings and Consequences: A Basis for Distinguishing Formative and Summative Functions of Assessment?, *British Educational Research Journal*, 22(5), pp. 537–548, http://dx.doi.org/10.1080/0141192960220502

Wilson, T., Schuwer, R. and McAndrew, P. (2010), *Collating Global Evidence of the Design, Use, Reuse and Redesign of Open Educational Content, Open Educational Resources*, Paper presented at the *2010 OER10 Conference*, 22–24 March 2010, Cambridge, UK.

Xie, H., Li, Q., Mao, X., Li, X., Cai, Y. and Rao, Y. (2014), Community-aware User Profile Enrichment in Folksonomy, Neural Networks, 58, pp. 111–121, http://dx.doi.org/10.1016/j.neunet.2014.05.009

14. Promoting Open Science and Research in Higher Education: A Finnish Perspective

Ilkka Väänänen and Kati Peltonen

This chapter presents the current state of open science and research in Finland. The Ministry of Education and Culture has established the Open Science and Research Initiative for 2014–17, which aims to promote the availability of open research information and open publication procedures. Along with this initiative, Finland aims to become the leading country for openness in science and research by 2017, covering a broad range of activities on many levels, and thus enabling the more effective utilization of research data and results for the greater benefit of society. Finnish Higher Education Institutes (HEIs) play an important role in fulfilling this vision. In this contribution we investigate Finland's open science and research framework by examining Lahti University of Applied Sciences as a case study of the implementation of open science and research (OSR) policies. As this example shows, the implementation of OSR policies is an iterative development process through repeated cycles in which raising awareness, sharing knowledge and building networks and capacity development are central issues in the creation of an open working culture for an HEI, and which is needed to achieve strategic goals and to increase the impact and quality of research.

     http://dx.doi.org/10.11647/OBP.0103.14

Introduction

The open education (OE) movement is built around the idea of open society and free sharing and the use of knowledge and educational resources. This movement is rooted in various historical backgrounds starting from the age of Enlightenment and the work of educational philosophers and reformists like Rousseau, Pestalozzi, Montessori and Dewey, who all advocated the open classroom, freedom and equality of learners and openness to experiences as essential elements in learning (Peter and Deimann, 2008). Since these early days, the ideals of open education have assumed new meaning and thrust by the invention of the internet and the rise of the open knowledge movement which translated in the rapid expansion in and the expansion of open and distance learning (Atkins, Brown and Hammond, 2007).

Today, open education can be seen as an umbrella concept covering a number of projects revolving around "openness" in the digital world, such as Open Educational Resources, open source, open access, open science, open archiving and open publishing (Peters, 2008; Peter and Deimann, 2013). Open Educational Resources (OER) refer to teaching, learning and research materials that are released under non-proprietorial licenses allowing for their free access and reuse (Atkins *et al.*, 2007). The basic idea informing OER is that all knowledge should be freely shared and disseminated (Yuan, MacNeill and Kraan, 2008). On a larger scale, this approach and term was adopted in a United Nations Educational, Scientific and Cultural Organization (UNESCO) meeting in 2002, which was seen as a starting point for the OER movement (D'Antoni, 2009; Atkins *et al.*, 2007). According to the definition provided by the Organization for Economic Cooperation and Development (OECD, 2007, 10), OER refers to "digitised materials offered freely and openly for educators, students, and self-learners to use and reuse for teaching, learning, and research". This approach to learning has its roots in the Open Source Movement, i.e. the provision of computer software that is publicly accessible and can be openly modified and shared, which started in the 1980's alongside the GNU free operating system project lead by Richard Stallman, the current president of the Free Software Foundation (Stallman, 2002).[1]

---

1   The GNU operating system is a complete free software system, upward-compatible with Unix. GNU stands for "GNU's Not Unix". Richard Stallman made the Initial

Open access, a term which was given currency with the Budapest Open Access Initiative of 2002,[2] refers to the free online availability of scientific knowledge and research outputs e.g. research articles, academic monographs and textbooks. Open science, following the definition given by Wikimedia, can be described as "the movement to make scientific research, data and dissemination accessible to all levels of an inquiring society, amateur or professional. It encompasses practices such as publishing open research, campaigning for open access, encouraging scientists to practice open notebook science, and generally making it easier to publish and communicate scientific knowledge".[3] This movement promotes a more efficient use of research results and data leading to increased open innovations (European Commission, 2015).[4] Open science encompasses open archiving (the practice of uploading of scholarly research papers into networked repositories which are openly accessible to all), as well as open access publishing. Under the EU research and innovation funding program Horizon 2020, open access to publications is now mandatory. The European Commission launched a pilot project to open up publicly funded research data available from 2013 onwards. In 2015, the Competitiveness Council adopted Council Conclusions on open, data-intensive and networked research as a driver for faster and wider innovation (Council of the European Union, 2015) in which it stated that member states like Finland look forward to the possible development of action plans or strategies for open science.

Open science and research (OSR) principles are encouraged by the Organization for Economic Co-operation and Development (OECD) and EU policy makers. Governments are key players in developing national OSR policies, as these guide the initiatives adopted at university level worldwide.

Announcement of the GNU Project in September 1983. A longer version called the GNU Manifesto was published in March 1985. See https://www.gnu.org/gnu/gnu-history.en.html

2   See http://www.budapestopenaccessinitiative.org. For a list of further declarations with links to the relevant documents and further resources see http://sparceurope.org/statements

3   https://en.wikipedia.org/wiki/Open_science#Organizations_and_projects_of_open_science

4   The European-funded project Facilitate Open Science Training for European Research (FOSTER, https://www.fosteropenscience.eu) has developed an open science taxonomy as an attempt to map the open science field.

In "A New Start for Europe: Opening up to an ERA of Innovation" Conference 2015, Carlos Moedas (2015), Commissioner for Research, Science and Innovation at the European Commission, stated: "We are moving into a world of open innovation and user innovation. A world where the digital and physical are coming together. A world where new knowledge is created through global collaborations involving thousands of people from across the world and from all walks of life". He went on to identify Open Innovation, Open Science and Openness to the World as the three strategic priorities for EU research.

Open innovation is about widening the involvement of a wide range of groups, from users to governments and civil society, into the process of creating and providing open digital content. Openness is needed in order to capitalize on the results of research and innovation. This meant creating the right ecosystems, increasing investment and bringing more companies and regions into the knowledge economy.

Open science describes the transformations in the way research is being performed: researchers collaborate and knowledge is shared so that everybody can contribute to scientific advancements through a more effective use of research results. Open science represents a systemic change in the *modus operandi* of science and research as the principle of "openness" affects the whole research cycle and its stakeholders: by requires transparency and facilitating networking and collaboration, open science shifts research from the "publish or perish" mantra to a knowledge-sharing ideal. Open science is also about making sure that science serves innovation and growth. It guarantees open access to publicly-funded research results and the possibility of knowledge sharing by providing infrastructures. Facilitating access to research data also encourages its re-use outside academia. For example, companies, and particularly small and medium-sized enterprises (SMEs), can access and re-use data, infrastructures and tools easily and at a reasonable cost, thus accelerating the implementation of ideas for innovative products and services.

Openness to the World means global scientific collaboration. It is not sufficient to only support collaborative projects; we must enable partnerships between regions and countries. Challenges in areas like energy, health, food and water are global challenges which can only be tackled through international collaborations.

Several countries of the OECD are adopting policies to promote open science and research including Finland, and Finnish Higher Education Institutes are playing an important role in the implementation of OSR. We analyze here the case of Lahti UAS to uncover the challenges and benefits of translating the principles of open science into the practice of university research within and beyond academia.

An Open Science and Research Framework in Finland

In 2014, the Finnish Ministry of Education and Culture (EduMin) established The Open Science and Research (OSR) Initiative for 2014–17, which aims at fostering the openness and quality of research as well as promoting the faster transfer and greater visibility of information (Forsström, 2014). In Finland open research refers to adopting practices available to anyone in research including free access to research results and raw data, methods which are published openly and it signifies free availability of research publications and the utilization of accessible standards in terms of quality of research. Along with this initiative, Finland aims at becoming the leading country for openness in science and research by 2017. "Openness" covers a broad range of activities on many levels with the common goal of achieving a more effective utilization of research data and results for the greater benefit of society. The ambition is to promote the trustworthiness of open science and research and to incorporate them into a whole research process, thus improving the visibility and impact of science throughout Finland's innovation system. This involves public and private stakeholders such as companies, business angels and funding bodies, universities and other research organizations. By supporting the culture of open science within the research community, society's awareness of open science will increase. The overall goal of this initiative is to boost the competitiveness and quality of the Finnish research system. According to recent global innovation surveys (Schwab 2013; Dutta, Geiger and Lanvin 2015; Dutta, Lanvin and Wunsch-Vincent 2015), Finland is ranked among the top 10 countries in innovation and competitiveness. However, in order to maintain this position and to strengthen Finland's competitiveness, the impact and visibility of both science and research need to be boosted. This requires more transparent and collaborative actions between various stakeholders in the Finnish research and innovation system (Forsström, 2014).

The Open Science and Research Initiative also aims at creating a sustainable information infrastructure and a variety of sophisticated tools and methods that will promote the long-term availability and accessibility of results (e.g. long term data storage system). In practice, the aim is to provide researchers with specific knowledge about how they can implement openness. Open science is promoted by directing special attention to three central constituents that complement each other: open scientific publications, open research data and open research methods, all of which have their corresponding storage facilities, metadata and access services. Furthermore, cutting-edge research environments, advanced skills and knowledge, comprehensive guidelines and other diverse support services and tools are included in the initiative.

The initiative also entails closer international collaborations for the possibilities and outcomes of open science are likely to be widely utilized both at a national and international level. In the Finnish research system, HEIs are very important. The Finnish higher education system is a dual system consisting of fourteen academic universities and twenty-four universities of applied sciences (UAS) (Melin *et al.*, 2015). In this research system, the task of the academic universities is to conduct scientific research, whereas the role of the UAS is to carry out practice based applied research, development and innovation (RDI) activities in close co-operation with local stakeholders.

Finland`s OSR Vision 2017 is "Open research leads to surprising discoveries and creative insights" (Ministry of Education and Culture, 2014, p. 13). The aim is that research data and materials will move freely throughout society from one researcher or research group to another, between disciplines, to innovative businesses and to decision-makers and citizens. It is intended that information flow will be facilitated by clear policies and best practices, and by providing services to safeguard the availability of scientific and research results. Openness is seen as a joint operating model which combines operations between business and research, and between HEIs and the private sector, and that gives Finnish research a competitive edge in the international arena.

The key objective of the Finnish Open Science and Research Roadmap 2014–17 (Ministry of Education and Culture, 2014, p. 14) is to publish research results, research data and the methods used, so that they can be examined and used by any interested party. Open science includes practices such as promoting open access publishing, publishing research materials on open platforms, harnessing open-source software and open standards, and the public documentation of the research process through the act of recording reflective notes about what is learnt from the data i.e. "memoing".

The roadmap will be implemented via four sub-objectives (Ministry of Education and Culture, 2014, pp. 14–18) which are: 1) Reinforcing the intrinsic nature of science and research: openness and repeatability increase the reliability and quality of science and research; 2) Strengthening openness-related expertise: those working in the Finnish research system know how to harness the opportunities afforded by openness to boost Finland's competitive edge; 3) Ensuring a stable foundation for the research process: good, clear, basic structures and services will enable new opportunities to be harnessed at the right time thus ensuring a stable basis for research; and 4) Increasing the societal impact of research: open science will create new opportunities for researchers, decision-makers, business, public bodies and citizens.

VISION
Open research leads to surprising discoveries and creative insights

Research data and materials move freely throughout society; from one researcher or research team to another, between disciplines, to innovative businesses, and to decision-makers and citizens. Information flow is facilitated by clear policies and best practices, and by providing services to safeguard the availability of scientific and research results. Openness is a joint operating model. Openness has given Finnish research an international competitive edge.

1. Reinforcing the intrinsic nature of science and research	2. Strenghtening openness-related expertise	3. Ensuring a stable foundation for the research process	4. Increasing the social impact of research
Openness and repeatability increase the reliability and quality of science and research.	Those working in the Finnish research system know how to harness the opportunities afforded by openness to boost Finland's competitive edge.	Good, clear basic structures and services enable new opportunities to be harnessed at the right time and ensure a stable basis for research.	Open science creates new opportunities for researchers, decision-makers, business, public bodies and citizens.

Figure 1. The vision for 2017 and the objectives of The Open science and Research Initiative. Image from The Ministry of Education and Culture's Open Science and Research Initiative (2014), CC BY 4.0

According to the OSR Initiative, the main activities that will enhance the open science and research principles of research and education organizations in Finland are the following:

- Openness as a part of organizational strategies
- Open and collaborative working culture
- Clear guidelines for publishing research results, licensing and immaterial property rights (IPR) questions
- Clear descriptions of the liabilities and rights of a researcher regarding openness
- Developing knowledge, skills and expertise related to OSR
- Supporting the utilization of shared service infrastructures
- Exploitation of local quality systems
- Fostering interoperability
- Increasing preconditions for research reproducibility
- Introduction and implementation of services that support openness, availability, visibility and utilization

Finland has several strengths that facilitate the implementation of its Open Science and Research Roadmap: Finland is one of the leading countries with regard to investments in R&D as a percentage of GDP; according to many indicators, Finland's infrastructures for science and research are of high quality; indicators show Finland has excellent skills and infrastructure for promoting innovation; Finland aims for equality in its researchers' working environments; the Finnish population is highly educated; Finland has an extensive library network and is the world's leader in library usage and the societal appreciation of libraries; Finland's scientific libraries are proactive in organizing events and exhibitions, and are continually increasing their own publishing activities; people in Finland respect science and research and are interested in the results of research; second only to Iceland, Finland has the most researchers per capita; research institutions and universities are linked by a comprehensive network and are engaging in closer cooperation; Finland is launching many initiatives that support research objectives on many fronts, such as furthering open government and initiatives targeting the availability of mass data and public administration information; and

Finland's national structures are advanced and include those inherited from previous initiatives (Academy of Finland, 2012; Melin *et al.*, 2015, p. 38).

The Ministry of Education and Culture in Finland published a study (Melin *et al.*, 2015, p. 38) highlighting the strengths of research in Finland: several important reforms have already been made, including an autonomy reform and new acts for universities and for UASs, which gave them an independent legal personality. It separated HEIs from the state and they had the choice of becoming either corporations subject to public law or foundations subject to private law. Furthermore, an important step towards a more transparent funding stream for UAS has been taken with the recent reform of UASs; academic leadership has also been strengthened through the reforms, such as increased connections to wider society, for example, through the inclusion of external members on HEI boards; lastly, mergers between HEIs have contributed to there being slightly fewer HEIs and better centralization, which means greater productiveness relative to cost. There is also a well-developed innovation system according to the Innovation Union scoreboard, while the strong connection between UASs and regional business aids research, as does the regional coverage of the UASs.

The same study (Melin *et al.*, 2015, p. 38) noted the weaknesses of research in Finland: there are only a few internationally top-ranked HEIs; there exist barriers towards transfer across the dual systems for students; only a small amount of foreign academic staff are recruited by HEIs; the HEI landscape is scattered with many HEIs, some of which are quite small; the level of internationalization in the system as a whole is low; and there is an underdeveloped level of cooperation between universities and UASs; there are legal barriers towards deeper cooperation and mergers between universities and UASs; and the innovation system does not contribute sufficiently to the commercialization of knowledge and the creation of new jobs. The study by Melin *et al.* (2015) proposed an increase in open research infrastructure cooperation on the European level in order to contribute to open science within European infrastructure networks, such as the Long-Term Socio-Ecological Research.

The Role of Higher Education Institutes in Promoting OSR Initiative

The Finnish higher education system consists of two complementary sectors: universities of applied sciences (UAS) and universities. The mission of universities is to conduct scientific research and provide instruction and postgraduate education based upon it. Universities of applied sciences train professionals in response to labor market needs and conduct RDI which supports instruction and promotes regional development in particular. Such universities are multi-field regional institutions focusing on contacts with working life and on regional development.

All HEIs have an essential role in fulfilling the OSR vision because they are in charge of delivering educational and research activities which benefit society in social, economic and cultural ways. The OSR Initiative challenges the Finnish HEIs to adopt and apply the open science and research principles of the OSR Initiative in their policies, operations and practices. As a result of the launching of the OSR Initiative, the HEIs in Finland are currently conducting university level policies and guidelines in order to make what OSR means in the context of research and teaching visible. These policies address why openness of research is important and give instructions concerning open research methods and open access publishing. At the same time, HEIs are planning and developing services and infrastructures as well as providing training for researchers related to data management planning and data preservation. From a teaching perspective, OSR means that open research results should be more rigorously applied as a teaching material and also new teaching materials need to be openly released under open licenses. In order to achieve this, HEIs are offering guidance and support for teaching staff for the creation of online courses. Regional development is a statutory task of HEIs and by being the forerunners of open science in their regions, the HEIs could help local industries and businesses to benefit from these openly available research results. However, this does not happen automatically and requires that, firstly, the HEIs develop processes through which they are able to provide this kind of support for the other regional stakeholders and, secondly, HEIs need to communicate clearly what kind of services are available and how local stakeholders can take advantage of them.

Lahti University of Applied Sciences (Lahti UAS)

The following section presents Lahti University of Applied Sciences (Lahti UAS) as an OSR case study and discusses the challenges and possibilities surrounding the implementation of the policies of OSR in practice, focusing on openness within RDI activities.

Lahti UAS is a multidisciplinary higher education institute located in the city of Lahti in southern Finland. With over 5,000 students and approximately 400 full-time teaching staff, Lahti UAS employs about 70 part-time teachers from other academic institutions, business and industry.

Research and development (R&D) input in the Lahti region is low, amounting to only approximately 250 euros/resident, in contrast to the 3300 euros/resident input provided in Finland (the highest regional amount). Thus, in order to promote the strategic choice of RDI at Lahti UAS, RDI activities must be transparent, practice-based and respond to future needs. They must promote the region's growth, competitiveness, well-being and employment opportunities in the focus areas. RDI activities must also facilitate skills and knowledge transfer, emphasize an international dimension and value networks, especially in terms of multidisciplinary teams and authentic learning environments, which are typical to the mode-2 type of knowledge production identified by Gibbons *et al.* (1994). Then, research systems will become highly interactive and "socially distributed". This kind of mode-2 knowledge is produced "in the context of application by so-called trans-disciplinary collaborations. Moreover, scientists are more reflexive and they operate according to different criteria in terms of quality when compared with the traditional disciplinary mode. Lahti UAS has to ensure that open science develops in the right way to contribute to the common effort to make both Finland and the Lahti region more competitive while maintaining excellence in science. This means that regional development can no longer rely solely on a tradition of innovations stemming from research, but instead an open innovation model needs to be applied more efficiently.

The practice-based innovation model is characterized by market-led thinking and company-driven challenges that work as triggers for innovation and practice-based innovation tools. A special user-driven model of action for R&D and innovation has been developed by university researchers in the Lahti region, based on the needs of local companies. Its strengths and characteristics are the fast application and commercialization of ideas, and it is an efficient means for attracting international expertise to support development. The companies in the region have successfully applied this model within their businesses (Harmaakorpi and Tura, 2012).

There are 380 staff working for 5,300 students studying within Lahti UAS at BSc or MSc level. Lahti UAS is an innovative partner in regional RDI and one of its statutory tasks is to conduct RDI activities for the benefit of the employment sector, regional development and Lahti UAS education. In addition, it promotes regional competitiveness in close cooperation with the local employment sector and provides students with multidisciplinary real-life business and industry projects to work on. This means that the RDI activities are work-related and aim at finding, developing and producing new or improved products, production systems, and methods and services for the region's needs. Lahti UAS operates in the global innovation system as part of the regional innovation ecosystems of the wider Helsinki metropolitan area and Päijät-Häme. This regional development is then further integrated into international cooperation as global challenges are also attached to Lahti and surrounding region. The Lahti UAS RDI program for 2016 to 2018 is based idm. to the EU's growth strategy (European Commission, 2010), whose priorities are to make the EU a smart, sustainable and inclusive economy that has high employment levels, high productivity and social cohesion.

The mission of Lahti UAS is to educate students so that they become competent professionals and promote the competitiveness of the region. The vision of Lahti UAS for 2020 is to be insightful, experimental and exploratory, becoming an international builder of future learning and a prime mover in creating regional growth. In addition to the vision and the mission, the following values also guide our RDI activities: joy of mutual exploration, the facilitation of insightful learning experiences, valuable work, expertise and success (Lahti University of Applied Sciences, 2015).

Openness in RDI Activities in Lahti UAS

As a part of the OSR initiative, the current state of the open working culture in Finnish HEIs (including Lahti UAS) was surveyed in 2014–15. This survey was carried out in two phases. In December 2014, all HEIs` web pages were assessed in terms of how openness was embedded in their strategies and working cultures and what kind of instructions and guidelines concerning openness were offered to the researchers in each organization. In February and March 2015, this assessment was complemented by a questionnaire in which the representatives of HEIs were asked to describe their level of engagement in activities fulfilling the objectives of the OSR initiative in greater detail, whilst also stating what policies and instructions guided these activities. Furthermore, the HEIs were asked to describe how the organizational knowledge and expertise of the OSR Initiative had grown, as well as how the OSR initiative had enhanced regional cooperation in terms of research infrastructures.

Based on that survey, the Finnish EduMin published an analysis (available only in Finnish) in September 2015 in which the HEIs were evaluated against four level criterions and then rated based on the results of five categories (uncontrolled, partial, specified, managed and strategic). The survey results show that over 50% of HEIs are currently actively enhancing OSR, though none of the HEIs reached the highest level and only two universities reached the second highest level. Generally, the academic universities scored higher than the universities of applied sciences which were all scored within the two lowest levels. Although all Finnish HEIs are based on the Government Program and the operative and financial plans of the Ministry of Education and Culture, not many explicitly mentioned openness as one of their core values. Only a few universities were found to be strongly engaged in promoting an open working culture.

Lahti UAS received its highest rating, a three, for the category of how well openness was incorporated into its university strategies. However, based on the average of all its scores, Lahti UAS was ranked on level four, indicating that the university is committed to promoting OSR and that preliminary steps in developing an open working culture have been taken, although that needs to be strengthened and openness as a working practice needs to be publicly encouraged and broadened.

Implementing the OSR Policies in RDI Activities in Practice

For Lahti UAS, promoting OSR and building an open working culture are the key development tasks for RDI activities in 2015 and 2016. Applying and embedding the OSR principles into RDI activities will involve both hard and soft elements. The hard elements include strategic and directive guidelines for RDI activities. The soft side stresses that it is essential to engage and familiarize the RDI staff members with the objectives and guidelines of the OSR Initiative and to build a shared understanding about what openness means with regard to RDI activities as well as the need to strengthen the staff members' openness-related expertise.

Several different initiatives are being undertaken to implement these OSR recommendations in Lahti UAS, and here we present the three main steps: the RDI program, OSR principles workshop and OSR Implementation action plan. As a first step, the Lahti UAS RDI program for 2016 to 2018 was revised during the fall of 2015 in a collaborative working process with the RDI staff members and the Lahti UAS board. It is a strategic policy document offering guidelines for RDI activities. As a result of this process, openness has been highlighted as one of the cornerstones of the RDI activities (Figure 2).

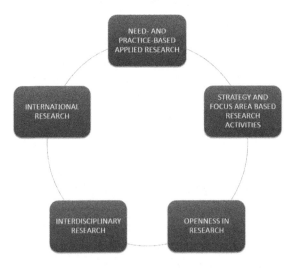

Figure 2. The cornerstones of RDI activities in Lahti UAS

As a second step, a workshop for teaching and RDI staff was arranged in December 2015 in order to build a shared understanding of the OSR principles with a larger audience. The aim of this workshop was to offer basic information about OSR and to debate what OSR means in everyday practices — with regards to both teaching and RDI activities. Over 45 staff members participated in the workshop and raised questions related to OSR. The main questions and challenges relevant to RDI were matters such as how to increase openness in the planning of research projects, how to operate using the data gathered from private company projects, how to deal with IPR issues, how to deal with research ethics and research permit issues, how to decide what research data is worth preserving for further research purposes and where and in which format the data should be saved and how the research data could be measured so that it can be reused. Additionally, staff members asked for more information and clear instructions on OSR issues e.g. concerning open access publications. In order to meet this need, the Lahti UAS administration ensured that the staff knew where to access OSR materials, such as the Open Science and Research Roadmap 2014–17, the Handbook of Open Science and Research, as well as the revised instructions of the Finnish Ministry of Education and Culture concerning the gathering of publication data.

As a third step, an OSR Implementation action plan for Lahti UAS for 2016 was accepted by the board of directors of Lahti UAS in January 2016. It involves several steps focusing on increasing the OSR expertise in Lahti UAS, such as staff training and building services and guidance for open publishing and open data management. One major issue raised at the workshop and training sessions was how authors can provide open access to their work. One way is to publish it and then self-archive it in a repository where it can be accessed for free. Some publishers require delays or an embargo before research put into a repository can become open access. In addition to implementing OSR principles for publication, there is also the implementation of OSR principles in RDI activities, and this requires further training. Lahti UAS representatives have attended workshops and seminars arranged by the OSR initiative and staff members have also participated in the work of the Open Science and Research Strategy Group and the Research Data Long-term Preservation Group, in order to gain the knowledge and expertise needed to develop and establish openness-related practices within Lahti UAS.

It is also necessary to develop research infrastructures and service processes that enable the storage and replicability of research data. During the fall of 2015, Lahti UAS RDI staff members and staff members from the academic library mapped the potential data material and available research data storage services, with the pilot project to test the service processes and data storage being completed in 2016. The action plan includes a road map devised to build the OSR, improve the way the OSR is structured, develop OSR activities and procedures that staff members engage in, ensure that the core values of Lahti UAS are realized in the OSR culture and the style of OSR leadership adopted, clarify who reports to whom and advance the actual OSR skills and competencies of the employees working for Lahti UAS.

Conclusion

As an umbrella concept, Open Education forms the basis for many different streams of openness of knowledge and learning. Though these streams address different perceptions, they all stem from the core idea of open access and the sharing of knowledge as well as a collaboration between different actors on producing and building upon shared knowledge.

Maintaining and boosting the competitiveness of the research and innovation systems while preserving accessible and shared materials and knowledge is essential to OER, which also requires the faster transfer of knowledge gained through increased and expanded access to research results and data. In addition, the OER movement has highlighted the importance of enhancing, retaining, revising, redistributing and reusing such educational resources (Jensen and West, 2015, pp. 215–218).

As it is crucial to advance open science on all levels — regional, national, European and global — the mutual responsiveness of all key stakeholders involved is required, be they organizations performing research or organizations and businesses funding research and businesses. Consequently, a review of how science is evaluated, the creation of new research funding mechanisms and alternative ways of publishing are also required. Secondly, we need to create an open science environment that is friendly to both science and business. Thirdly, open science should be an inclusive process. We need to stimulate further engagement with open science stakeholders: ranging from individual researchers to universities, from start-ups to large companies. Open science is also about making sure that science becomes more responsive to socio-economic and public demands, while enabling faster innovation.

This chapter focused on an Open Science and Research (OSR) perspective and discussed it in the context of Finnish higher education. As discussed above, Finland is one of the leading countries for incorporating OSR initiatives into whole research and innovation systems. HEIs, including the universities of applied sciences, play a central role in adopting OSR principles in their research practices. The current development and future trends of open education, open science and OER provide many opportunities and challenges for HEIs.

In this contribution we presented the OSR architecture framework of Finland and illustrated the main findings in terms of implementing the OSR principles in practice by presenting Lahti UAS's OSR development work as a case study. The implementation of open science and research policies is an iterative development process through repeated cycles in which raising awareness, sharing knowledge and building networks and capacity development are central issues in the creation of an open working culture for an HEI, and which is needed to achieve strategic goals and to increase the impact and quality of research.

The Lahti UAS case provides an example of open science and research at work. The process began with an analysis and evaluation of the institution's situation and potential. Government guidance ensured that the process became established in each higher education institute. The case study of Lahti UAS also indicates that a UAS that is given an average rank regarding how well openness was incorporated into its strategies and how strongly it is committed to promoting OSR still needs to continually and systematically strengthen its open working culture.

References

Academy of Finland (2012; 2016), The State of Scientific Research in Finland 2012, in L. Treuthardt and A. Nuutinen (Eds.), *Publications of the Academy of Finland 6/12*, Helsinki: Academy of Finland, http://www.aka.fi/globalassets/ awanhat/documents/tieteentila2012/en/the_state_of_scientific_research_in_ finland_2012.pdf

Atkins, D. E., Brown, J. S. and Hammond, A. L. (2007; 2015), *A Review of the Open Educational Resources (OER) Movement: Achievements, Challenges, and New Opportunities*, http://www.hewlett.org/uploads/files/ ReviewoftheOERMovement.pdf

Council of the European Union (2015), *Council Conclusions on Open, Data-intensive and Networked Research as a Driver for Faster and Wider Innovation*, 8970/15 RECH 141 TELECOM 119 COMPET 228 IND 80, http://data. consilium.europa.eu/doc/document/ST-9360-2015-INIT/en/pdf

D'Antoni, S. (2009; 2015), Open Educational Resources: Reviewing Initiatives and Issues, *Open Learning: The Journal of Open, Distance and E-Learning*, 24, pp. 3–10, http://dx.doi.org/10.1080/02680510802625443

Dutta, S., Geiger, T. and Lanvin, B. (Eds.) (2015; 2016), *The Global Information Technology Report 2015*, Geneva: World Economic Forum, http://www3. weforum.org/docs/WEF_GITR2015.pdf

Dutta, S., Lanvin, B. and Wunsch-Vincent, S. (Eds.) (2015; 2016), *The Global Innovation Index 2015: Effective Innovation Policies for Development*, Fontainebleau, Ithaca and Geneva: Cornell University, INSEAD and WIPO, https://www.globalinnovationindex.org/userfiles/file/reportpdf/gii-full-report-2015-v6.pdf

European Commission (2010; 2016), *Communication from the Commission Europe 2020: A Strategy for Smart, Sustainable and Inclusive Growth*, Brussels, http://eur-lex.europa.eu/LexUriServ/LexUriServ.do?uri=COM:2010:2020:FIN:EN:PDF

European Commission (2015; 2016), *Validation of the Results of the Public Consultation on Science 2.0: Science in Transition*, http://ec.europa.eu/research/ consultations/science-2.0/science_2_0_final_report.pdf

Forsström, P-L. (2014; 2015), *The Intention of Open Science and Research Initiative in Finland*, https://avointiede.fi/documents/10864/35689/The+intention+of+O pen+Science+and+Research+initiative+in+Finland.pdf/6e84a2f4-2881-4a9b-bb70-5e0f8974262a

Gibbons, M., Limoges, C., Nowotny, H., Schwartzman, S., Scott, P. and Trow, M. (1994), *The New Production of Knowledge: The Dynamics of Science and Research in Contemporary Societies*, London: Sage.

Harmaakorpi, V. and Tura, T. (2012; 2015), Towards Smart Specialisation — The Lahti Region, *Nordregio News*, 5, http://www.nordregio.se/en/Metameny/ Nordregio-News/2012/Smart-Specialisation/Case

Jensen, K. and West, Q. (2015), Open Educational Resources and the Higher Education Environment, A Leadership Opportunity for Libraries, *College and Research Libraries*, 76, pp. 215–218.

Melin, G., Zuijdam, F., Good, B., Angelis, J., Enberg, J., Fikkers, D. J. and Zegel, S. (2015), Towards a Future Proof System for Higher Education and Research in Finland, *Reports of the Ministry on Education and Culture*, Department for Higher Education and Science Policy, 11, Finland, http://www.minedu.fi/export/sites/default/OPM/Julkaisut/2015/liitteet/okm11.pdf?lang=en

Ministry of Education and Culture (2014; 2015), Open Science and Research Leads to Surprising Discoveries and Creative Insights, Open Science and Research Roadmap 2014–2017, *Reports of the Ministry of Education and Culture*, Department for Higher Education and Science Policy, Science Policy Division, 21, Finland, http://www.minedu.fi/export/sites/default/OPM/Julkaisut/2014/liitteet/okm21.pdf?lang=en

OECD (2007; 2015), *Giving Knowledge for Free: The Emergence of Open Educational Resources*, Centre for Educational Research and Innovation, http://www.oecd.org/edu/ceri/38654317.pdf

Peters, M. A. (2008, 2015), The History and Emergent Paradigm of Open Education, in Michael A. Peters and Rodrigo G. Britez (Eds.), *Open Education and Education for Openness*, Educational Futures: Rethinking Theory and Practice, 27, Rotterdam: Sense Publishers, pp. 3–16, https://www.sensepublishers.com/media/729-open-education-and-education-for-openness.pdf

Peter, S. and Deimann, M. (2013), On the Role of Openness in Education: A Historical Reconstruction, *Open Praxis*, 5, pp. 7–14, http://dx.doi.org/10.5944/openpraxis.5.1.23

Schwab, K. (Ed.) (2013; 2016), *The Global Competitiveness Report 2013–2014: Full Data Edition*, Geneva: World Economic Forum, http://www3.weforum.org/docs/WEF_GlobalCompetitivenessReport_2013-14.pdf

Stallman, R. (2002), *Free Software, Free Society: Selected Essays of Richard M. Stallman* (intr. Lawrence Lessig; ed. Joshua Gay), Boston: GNU Press/Free Software Foundation, Inc.

Yuan, L., MacNeill, S. and Kraan, W. (2008; 2015), Open Educational Resources — Opportunities and Challenges for Higher Education, *Educational Cybernetics: Reports*, Paper 1, http://ubir.bolton.ac.uk/290/1/iec_reports-1.pdf

15. Credentials for Open Learning: Scalability and Validity

Mika Hoffman and Ruth Olmsted

In this contribution we advocate separating credentialing from the learning process as a path to greater scalability and better measurement of what independent learners learn from OER. We address the challenge of matching/aligning OER offerings with standardized exams as a way for independent learners to access academic credit, and explore ways to achieve consensus among educational institutions about what academic credit means and which types of evidence to accept in terms of learning that occurred outside a particular institution. We begin the chapter with an overview of credit by examination, contrasting the standardized testing approach with the classroom teaching approach to academic credit. We briefly describe our process for creating exams and the accompanying materials that make clear to potential test-takers what the learning objectives are. We then define a method for building the bridge between OER and the exam. Finally, we discuss the policy issues of accepting exams for credit and envision a future in which learners can receive transferable credentials in a cost-effective, efficient and valid manner.

http://dx.doi.org/10.11647/OBP.0103.15

OER and Academic Credit

The growth of Open Educational Resources (OER) has sparked an interesting and productive discussion about how OER might be used to expand learners' options for earning academic credit without traditional instruction (see, for example, Conrad and McGreal, 2012; Camilleri and Tannhäuser, 2012). The discussions tend to begin with OER and examine how best to grant credit for learning based on that OER. This chapter examines the issue from the other direction: for learners planning to sit for an existing examination for credit, how can those learners best find OER that covers the material they need to master the subject of the examination? As a corollary, how can higher education institutions (HEIs) encourage the validation of independent learning through scalable examinations to take advantage of the scalability of OER? What are known in the US as standardized exams (that is, exams produced for use across multiple institutions) have long served as vehicles for academic credit in the US. They are scalable, flexibly scheduled and cost-effective — but they exist outside of any context of formal classroom instruction and are not tied to a specific HEI, so learners are left to choose their methods of attaining knowledge independently, and may sometimes fail to recognize that their studies have been incomplete. In addition, debate continues in many US HEIs and other organizations that look for a university credential over how and whether to accept particular types of evidence of learning that occurred outside a particular institution. The authors come from the perspective of a US institution that has been in the forefront of prior learning assessment and adult degree completion for more than 40 years. We address three main issues: the concept of what academic credit means, the mechanisms by which OER-based independent learning can fit into a system of large-scale examinations and the need for a common understanding and standard guidelines for accepting and awarding credit by examination in recognition of independent learning.

The Meaning of Academic Credit

Credit by examination as practiced in the US has grown in a different direction from the assessment practices of the UK and many European countries, where sitting for a comprehensive exam represents a milestone in one's degree program. Two primary approaches to academic credit have bifurcated in the US: one focused on testing detached from specific HEIs, and one focused on teaching, which is predominant on traditional campuses.

The testing approach seeks to make rigorous examinations more scalable and reliable than individually-rated program-specific exams can be. Robust standardized exams are built to measure the desired outcomes (usually in chunks corresponding to what would normally be expected in a one-semester course), regardless of how the student learned the material. All candidates for a similar qualification sit for the same examination, so that their learning of, for example, a term's worth of calculus can be compared on some objective basis. Although many in the US decry the current (over)use of standardized tests in primary and secondary education, standardized subject tests are rooted in American traditions of accessibility, equality and mass production, and evolved in the mid-nineteenth century as a way to promote equality and fairness in compulsory education (US Congress, Office of Technology Assessment, 1992). US examples of the use of standardized exams in higher education date to the middle of the twentieth century, and include the College Level Examination Program (CLEP), the UExcel and Excelsior College Examinations programs, and the DANTES Subject Standardized Tests (DSST). All these exams are designed to be used for academic credit in lieu of participation in a university course, have undergone review by national agencies similar to, but exclusive from, the regional accrediting bodies that certify colleges and universities, and are widely used for that purpose in the US. Note that these are not the same as exams designed by one institution's faculty for use in determining course placement at that institution; the standardized exams are designed by testing specialists and psychometricians along with subject-matter experts for use at any institution. Hundreds of thousands of students in the US earn at least some of the credit they need for a degree using such exams every year, saving money on tuition fees and earning credit on their own schedule (Council for Adult and Experiential Learning, 2010).

The teaching approach relies on ensuring that the academic content is well taught, with measurement of what is learned relying on multiple measures in the context of a course, sometimes but not always culminating in a comprehensive high-stakes final/terminal exam. The emphasis in this approach is on instruction; measures of quality in academia rely heavily on how engaging the learning process is and how well-aligned the learning materials are with outcomes, with less attention paid to whether the individual assessments provide good measurement of the outcomes. This approach certainly involves testing, but testing is typically treated as secondary in importance to quality of instruction (see, for example, MarylandOnline, Inc. (2014)). In the US, the backbone of the system is the Carnegie credit hour, which defines one transcripted credit-hour as representing a course that met once a week for a 15-week semester, and required two hours per week of outside homework or lab work. Also contributing to this trend is the requirement from many US accreditors and government bodies that there be a certain amount of instructor-student interaction.

Consensus is growing, however, that defining the amount of learning, as the Carnegie hour does, in terms of the amount of time spent in class is inaccurate, at best, as it does not take into account directly what outcomes are actually assessed, and there is a growing desire among accreditors in American higher education to consider learning outcomes a more accurate measure than seat time (Laitinen, 2012). This has resulted in the rise of competency-based degree programs that typically assess specific competencies rather than aggregate grades from various assignments (Klein-Collins, 2012). Some programs still maintain a link to the Carnegie hour and many also still emphasize the quality of the learning experience, while others focus on the assessment, usually designing assessments specifically for the program (McClarty, 2015).

Independent and Open Learning as Preparation for Assessment

We turn now from the concept of credit to the learning students do to earn credit. The OER movement has sought to change what it means for information to be freely accessible, at least for those with internet access. Instead of educators or institutions making limited numbers of copies of material for specific groups of students, information can now be put on the web for anyone to find and access. The universe of independent learning opportunities and content curators has expanded rapidly. This universe includes both truly open resources, which anyone may share and modify, and resources that are free for anyone to access, but that are not open for modification and sharing, such as many Massive Open Online Courses (MOOCs). With this caveat, we will include MOOCs in our discussion of independent learning, as our emphasis is on free access for learners.

Even with more resources for study, however, there are two major challenges for independent learners: they still need exceptional self-direction and motivation, and earning academic credit for what they have learned is still not an easy process. Most learners would acknowledge that interacting with static material and having to interpret it alone is more difficult than learning with someone who can answer questions or guide learners to appropriate additional resources. But even for those who succeed in learning independently, opportunity to demonstrate that learning and be evaluated for academic credit remains limited. One limiting factor is the availability of credit-worthy assessments for whatever the learner learned; there are far more academic subjects than there are high-quality and scalable assessments, and even if an assessment is available in the general subject area, it may be hard to know whether the resources the learner used actually match the exam content. The other limiting factor is the prevalence of the teaching approach to credit: in this model, assessment and instruction are so closely tied that many institutions find it hard to imagine unbundling them. Processes for awarding transfer credit, accepting standardized examinations for credit and using other methods of awarding credit for prior learning are all permeated by the idea that the credit-granting institution "owns" the definition of credit at that institution and by the accompanying assumption that no one else can assess learning just the way that institution would (see Ferrari and Traina, 2013; Conrad and McGreal, 2012; Camilleri and Tannhäuser, 2012; European Commission, 2015; FitzGibbon, 2014). We will discuss these two barriers in turn, beginning with the problem of linking OER to assessment.

Linking OER to Assessment

As mentioned above, the assessment challenge is that assessments tend to be either individualized and thus unlikely to be reliable, or large-scale and thus not tailored for the particular individual's learning. We leave aside the topic of individualized assessments here; our focus is on assessments that can be scaled to the broad needs of many independent learners. The particular challenge of batteries of exams such as those in the College Board's College Level Examination Program, Prometric's DANTES Subject Standardized Tests and Excelsior College's UExcel exams is that although the purposes for each examination are clear and the learning outcomes to be measured/demonstrated are defined, it may not be clear to a learner whether a given learning resource is going to be sufficient during the preparation phase. Coming at the question from the other side, it may not be clear to exam developers exactly what a given learning resource contains without going through the entire resource. Given the number and depth of resources available, this is impractical, particularly for resources that are entire courses, such as MOOCs. If HEIs are to recommend the pairing of OER with credit by exam, they need some efficient way to help learners identify appropriate resources. For example, learners may come with different areas of strength. Those with practical experience may need to learn or review the theoretical basis of the subject in order to do well at a college-level exam, whereas others may need a complete open online course, not just a refresher in specific topics.

The ideal approach to selecting appropriate open learning for credit-by-exam preparation, then, is to consider both the learner and the content. As a practical matter, no educator can prepare a complete list of the various configurations of material that would be ideal for each learner. Rather, we can be transparent about the learning objectives of the material and provide information about how the material is accessed and presented, to help learners make informed decisions.

We speak from the perspective of Excelsior College, an American institution with a global student body that has been a pioneer in prior learning assessment (PLA, also known as recognition of prior learning, or RPL), especially credit by examination. Excelsior College helps learners and HEIs understand its exams by publishing the knowledge and skills that are assessed and a detailed content outline that serves the same purpose as a syllabus in a traditional course. Over the years, while speaking encouragingly of "being your own teacher", we have experimented with learner support offerings such as workbooks and learning packages, and we have fought a constant battle with "test prep" providers who typically stay at the lowest cognitive level with materials such as flashcards and drills rather than providing materials that truly enable learners to meet the learning objectives. The advent of Open Educational Resources has provided a welcome opportunity to recommend free resources to our students, who tend to be lower income and working full time and do not always feel they can afford textbooks.

Excelsior developed a standard system for reviewing the match between OER and the learning outcomes of its exams: we ask a subject-matter expert (SME) to go through each content area in our test specifications document and to comment on whether the OER covers the entire content of the exam or a defined portion of it.

Our SMEs, usually two or three of them, examine the match from several different perspectives: the degree to which specific learning outcomes match, the degree to which individual elements mentioned in the detailed content outline of the exam are covered in the open course, and — much more difficult to assess — the weighting and cognitive level match between the expectations of the exam blueprint and the learning provided. We provide a rubric for rating the match on each aspect as excellent, acceptable or deficient. We provide space for comments, and acknowledge the possibility that some element of content will be in the course but not in the exam content outline, as well as the other way around. An example of a partial rubric is represented in Figure 1.

Content Area	Full Match	Covers Major Topics	Missing 1 or more major topic - which?	Do Resources prepare student for exam?	Comments
I. Overview of Statistics					
A. Descriptive vs. inferential statistics (populations–samples, parameters–statistics)	x	x		x	
B. Uses and misuses of statistics	x	x		x	
C. Counting and measuring					
1. Measurement scales (nominal, ordinal, interval, ratio)		no	all	no	not covered
2. Discrete vs. continuous variables	x	x		x	
D. Collection of data (random samples, probability samples, samples of convenience)			prob. sample	For topics covered	

Figure 1. Sample Segment of a Completed Match Review Rubric
Source: Mika Hoffman and Ruth Olmsted; Excelsior College

This granular approach, identifying matches at the outcome and content-area level, provides opportunities for learners to tailor the level of "instruction" to their individual needs: they can use both full courses and a variety of modules to craft a program that will build or bolster the competencies they will demonstrate on the exam. With the variety of OER available, however, a list considering content alone will not capture the full extent of the possibilities that OER offers. So, we take several dimensions other than content into account as we evaluate

OER's suitability as support for learning for particular exams: is the material presented at a college level? How user-friendly is the OER? Are there specific access concerns?

We have found that the project has led to interesting collaboration opportunities: OER resource developers can revise their work to fill some gap we found upon initial review or proactively look at our content outlines and learning outcomes as they develop their resources. And we solicit feedback from exam takers about the quality of the match as well, so that learners, resource developers and exam developers all put the learning at the center and participate in the bold endeavor of assisting post-traditional learners in their quest to better themselves through higher education qualifications.

Independent Learning within the Content-Centered Approach

Our approach separates the assessment of learning from the learning process and considers both to be essential, but different, facets of a process in which learners achieve learning outcomes. This content-centered — rather than teacher-centered or learner-centered — approach is different from most modern, organized education and is the foundation of the testing approach to credit. It arises from the idea that learning materials and exams both start with the question of what we think learners need to learn — the learning outcomes. Exam developers then proceed to spend a great deal of time and effort on assessing those outcomes, not worrying about how learners acquire the knowledge, while resource developers tend to focus attention on enabling learners to achieve the outcomes and only touch lightly on assessment. In our view, this is as it should be: experts in inculcating knowledge and experts in assessment focus on their areas of expertise, with the common thread of the learning outcomes linking their efforts to provide a positive outcome for the learners. Although this sort of disaggregation is not widespread, it is potentially very useful as a means of promoting the use of OER. The Open Educational Resources Universitas (OERu), an international higher-education consortium, spells out the elements of education in the context of how partner institutions can maximize efficiency (Conrad, Mackintosh, McGreal, Murphy and Witthaus, 2013, p. 13):

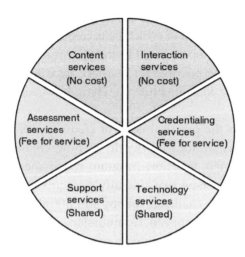

Figure 2. How to maximize efficiency. Image from Conrad, Mackintosh, McGreal, Murphy and Witthaus, 2013, CC BY-SA

A major benefit to learners is that they can choose learning materials that are appropriate for them, knowing that those materials will help them toward a credential. This is a matter of input and output. The existence of a robust measurement of the output — what is actually learned — can actually make the selection of inputs more personalized, provided appropriate boundaries are in place between the provider of prep material and the developers of the secure examinations. The disentangling of inputs and outputs allows us to accommodate different students' needs and quirks, because what they actually learned (maybe from experience, leisure reading, passionate pursuit of a topic or even just reading a more diligent classmate's notes and papers) is tested in a single, comprehensive measure that is carefully designed to reflect all the desired learning outcomes.

Accepting and Awarding Credit for Independent Learning

This dissociation of instruction from assessment runs counter to deeply ingrained views of what constitutes good education, which gives rise to the second of the barriers facing learners using OER to prepare for taking independent exams: credentialing. We have matched OER to several dozen exams, all of which bear credit at Excelsior College. But in keeping with the spirit of OER and the scalability of standardized exams, it should be possible for learners anywhere to use the exams for credit at their local institutions. Here, however, there are several challenges.

First, there is the practical issue of credit transfer generally. There is great diversity around the world in how credit is counted, how outcomes are stated, and how program requirements are built. From an international perspective, identifying equivalencies in level and amount of credit is a challenge for any sort of transfer (Commonwealth of Learning, 2010; European Commission, 2015; FitzGibbon, 2014). Even within a given country, identifying equivalencies can be difficult. At our institution, we have made the decision to standardize our exam development on the American 3-credit course (see definition of the Carnegie hour above), so we are both constrained and challenged to provide sufficient learning output definitions to convincingly test mastery of three credits' worth of knowledge. But many competency-based programs do not work within that framework, and universities outside North America also use different systems for which there may not be easy equivalents. Here again, working toward clear and publicized outcomes can help. Just as a course developer can stack up learning outcomes to make a 3-credit course, it is possible to stack up the same learning outcomes to define and demonstrate competencies, or move from course-level goals, to the major level, to the entire degree level. This idea is not so different from the kind of degree map or status report students built with academic advisors to make sure all requirements are being fulfilled. This stacking or mapping is not usually shown explicitly on an institution's transcript but some competency-based programs are moving in this direction, and quite a few institutions' competency-based degrees define their competencies not so differently from typical general education distribution requirements. Schools all over the United States have databases full of cross-listings of what course meets which requirement. All this indicates that the day may be coming when we are able to map exam outcomes to a set of competencies rather than just "equivalent to a three-credit course in X".

Even with a mechanism for credit transfer in place, however, the larger barrier arises from the teacher-centered model: most institutions assume that assessment is the responsibility of the institution granting the credential, indicating a lack of trust that any other organization could adequately determine whether that institution's students meet standards. This assumption gives rise to many barriers for the acceptance of credit-by-exam as evidence of learning. For example, Camilleri, Haywood and Nouira (2012) outlined a number of possible scenarios for a student wishing to use OER for credit (see Figure 3).

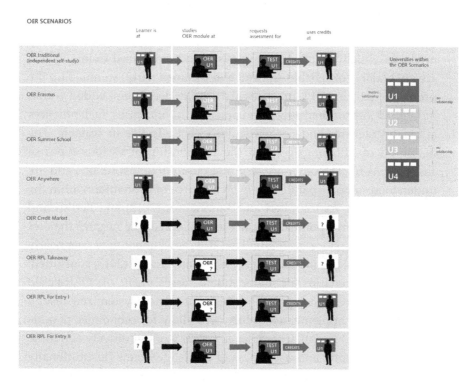

Figure 3. OER Scenarios. Image from Camilleri, Haywood and Nouira (2012), CC BY-SA 3.0

The scenarios with stars are the favored ones: all involve assessment by the credit-granting institution or a trusted partner. Camilleri and Tannhäuser (2012) expanded on this model, noting: "The necessary conditions for all the scenarios to be viable are that the self-study materials are placed online for general access, and that those materials are sufficient in scope and quality of content, and required associated activities, to enable a learner to acquire the competences defined in the expected learning outcomes, and that *a university is able to use them to guide the assessment* of those learner competences" (p. 31, our emphasis). Note that the assumption is that the university is responsible for the assessment. Even though the scenarios include one in which assessment, learning, and credit are at separate universities, this situation is noted as problematic, and recognition of prior learning (PLA/RPL) is put forth as a more useful model.

Indeed, PLA/RPL is a very common model for granting credit for learning gained through OER, as it allows credit-granting institutions to tailor the assessment to their own requirements. The problem is that this model essentially returns to the days of individualized exams, which are not scalable or reliable. Conrad and McGreal (2012) summed up the problem: "Existing RPL practices are usually deeply embedded within individual institutional policy and practice. In some cases, such practices are labor-intensive and not particularly cost-effective or scalable. The definition of RPL practices and the relationship of various types of assessments to each other are also often unique to institutions and are understood to be disparate and even a source of contention within the field" (pp. 2–3). As Camilleri and Tannhäuser (2012) and Ferrari and Traina (2013) have pointed out, the lack of scalability negates the cost savings of OER, since individualized RPL assessment may cost nearly as much as a full traditional course. Ferrari and Traina (2013) concluded: "Thus, this scenario [of independent assessment of OER-based learning] will remain marginal unless automated/systemized testing procedures are implemented, which will allow for economies of scale to be generated" (p. 30). Conrad *et al.* (2013) wrote positively about the potential scalability and usefulness of challenge exams (institutionally developed exams that a student can pass to validate knowledge and bypass an actual course) but noted that the practice of awarding credit this way is not widespread; again, the teacher-centered model, assuming that assessment and instruction are inseparable, leads to discomfort with the idea of granting credit based solely on any external exam, even the institution's own.

A further consequence of the teacher-centered model is that institutions of higher learning vary widely with respect to the amount of credit from any outside sources that can be transferred in, and what kind of evidence of "prior learning" they accept. It is understandable that when colleges and universities are competing with each other for students, they want to differentiate themselves and their programs, and directly granting credit based on anyone else's evaluation, even if the HEI granting the credit is accredited by the same body, undermines the uniqueness of those programs. Many may feel that accepting outcome-based assessments, or even requiring certain outcomes, impinges on academic freedom (FitzGibbon, 2014). On a more practical level, in the absence of national standards for the content of specific courses, institutions are legitimately concerned that a student who transfers in, for example, three credits of first-semester calculus, will not have learned the same thing that students at that institution learn in the course, and thus may not be prepared for that institution's second-semester calculus course. It is unrealistic to expect that every institution anywhere in the world would accept any specific exam-based validation of OER learning. However, there are opportunities for institutions to do more than they are currently doing; particularly as more adult students seek to complete a degree, institutions that welcome prior learning assessment including credit-by-exam may attract more students and improve persistence rates (Council for Adult and Experiential Learning, 2010).

In summary, credentialing learning via independent assessment faces both the practical challenges of translating what the assessment is measuring and philosophical challenges arising from a view that instruction, assessment and credentialing should belong together. Although we believe that independent assessment disaggregated from OER-based learning is a powerful and legitimate way for learners to earn credentials, we need to examine the root of the problem a little more closely.

Credit-worthy Assessment

The desire to link instruction and assessment and the lack of trust of other people's assessments or other institutions' credit both arise from a widespread lack of understanding about how to evaluate the quality of assessments. It is certainly reasonable that if an institution cannot determine whether an assessment truly measures the important outcomes to the standards the institution requires, it is not going to want to use the results of that assessment. Test-taker authentication is one issue that institutions point to (it can be set up to allow valid assessments to be associated with OER, although such measures almost inevitably render the OER no longer free) but it is not the only measure of assessment quality. It is also important for the assessment to provide tasks that actually measure the outcomes to the right level. Many people assume that certain types of tasks, notably multiple-choice, cannot possibly measure college-level outcomes (Camilleri and Tannhäuser, 2013; Ferrari and Traina, 2013; Witthaus *et al.*, 2015). This is an oversimplified view of assessment; in the hands of skilled assessment professionals, virtually any type of task, even multiple-choice, can provide useful information about learning outcomes, even at higher cognitive levels, and machine-scored task types can provide excellent reliability and fairness compared to subjectively rated types. Witthaus *et al.* (2015) provide an overview of assessment "robustness" that conflates task type and security: although their main point is that assessment robustness correlates with formality of recognition, which is an important point to make, it is unfortunate that scholars working to understand the relationship between assessment and credentialing are not diving deeper into understanding assessment quality. Returning to our content-centered model, assessment is a specialization of its own and many in the field of education do not understand how to build and justify high-quality assessments. This is why the high-stakes, standalone verification of learning is better done through experts in assessment rather than through experts in instruction who may not know how to build assessments to the standards needed for those stakes. Note that this does not mean that instructors are incompetent at assessment: validity in assessment is determined in the context of the use of the scores (American Educational Research Association, American Psychological Association and National Council on Measurement in Education, 2014), and what may work perfectly well for a unit test or even a final exam in the context of other input may not provide valid evidence of learning for a standalone credit-bearing exam. Professionally run testing programs publish validity arguments or evidence to support the use of their test scores.

Putting the Pieces Together

Credit for MOOCs?

Given this context-driven view of validity, consider the assessments currently existing as part of OER. In many cases, the assessments are the same as those created for the "traditional" version of the course, or modelled after similar assessments. While there may be nothing wrong with these assessments in their original contexts, their validity needs to be determined afresh in the new context. Without identity verification, for example, the assessments are not valid, for they do not link the mastery of the learning outcomes with any particular student. And even when attempts are made to insert identity verification, such as by having a proctored final exam, if this final exam has only one form, so that the content quickly becomes known, or if it does not cover all the outcomes, the results will still be inadequate as the only evidence for granting credit.

One of the big questions swirling around any discussion of open education has been "Should credit be granted for MOOCs?" This is the wrong question. "Should credit be granted for what students learn in MOOCs?" provides better focus. No one asks whether credit should be granted for library books, or for Wikipedia. People ask whether MOOCs should be treated just like traditional courses because MOOCs look so similar to traditional courses, and thus people think they could be similar in other respects as well.

In response to the credit-for-MOOCs question, two US organizations, the American Council on Education (ACE) and the National College Credit Recommendation Service (NCCRS), have evaluated selected MOOCs using the same standards to which they have reviewed corporate and military training and other courses offered by "non-collegiate" organizations. For both agencies, their historic standards for evaluating "courses" are different from their standards for evaluating "exams". For courses, they rely on the qualifications of the instructors and the existence of systems for tracking individual participation and performance. These evaluators have treated MOOCs and course-like OER such as the offerings of the Saylor Foundation as courses, because they provide instruction and at some level "look like courses". To address the online, anonymous format of such offerings, ACE and NCCRS have required the course providers to add identity verification, discussion facilitators, and challenge questions, as well as a proctored final exam, to provide assurance that the student being awarded the credit is the one who actually learned something. But since ACE and NCCRS do not hold assessments within courses to the standards required for validity in the context of massive numbers of learners, we believe such course credit is still less reflective of mastery of learning outcomes than an exam with multiple forms that is expressly designed to assess the outcomes of an entire college course.

Consider what it is about traditional courses that provides the credible assurance of learning. US regional accrediting agencies will look for three things: the course has learning outcomes; students in traditional courses are known to the instructor; and the instructor provides assessments of learning linked to those individual students and to the learning outcomes: essays, performance in labs, class participation, projects, and/or proctored quizzes and exams. MOOCs typically have learning outcomes, but lack the other two requirements. It is not currently possible for a MOOC to provide individually verified assessment performance and still remain free. Identity verification must be done on an individual basis, and establishing the validity of assessments at a large scale is typically too costly for a free course to provide. So "granting credit for MOOC learning" directly is not feasible, and in fact, trying to modify MOOCs or other OER so that credit can be associated with them directly undermines the very openness and accessibility of the learning resources. All this is a result of thinking that instruction and assessment are inseparable.

But once instruction and assessment are separated, granting credit for the learning obtained through MOOCs or OER becomes feasible. Assessment and identity verification need not be bound up in the instructional elements of a learning experience. Indeed, the argument can be made, and is made by advocates of competency-based programs, that assessment of knowledge not tied to the idiosyncrasies of any individual's instruction is superior to assessment that may depend too much on assumptions that students were paying attention in class.

Solutions and Recommendations

Good assessments are available: established credit by examination programs are run by professionals who have spent a career learning the principles of assessment validity and how to apply them to build, administer, and score a test. What is needed is for institutions to understand the content and outcomes covered and trust the evidence of validity supplied by the exam programs.

We believe that large-scale professionally produced exams are a good fit for a considerable amount of the learning from OER and MOOCs. For relatively common subjects such as Statistics, learners accessing their learning at no cost can gain credentials at a low cost. The activity of learning needs to be conceptually disaggregated from the activity of assessing what has been learned; the credential is granted through the linking of the learning outcomes to the assessment and the learner. It is up to any given credit-granting institution, of course, to determine whether to grant credit, so it is incumbent upon assessment professionals to provide them with the information they need. It is also incumbent upon credit-granting institutions to have clear, rational, coherent, and transparent policies for acceptance of standardized credit by exam. The match of independent assessments with learning that can be gained through OER will enable massive numbers of people who previously might not have had access to higher education to gain not only learning, but credentials that they can use to further their careers and better their lives.

As institutions consider transfer and articulation policies, the issue of how learning was attained continues to be given a great deal of importance, even when there is credible assessment linked to learning outcomes (Camilleri and Tannhäuser, eds., 2012). Higher education institutions need to consider learning outcomes as a basic building block, and determine their transfer and PLA/RPL policies based on which learning outcomes can be appropriately represented by credentials from elsewhere, and which ones they feel need to be assessed internally. Further, adoption of something like the UK Quality Code's [Chapter B6] Indicator 2, regarding transparency of assessment policies, by institutions everywhere would assist students in making informed decisions about their own educational paths. In turn, makers of exams need to be transparent about the learning outcomes and content areas addressed by the exam, and to make their validity arguments clear and transparent as well. And institutions need to understand the basics of what makes good validity evidence: an excellent resource is McClarty and Gaertner (2015), which, although focused on competency-based education, provides a good explanation of assessment concepts as they apply to disaggregated assessment. Together, these elements will provide institutions with the tools they need to readily evaluate external assessment evidence that students may bring for credit.

References

American Educational Research Association, American Psychological Association and National Council on Measurement in Education (2014), *Standards for Educational and Psychological Testing*, Washington: American Psychological Association.

Camilleri, A., Haywood, J. and Nouira, C. (2012), *Giving Credit for OER-based Learning*, Paper presented at UNESCO World Open Educational Resources Congress, Paris, http://www.unesco.org/new/fileadmin/MULTIMEDIA/HQ/CI/CI/pdf/themes/nouira.pdf

Camilleri, A. and Tannhäuser, C. (Eds.) (2012), *Open Learning Recognition: Taking Open Educational Resources a Step Further*, European Foundation for Quality in e-Learning, http://efquel.org/wp-content/uploads/2012/12/Open-Learning-Recognition.pdf

Commonwealth of Learning (2010), *Transnational Qualifications Framework for the Virtual University for Small States of the Commonwealth*, Vancouver: Commonwealth of Learning, http://www.colfinder.org/vussc/VUSSC_TQF_document_procedures_and_guidelines_Final_April2010.pdf

Conrad, D., Mackintosh, W., McGreal, R., Murphy, A. and Witthaus, G. (2013), *Report on the Assessment and Accreditation of Learners Using OER*, Vancouver: Commonwealth of Learning, http://oasis.col.org/bitstream/handle/11599/232/Assess-Accred-OER_2013.pdf?sequence=1&isAllowed=y

Conrad, D. and McGreal, R. (2012), Flexible Paths to Assessment for OER Learners, *Journal of Interactive Media in Education*, 2 (p. Art. 12), http://jime.open.ac.uk/articles/10.5334/2012-12

Council for Adult and Experiential Learning (2010), *Fueling the Race to Postsecondary Success: A 48-institution Study of Prior Learning Assessment and Adult Student Outcomes*, http://www.cael.org/pdfs/PLA_Fueling-the-Race

European Commission (2015), *ECTS Users' Guide 2015*, http://ec.europa.eu/education/library/publications/2015/ects-users-guide_en.pdf

Ferrari, L. and Traina, I. (2013), The OERTest Project: Creating Political Conditions for Effective Exchange of OER in Higher Education, *Journal of e-Learning and Knowledge Society*, 9(1), pp. 23–35, https://www.learntechlib.org/j/JELKS/v/9/n/1

FitzGibbon, J. (2014), *Learning Outcomes and Credit Transfer: Examples, Issues, and Possibilities*, Vancouver: British Columbia Council on Admissions and Transfer, http://www.bccat.ca/pubs/Learning_Outcomes_and_Credit_Transfer_Feb2014.pdf

Klein-Collins, R. (2012), *Competency-Based Degree Programs in the U.S.*, Chicago: Council for Adult and Experiential Learning, http://www.cbenetwork.org/sites/457/uploaded/files/2012_CompetencyBasedPrograms.pdf

Laitinen, A. (2012), *Cracking the Credit Hour*, New America Foundation and Education Sector, http://www.cbenetwork.org/sites/457/uploaded/files/Cracking_the_Credit_Hour_Sept5_0.pdf

MarylandOnline, Inc. (2014), *Quality Matters Higher Education Rubric*, 5th edn., https://www.qualitymatters.org/rubric

McClarty, K. N. and Gaertner, M. N. (2015), *Measuring Mastery: Best Practices for Assessment in Competency-based Education*, American Enterprise Institute, Center on Higher Education Reform, https://www.aei.org/wp-content/uploads/2015/04/Measuring-Mastery.pdf

US Congress, Office of Technology Assessment (1992), *Testing in American Schools: Asking the Right Questions*, Washington: US Government Printing Office, http://govinfo.library.unt.edu/ota/Ota_1/DATA/1992/9236.PDF

Witthaus, G., Childs, M., Nkuyubwatsi, B., Conole, G., Inamorato dos Santos, A. and Punie, Y. (2015), An Assessment-recognition Matrix for Analysing Institutional Practices in the Recognition of Open Learning, Open Education Europa, *eLearning Papers*, 40, http://www.openeducationeuropa.eu/en/article/Assessment-certification-and-quality-assurance-in-open-learning_From-field_40_1

16. Open Education Practice at the University of Southern Queensland

Ken Udas, Helen Partridge and Adrian Stagg

The University of Southern Queensland (USQ) has a strong social justice ethos. Based on this ethos, USQ is seeking to re-position and re-conceptualize itself as a university grounded in the principles of openness and open education. This chapter describes the experiences of USQ as it strives to build a culture of openness and agility and investigates the activities undertaken by USQ including the issues, barriers, challenges and opportunities faced. The chapter concludes with a discussion of the key lessons learnt from USQ's journey to more fully embrace Open Educational Practice and culture.

http://dx.doi.org/10.11647/OBP.0103.15

Introduction

This contribution describes the experiences of the University of Southern Queensland (USQ) as it strives to build a culture of openness and agility. The aim of this chapter it to give a comprehensive overview of one university's journey to re-position and re-conceptualize itself for openness, including the activities undertaken and the issues, barriers, challenges and opportunities faced. USQ is a regional Australian university offering a broad range of academic programming at the undergraduate and postgraduate levels. It has been a leader in distance learning since the 1970s and currently 75% of the University's 28,000 students undertake their studies via online or distance modes. The University has a strong ethos and reputation for serving people that are generally under-represented in higher education. Its student population includes part-time working students, people from socioeconomically disadvantaged backgrounds, and from remote and rural areas. With a strong social justice ethos it is therefore not surprising that USQ is seeking to embrace the principles and practices of openness and open education. We begin with a brief review of relevant literature before providing an overview of USQ with specific focus on the evolving focus and support for Open Educational Practice. The chapter concludes by discussing USQ's key lessons learnt and the next steps.

Literature review

Open Educational Practice (OEP), like online learning, has the potential to transform higher education learning and teaching (Bossu, Bull and Brown, 2012). OEP refers to the teaching techniques that draw upon open technologies and high-quality open educational resources (OER) in order to facilitate collaborative and flexible learning (Beetham, Falconer, McGill and Littlejohn, 2012). OER, which are defined as "teaching, learning and research materials that make use of appropriate tools, such as open licensing, to permit their free reuse, continuous improvement and repurposing by others for educational purposes" (Orr, Rimini and Van Damme, 2015, p. 17) are a key mechanism for this collaboration. The broader term OEP includes Open Access Publishing (OA), Free and Open Source Software (FOSS), open policy, open textbooks, open data, open research and, more broadly, open education.

OEP has been perceived as response to the need for affordable, equitable access to education and as a way for institutions to meet the rising demand globally for university education (Bossu, Brown and Bull, 2012). Whilst open education can be pursued for on-campus degree programs, the benefits have been discussed primarily for distance and online education as a way of broadening access to students whilst potentially reducing the costs associated with studying at university (Scanlon, McAndrew and O'Shea, 2015). Open education could provide lower- or no-cost resources to support education in rural and remote communities, and also empower learner-centered educational approaches that build contextual cultural competencies within specific student cohorts (Willems and Bossu, 2012).

When compared to initiatives and engagement with open education in countries such as Canada, North America and the United Kingdom; Australian open practice is still maturing (Bossu and Tynan, 2011). The three current key focus areas arising from the global literature with particular application to the Australian context are (1) policy frameworks, (2) open textbooks and (3) formal support for staff capacity-building. It will be demonstrated that the University of Southern Queensland, through exploratory and developing initiatives, is addressing these priority areas.

Global challenges for the open education movement are mirrored in the Australian environment, although some factors are of particular concern nationally. The lack of practitioner adoption globally has been attributed to low awareness, a perceived lack of quality in open resources, low interest in investing time to author OER, an absence of extrinsic motivators such as institutional reward and recognition programs, and a lack of formal institutional-level support to build staff capacity (Bossu, Bull and Brown, 2012).

In the Australian higher education sector, there is also a lack of regulatory frameworks or policy relating to, or supporting OEP (Bossu and Fountain, 2015), a lack of evidence- and practice-based research (Stagg, 2014) or empirical research about the impact of openness on the sector (Murphy, 2012), and a rising need to reconcile government and institutional copyright policy frameworks with the environment required to fulsomely engage with Open Educational Practice (Padgett, 2013).

In order to create an environment where taxpayers experience transparency in government processes (as appropriate) and access to publicly-funded research outcomes, the Australian Government has adopted open principles to license government data (ANDS, 2015), encouraged the selection of open source software in the first instance (Australian Government, 2011), funded open data sets (ANDS, 2015), a National Digital Learning Resource Network (Education Services Australia, 2012), and a nascent Open Access and Licensing Framework (AusGOAL, 2011).

Despite these initiatives, there has been no mandate, nor even a consolidated approach to open educational policy in Australian higher education. Some Australian institutions have enacted policy linking engagement with OEP to formal recognition and promotion (UTas, 2014) whilst many others have purely focused on open research outcomes and data with little attention to learning and teaching.

There is strong conceptual alignment between the goals of OEP and the recent "Keep it Clever" statement on education (Universities Australia, 2015), but, as yet, explicit discussion about this alignment has been absent. The "Keep it Clever" policy document contextualizes the discussion by stating that educational investment is directly linked to future positive economic growth and international competitiveness (Universities Australia, 2015). In order to do so, it calls for "a new *social contract* with the Australian public" (p. 4, own emphasis). If the term "social contract" is used in a historically philosophical sense, this policy document is both conceptually aligned and politically sympathetic with openness. The principles outlined in the statement refer to:

- Accessibility — that Australians should be able to readily access a university education;

- Affordability — that the cost of higher education should not be such that it excludes segments of Australian society;

- Quality — which refers to the international quality of both teaching and learning, and research endeavors;

- Research capability — in that universities have a broader societal role in the generation of knowledge;

- Resourcing — especially calls for sustainable models of education; and

- Accountability — infers not only accountability but transparency for the return on investment for taxpayer funds (p. 5).

Open education systems can be leveraged to influence positive outcomes indexed against all these criteria, however the systems are not referenced within the document. This perhaps illustrates a stark gap in national advocacy and political lobbying for open education in the Australian landscape.

The use of "new social contract" in the preamble (p. 4) invites deeper exploration of the status of open education in the proposed educational future. The foundation of the social contract is that, in order to achieve security and a civil good, citizens willingly cede some individual freedoms to the state (Hobbes, 1651) — although Hobbes did admonish citizens to be wary of submitting to systems that did not serve the ideal of "public good". In this way, the social contract is further aligned with Bakunin's collectivist anarchy movement of the mid-1800's, which respected the differences of individuals within society, but called for societal equality and equity of access to "social rights" that included education (Masters, 1974). If one considers the assertion by open practitioners (McKerlich, Ives and McGreal, 2013) that current educational models and copyright policy frameworks are insufficient to meet the demands of equitably-accessible twenty-first century education, then the "new social contract" needs to strongly incorporate aspects of openness.

One could even posit that national openness is a response to ideals that do not reflect those ideals of "social good", and that the change enacted by open practitioners is an approach consistent with Hobbes' admonishment, by opening a traditionally closed and opaquely accountable sector. These goals are consistent with both the policy statement and open education overall and exploring these in more detail provides a basis — both practically and philosophically — for policy-supported practice.

The *Keep it Clever* policy statement, like the previous *Review of Australian Higher Education* (Bradley, Noonan, Nugent, and Scales, 2008) espouses values that are conceptually and practically aligned with open education — although the latter was far more proscriptive in setting targets for the Australian sector in terms of participation and inclusion. If the *Keep it Clever* principles are examined through an open lens, the potential for OEP to be woven into national mechanisms becomes explicit.

Accessibility and *affordability* are conceptually underpinned by social inclusion and the removal of barriers to a university education.

Participation in higher education (especially for indigenous, rural and remote, and low socio-economic status students) has featured in public educational policy since the early 1990's, and arguably there has been little overall success during this time period (Gale and Mills, 2013). OEP provides a way to leverage reduced-cost or free learning resources (especially in terms of textbooks), which addresses a significant access barrier for Australian students. Likewise, authentically open courses can provide students with a transparent view of university education and even assist students to transition into their first year by "demystifying" "university education — a key component of nationally recognized transitional pedagogy (Kift, Nelson and Clarke, 2010).

There are claims that by providing international access to OER that the *quality* of learning and teaching resources can be improved. A transparent teaching environment provides access to others' work, which can be translated and synthesized into local teaching practice contexts by both educators and students (Bossu and Tynan, 2011).

Australian *research capacity* can be enhanced by opening access to research data and published output with the realization that data sets and publications can become OER when used for learning and teaching purposes. Increased access to Australian research and data has the potential to broaden collaboration (especially internationally and cross-discipline), provide replicable or comparative data sets and also build a strong foundation for future research.

The aforementioned need for sustainable educational systems in the face of rising demand will need appropriate *resourcing*. Whilst open business models are still maturing (Butcher and Hoosen, 2011), open institutions are re-evaluating the balance between open content and commercialization. Additionally, the notion of reputational capital in higher education — gained through transparency and openness — is gaining traction. Whilst universities have traditionally focused on commercializing research output there is a growing acceptance of the societal role of universities in knowledge construction. The traditionally espoused value of knowledge construction and dissemination is transitioning to an enacted value — in part due to the role of openness.

Given the publicly funded nature of education, a level of *accountability* should be expected in both research and learning and teaching. Open education systems have the potential to make the teaching resources and, in a small part, the learning experience, transparent to the sector.

The current weakness in open rhetoric internationally has been practicality (or a lack thereof). Evidence exists demonstrating that OEP is, after ten years, neither widespread nor well-known (Conole, 2013), and is far from mainstream practice (Lane and McAndrew, 2010). This is certainly the case in Australia.

One of the key areas requiring significant development is internal staff capacity building. Staff capacity development is essential to successful engagement with OEP as there are inherent complexities that have been mostly unexplored through empirical research (Stagg, 2014).

A review of institutional websites shows that many universities currently have a general information webpage about open resources — accessible to both staff and students — and that enquiries are directed to the library. Open access to research and providing information supporting open publishing models appears far more frequently. The University of Southern Queensland and the University of Tasmania were the only institutions that had visible resources contextualized for the learner (whether staff or students) to explicitly guide the user through the use of open resources and the possible benefits to teaching and learning practices. This approach mirrors the maturation of the open discourse internationally; initiating intended change through a focus on access to resources and the subsequent realization that this was an insufficient catalyst alone.

This perception is perhaps exacerbated by open education research, which often over-simplifies the practitioner experience in (re)using OER by either presenting the activity as a linear process or using lead-in fictional use cases that exemplify "best experience" rather than ones grounded in the complex reality of reuse (Wenk, 2010). This further illuminates a professional development gap at the institutional and sector level in Australia.

Any attempt to promote sustainable engagement with open education needs to acknowledge staff learning challenges and offer a mechanism to frame strategic responses grounded in institutional needs, which has yet to occur in an holistic, integrated manner in Australian higher education.

The University of Southern Queensland

The University of Southern Queensland (USQ) is based in Toowoomba, Queensland, Australia, with campuses also in Springfield and Ipswich. The institution was established in 1967 as the Queensland Institute of Technology (Darling Downs). In 1971, it became the Darling Downs Institute of Advanced Education, then the University College of Southern Queensland in 1990 and finally the University of Southern Queensland in 1992. In less than fifty years, USQ has become a prominent teaching and research institution providing education worldwide. In its short history, USQ has grown rapidly in size and complexity.

USQ consists of five divisions: (i) Academic Division has overall responsibility for the University's academic program portfolio; its continuous improvement, and its quality delivery across all campuses; (ii) Academic Services Division supports the learning, teaching and research needs of the University; (iii) Research and Innovation Division coordinates the University's research agenda; (iv) Students and Communities Division is responsible for supporting the student experience and building relationships with current, future and past student communities; and (v) University Services Division has oversight of University finance, human resources, sustainable business management and improvement and campus services.

USQ's Academic Division consists of two faculties: the Faculty of Business, Education, Law and Arts (BELA) consists of six schools: (i) School of Arts and Communication; (ii) School of Commerce; (iii) School of Law and Justice; (iv) School of Linguistics, Adult and Specialist Education; (v) School of Management and Enterprise; (vi) School of Teacher Education and Early Childhood. The Faculty of Health, Engineering and Sciences (HES) consists of six schools: (i) School of Agricultural, Computational and Environmental Sciences; (ii) School of Civil Engineering and Surveying; and (iii) School of Nursing and Midwifery; (iv) School of Health and Wellbeing; (v) School of Mechanical and Electrical Engineering and (vi) School of Psychology and Counselling. In addition, USQ has three colleges: the Open Access College, College for Indigenous Studies, Education and Research, and the Queensland College of Wine Tourism. The University has three research institutes:

- Australian Digital Futures Institute (ADFI).
- Institute for Agriculture and the Environment (IAgE).
- Institute for Resilient Regions (IRR).

USQ has a diverse student population, including undergraduate and postgraduate students from more than 100 countries, with more than 80 nationalities. The current student enrolment is approximately 28,000 and, of this total, more than 20,000 study off-campus by online/distance learning. Just over 54% of the students are female, over one quarter are classified as low socio-economic status and only 10% are first school leavers.

In 2013, 496 Higher Degree Research students, 4,433 Higher Degree Coursework and 14,930 Bachelor level students were enrolled at USQ. In 2013, over 5,000 international students were enrolled, with 1,797 students studying on-campus and the reminder studying outside Australia either through USQ Education Partners or directly with USQ.

The *USQ Strategic Plan 2016-2020* is built on three pillars — Education, Research, Enriched and Enterprise. The Plan guides the University in delivering its mission, which is "to lead in economic and social development through higher education and research excellence":

- **Education:** USQ successfully blends access with excellence and is a leading university for student experience and graduate outcomes.
- **Research:** USQ is internationally recognized for high impact research in our areas of research focus.
- **Enterprise:** USQ is a socially responsible and well managed enterprise with a work culture that promotes high performance and is reflective of our values.

USQ and the Conundrum of Openness

The topic of OEP can seem counter-intuitive. After all, it seems natural that the University would create value through limiting access to data, information and knowledge generating a market based on constraint. The internet of ideas makes information markets based on restriction very expensive to create and protect, while contributing and using the open market of ideas and artefacts potentially reduces a range of costs and may increase margins for the University's core product offerings.

As will be mentioned in the coming paragraphs, Openness is not an all or nothing proposition. Although one might argue that there is value that the University can derive from limitation (its credentials and patentable discoveries, for instance), but not from unnecessarily limiting access to the information it uses for the purposes of learning and teaching. Openness need not simply be accepted as an article of faith, but it must be accepted in the spirit of the principles that provide the contours of open practice. USQ has found an easy alignment between the historical mission (based on the notion of social justice and access) and the contemporary Open Educational Practice. For any institution, the question of *why* openness is an attractive proposition is a critical first step for purposeful engagement. In recent years, MOOCs (Massive Open Online Courses) were a high profile example of international engagement with perceived openness that was often neither connected nor beneficial to institutional goals or the enhancement of learning and teaching practice.

The following Openness Principles[1] are therefore guiding USQ's OEP endeavors:

---

1   The following are some of the resources that influenced the development of the proposed Openness Principles at USQ.
- AACU: Academic Freedom and Educational Responsibility (http://www.aacu.org/about/statements/documents/academicfreedom.pdf)
- AAUP: 1940 Statement of Principles on Academic Freedom and Tenure (http://www.aaup.org/report/1940-statement-principles-academic-freedom-and-tenure)
- AAUP: Academic Freedom and Electronic Communications (http://www.aaup.org/report/academic-freedom-and-electronic-communications-2014)
- Coase's Penguin, or Linux and the Nature of the Firm (http://www.benkler.org/CoasesPenguin.html)
- EDUCASUE Openness (https://net.educause.edu/elements/staff_web_pages/doblinger/openness.pdf)
- Free Cultural Works (http://freedomdefined.org/Definition)
- Future Learn (https://about.futurelearn.com/terms/openness)
- Human Rights Initiative (http://www.humanrightsinitiative.org/programs/ai/rti/articles/handbook_intro_to_openness_&_ai.pdf)
- Oxford Scholarship Online: The Information Society and the Welfare State: The Finnish Model (http://www.oxfordscholarship.com/view/10.1093/acprof:oso/9780199256990.001.0001/acprof-9780199256990)
- Open Government (http://www.opengovpartnership.org/about/open-government-declaration)
- Openness Index (https://wiki.jasig.org/display/2398/Openness+Index)
- Open Science Commons (http://sciencecommons.org/resources/readingroom/principles-for-open-science)
- Principles on Open Public Sector Information (http://www.oaic.gov.au/images/documents/information-policy/information-policy-agency-resources/principles_on_psi_short.pdf)
- Unisa Open (http://www.unisa.ac.za/default.asp?Cmd=ViewContent&ContentID=27755)
- WikiEducator (http://wikieducator.org/The_right_license/Free_cultural_works)

1. **Openness as Core to Education and Social Justice:** As an actor in the twenty-first century, USQ understands that education is practiced in a data, information, and knowledge ecosystem that is supported by technical and social networks. Our principal role as a university is to grow knowledge from more to more, while promoting social progress and social justice. Open access is a principal factor in the efficient and effective distribution of information for the growth of knowledge and promotion of critical and reflective education leading to civic capacity. We optimize our contribution to the open education ecosystem by supporting the use and creation of free cultural works that provide:[2]

   a. the freedom to use the work and enjoy the benefits of using it;

   b. the freedom to study the work and to apply knowledge acquired from it;

   c. the freedom to make and redistribute copies, in whole or in part, of the information or expression; and

   d. the freedom to make changes and improvements, and to distribute derivative works.

2. **Respect for the Traditions of the Academy:** Openness is a fundamental tenant of academic freedom and responsibility for the academy and the professoriate, striking at the very purpose of the University and its singular role in free societies.

3. **Do the Right Thing:** Opening up educational resources for use, re-use, and modification is a moral good and our academic, professional, and managerial staff along with our partners should look to contribute to the stock of open educational resources.

4. **Think of our Students:** Whenever possible the University should default to OEP to reduce the overall cost of receiving a high quality, accessible, and affordable education including the use of open textbooks, journals, course materials, other supplementary content, and technologies.

5. **Access and Distribution with Respect:** Individual learners, faculty, and visitors to our sites must feel confident that they can participate in a safe and secure environment for learning, which respects the content they generate as part of their learning.

6. **Default to Open:** We believe that opening access to educational resources is a moral good, and when permissions allow, we will contribute any content or translations generated by our academic,

---

2   http://freedomdefined.org/Definition

professional, and managerial staff and community for the purposes of learning, teaching, and scholarship as OERs under the Creative Commons Attribution (CC-BY) license.

7. **Lawful Practice:** Our partner publishers and content suppliers need to be able to make their own decisions about how their materials and contributions are used. For partners who request that we restrict free access to their content to a limited number or type of user, we respect their requirements and manage their content with the appropriate Digital Rights Management technology.[3]

8. **Alignment with Public Good:** The University of Southern Queensland is aligned with the broad goals and application of the Australian Governments Open Access and Licencing Framework (AUSGoal)[4] and Office of the Australian Information Commissioner's Eight Principles on Open Public Sector Information in the context of course materials and information management broadly:

   a. Open access to information — a default position.

   b. Engaging the community.

   c. Effective information governance.

   d. Robust information asset management.

   e. Discoverable and useable information.

   f. Clear reuse rights.

   g. Appropriate charging for access.

   h. Transparent enquiry and complaints processes.

9. **Agility and Agile Practice:** The University of Southern Queensland strives to be an "agile" organization through the adoption of agile management practices, for which Openness is an essential precondition.

Openness and Opportunities at USQ

The Openness movement is creating opportunities that challenge traditional business and education models and may accelerate the use and impact of information and communication technologies (ICT), new media, online education and distributed learning. Although USQ was an early leader in the OER movement, it has not taken full advantage of

---

3   https://www.libraryforall.org/openness-principles
4   http://www.ausgoal.gov.au

that position. That being said, it is still in a position, with appropriate leadership, to take uncommon advantage of opportunities and assert an international leadership position in a new order. This will take fortitude, bravery and willingness to experiment small, and fail early and often, while succeeding with confidence and making those successes really matter. Although OEP is a long-term journey that keeps renewing itself, we need to recognize that others have taken steps by formalizing open policies at the institutional level. Notable institutions include Lincoln University (NZ), Otago Polytechnic (NZ), Athabasca University (CA), the State University of New York (US) and many others.

By experimenting with and adopting open practice, we are practicing in ways that optimize the value we create through the generation, curation, use and reuse of information and knowledge assets. We will also promote meaningful collaboration that brings tangible benefits to the University, its learners, alumni and broader stakeholders. It helps us better engage with our social justice mission and, as a public university, provides us with a natural mechanism to maximize the value that every Australian can receive from their publicly funded university sector. Research among universities participating in some form of OEP has indicated that the priority of the benefits of openness are as follows:

1. participating in an international network of like-minded partners;
2. philanthropic mission/social justice; and
3. new business opportunities.

According to almost every education report available today, twenty-first century education will be different from the past. Our learners and our funders will expect (if they do not already) and we will witness increasingly (if we have not already) personalized, data driven and technology-enabled learning opportunities. We will participate in the continued disaggregation of educational services on the institutional level, and we will facilitate the re-aggregation of education on the personal level.

Although still under iterative development indicative of agile methodologies, unique educational processes enabled through Open Educational Practice are emerging within the OERu. This is evident in the growing embrace of OER and of courses collaboratively designed and developed by teams including content area specialists, educational technologists and instructional designers who are forging new approaches to learning and teaching scholarship. This same approach, supported through the pedagogy of discovery[5] lends itself to courses effectively designed through crowdsourcing, affinity grouping and distributed educational activities. OERu has proposed a formal program of Academic Volunteers International[6] that was used during USQ's first OERu course offering. The course was intended to support peer mentoring through critique and reflection and, more broadly, reflect a gradual shift toward learner-centered pedagogies and competency-based, outcomes-oriented approaches. Participation in twenty-first century education will require agile organizational management and governance, digital fluency and transparency that can only result from open processes and practices and freely available content. The internet and its presentation environment, the web, were architected to liberate information, not to impose barriers. The corporatization of the University demands creative and innovative approaches to a "market" that feeds on agility. Open education is the natural consequence of and catalyst for delivering education in such an environment and delivering in such an environment sits at the very center of USQ's learning and teaching strategy.

Current Openness Activities at USQ

During the past five years, the University of Southern Queensland has been building momentum in support of its commitment to OEP and OERs. Although OEP is not an *all or nothing* strategy, it is one that requires thoughtful engagement throughout the University. Fortunately, successful OEP adoption tends to have low reputational risk because adoption tends to be agile and incremental, so OEP can be integrated into existing operations without incurring additional and significant cost. However, because of its somewhat counter-intuitive nature, OEP requires discipline about how we make important strategic as well as

---

5   http://wikieducator.org/Kenya_national_symposium_on_open_education/
     The_pedagogy_of_discovery:_Using_OER_to_enable_free_range_learning

6   OERu Proposal for action for Academic Volunteers International http://
     wikieducator.org/OERu/2011.11_OERu_Proposal_for_action_for_Academic_
     Volunteers_International

operational decisions, the types of questions we ask of ourselves, and how we structure those questions. For example:

- how we build our intellectual property and copyright policy is important.
- how we identify, select and prescribe textbooks and whether we put the onus on explaining why we would assign an expensive proprietary text or other resource when open and free alternatives are available of similar quality.
- assuming open licensing first of all and then only retaining all reserved rights when there is a strong argument to doing so.
- assessing accurately the costs and risks associated with closing content and managing proprietary intellectual property.
- how can we incentivize high quality open scholarship and publication as appropriate.
- how can we recognize and incentivize creative reuse, sharing and the creation of high-quality localized or internationalized works.
- clearly stating and practicing our values relative to our use and distribution of publicly funded intellectual assets.

Although these are not the types of questions historically asked or the standards adopted and set, they have recently become much more clearly articulated in our work on an University IP policy, open textbook proposal and early stages of a green paper prompting an "open first" posture on educational content and learning technologies. We are recognizing that simply asking the questions, publicly and with conviction, helps promote critical thinking on the topic of openness, creativity and innovation. Fortunately, USQ was an early adopter of some aspects of open practice, which has generated a common identity for a small group of academic and professional staff that have been experimenting somewhat "under the radar". The open practice that has been pursued, although not fully embraced at the University, has been enough to garner a small reputation for USQ as being a progressive practitioner in the area.

The University's current initiatives and activities fall under five classifications:

1. Open Educational Resources
    a. active participation in the OERu.

b. the first Australian university to join and contribute courses to the Open Courseware Consortium (OCWC).[7]

c. faculty driven creation of an open textbook on Sports Physiology that includes contributions from dozens of internationally leading scholars who have made their contributions open for the text.

d. participation on an Office of Learning and Teaching (OLT) Seed Grant along with colleagues at the University of Tasmania to experiment with the development of micro Open Online Courses (MOOCs).

e. introduction of a USQ Open Textbook Grant Scheme in which, through a competitive process, university academics receive funds to use or develop an open text book.

f. introduction, in 2015, of a USQ eLearning Objects Repository (eLOR) that helped reduce barriers to sharing content internally within the University.

2. Open policy and practice

a. building a new capacity in open education environments to improve authoring and delivering quality through investment in better content management, intellectual property, licensing control and enhanced discovery.

b. establishment of a working party with representatives across the university to explore and articulate recommendations regarding open content licensing practices.

c. Launch of the USQ Open Practice website (http://www.usq.edu.au/open-practice) to provide a space to formally articulate and share USQ's commitment to openness.

d. having proposed and now developing a workflow and content management environment supporting open licensing for course materials.

3. Open research

a. building a new capacity to discover and index the discovery of open research reports on a global scale through investment in technology and expertise, taking advantage of structured repositories of public research and teaching materials that have not been adequately indexed by major search engines.

---

7 http://www.ocwconsortium.org/news/2007/07/university-of-southern-queensland-opencourseware

b. having developed relationships with USQ researchers to openly publish open research outputs that can be used across the curriculum for learning and teaching.

c. having a USQ ePrints repository to enable the sharing of research outputs to the broader national and international community.

4. Open source software

a. leadership in a collaborative project with the Open Source Initiative (OSI), Opman Group, Origin International Technology Law Group and the OER Foundation to develop and deliver an open course on Free, Libre and Open Works project management course.

b. first higher education affiliate with the OSI.

5. Open community participation

a. active participation in and creation of openly available resources for Open Access Week, OER Week and Information and Library Studies Week.

These efforts have built a sufficient capacity for the University to take the next step, but without committing to do so, the USQ academics will eventually run their course/s as open educators, find alternative pursuits at USQ or gravitate to universities and other organizations that value openness as a principle and innovate in their practices.

Change and Change Processes

As already mentioned, USQ has been involved with open educational resources and open education more broadly for longer than a decade. Some of our notable "firsts" included participation in the Open Courseware Initiative in 2007, the OERu in 2011 and, most recently, our affiliation with the Open Source Initiative in 2015. In very many ways, early involvement in openness by people like Professor Emeritus Jim Taylor on behalf of the University points to a very keen insight. He saw that openness potentially strikes directly at the core purposes of a university like USQ, which is committed to enhancing access to learning. OERu provided a perfect pilot for USQ. It provided a need to engage teachers in designing courses for an open environment, use of open content and serious consideration of an educational model based on credentials distributed among partner universities, course and content "owned" by a particular university, but freely available, and without a clear sustainability model. USQ initially sought to engage with openness through a series of small-scale, diverse projects. This approach was designed as a multi-pronged capacity-building and experiential learning strategy aiming for longer-term institutional normalization. The actualization of this strategy has been a more complex and resource-intensive undertaking.

We have become more active to incentivize engagement with a variety of openness activities, some of which have been described to simply illustrate how openness can liberate creativity. We have worked with a handful of teachers to rethink the idea of a textbook so it is not only open but is something fundamentally different than what proprietary distributors of texts are willing to provide. We have come to grips with the fact that it is difficult to *reposition* or *re-conceptualize* a university that is growing, financially sound and well led like USQ, principally because things are generally going well and there is a low sense of urgency. What we can do is reduce the barriers to experimenting with openness, use its language liberally, increase the viability of open options and make decisions that place open first.

Lessons Learnt and Next Steps

It is not good enough to simply espouse openness as an "institutional good". Openness needs to be useful, as well, and its value needs to be discovered and internalized locally, and in many cases individually. If openness can help teachers more easily design their course, students more affordably study, or the University be more creative and impactful in its curriculum, program design and course offerings then openness and open resources will more likely be adopted. We have learned that open practice by academic staff needs to be an individual decision but the University can reward and recognize open behavior and support experimentation.

In addition to sponsoring projects which are designed to promote open practices, making it easier to use open resources for course design and promoting open distribution through modelling our own practices, we are also ensuring that relevant university policies, such as Intellectual Property, explicitly recognize open practice and that software procurement processes are open source friendly and consideration is given to open technology standards and the consumption and creation of open file formats. The coming year will see an active effort to engender a university-wide dialogue about open practice as we launch a "green paper" for open consultation, which will lead to more formal statements about University commitment to open practice.

Conclusion

The University of Southern Queensland's approach to openness has been a decade-long steady march guided more by principle than opportunity. As a university we have for the most part stayed away from organizations and efforts that we perceive as *"fauxpen"* or engaging in *"open washing"*. We do not want to confuse the core meaning of open by introducing predatory marketing into the community. As an institution, we have also been rather pragmatic and are normally guided by efforts that we think will either have direct positive outcomes for students and members of the faculty, meet our educational goals, or promote a broader open culture at the University. The University has found that simply participating in genuine open activities and working with open organizations like the OER Foundation, OERu and the OSI help us refine our understanding of openness and our practice.

We believe that it is through thoughtful and methodical engagement that we are developing a culture in which openness is a natural impulse and those activities that promote closed culture and restrictions on the free flow of information, knowledge and culture are understood for what they are. The open impulse not only guides our decision-making as institutional leaders charged with crafting policy and resourcing decisions and as individual actors, but also promotes a culture with the capacity to continuously improve our practice and seriously consider the implications of agility.

References

AusGOAL (2011), *Australian Governments Open Access and Licencing Framework*, http://www.ausgoal.gov.au

Australian Government (2011), *Australian Government Open Source Software Policy*, Department of Finance and Deregulation, http://www.finance.gov.au/sites/default/files/australian-government-open-source-software-policy-2013.pdf

Australian National Data Service (2015), *Australian Research Data Commons*, http://www.ands.org.au/about-ands.html#ardc

Beetham, H., Falconer, I., McGill, L. and Littlejohn, A. (2012), *Open Practices: Briefing Paper*, JISC, https://oersynth.pbworks.com/w/page/51668352/OpenPracticesBriefing

Bossu, C., Bull, D. and Brown, M. (2012), Opening Up Down Under: the Role of Open Educational Resources in Promoting Social Inclusion in Australia, *Distance Education*, 33(2), pp. 151–164, http://dx.doi.org/10.1080/01587919.2012.692050

Bossu, C. and Fountain, W. (2015), Capacity Building in Open Education: an Australian Approach, *Open Praxis*, 7(2), pp. 123-132, http://dx.doi.org/10.5944/openpraxis.7.2.197

Bossu, C. and Tynan, B. (2011), OERs: New Media on the Learning Landscape, *On the Horizon*, 19(4), pp. 259–267, http://dx.doi.org/10.1108/10748121111179385

Bradley, D., Noonan, P., Nugent, H. and Scales, B. (2008), *Review of Australian Higher Education: Final Report*, Canberra: DEEWR.

Butcher, N. and Hoosen, S. (2011), *Exploring the Business Case for Open Educational Resources*, Vancouver: Commonwealth of Learning.

Conole, G. (2013), *Designing for Learning in an Open World*, 4, New York: Springer.

Education Services Australia (2012), *National Digital Learning Resource Network*, http://www.ndlrn.edu.au/default.asp

Gale, T. and Mills, C. (2013), Creating Spaces in Higher Education for Marginalised Australians: Principles for Socially Inclusive Pedagogies, *Enhancing Learning in the Social Sciences*, 5(2), pp. 7-19, http://dx.doi.org/10.11120/elss.2013.00008

Hobbes, T. (1651 [1982]), *Leviathan*, London: Penguin.

Kift, S., Nelson, K. and Clarke, J. (2010), Transition Pedagogy: a Third Generation Approach to FYE: A Case Study of Policy and Practice for the Higher Education Sector, *International Journal of the First Year in Higher Education*, 1(1), pp. 1-20, http://dx.doi.org/10.5204/intjfyhe.v1i1.13

Lane, A. and McAndrew, P. (2010), Are Open Educational Resources Systematic or Systemic Change Agents for Teaching Practice?, *British Journal of Educational Technology*, 41(6), pp. 952–962, http://dx.doi.org/10.1111/j.1467-8535.2010.01119.x

Masters, A. (1974), *Bakunin, the Father of Anarchism*, New York: Saturday Review Press.

McKerlich, R., Ives, C. and McGreal, R. (2013), Measuring Use and Creation of Open Educational Resources in Higher Education, *The International Review of Research in Open and Distance Learning*, 14(4), pp. 90-103.

Murphy, A. (2012), *Benchmarking Open Educational Practices in Higher Education*, in ASCILITE 2012: 29th Annual Conference of the Australasian Society for Computers in Learning in Tertiary Education: Future Challenges, Sustainable Futures, 25-28 November 2012, Wellington, New Zealand, pp. 25-28, https://eprints.usq.edu.au/22358

Orr, D., M. Rimini and D. Van Damme (2015), *Open Educational Resources: A Catalyst for Innovation*, Educational Research and Innovation, Paris: OECD Publishing, http://dx.doi.org/10.1787/9789264247543-en

Padgett, L. (2013), *Understanding Open Educational Resource Licensing in Australia*. Paper presented at the 25th ICDE World Conference on Open and Distance Education, Tianjin, China, 16-18 October 2013.

Scanlon, E., McAndrew P. and O'Shea T. (2015), Designing for Educational Technology to Enhance the Experience of Learners in Distance Education: How Open Educational Resources, Learning Design and Moocs are Influencing Learning, *Journal of Interactive Media in Education*, 2015(1), pp. 1-9, http://dx.doi.org/10.5334/jime.al

Stagg, A. (2014), A Continuum of Open Practice, *Universities and Knowledge Society Journal*, 11(3), pp. 152-165, http://dx.doi.org/10.7238/rusc.v11i3.2102

Universities Australia (2015), *Keep it Clever Policy Statement 2016*, https://www.universitiesaustralia.edu.au/news/policy-papers/Keep-it-Clever--Policy-Statement-2016#.V82RBGpTHIU

University of Southern Queensland (2016), *Strategic Plan 2016-2020*, http://www.usq.edu.au/about-usq/about-us/plans-reports/strategic-plan

University of Southern Queensland (2015), *USQ Educational Experience Plan*, http://www.usq.edu.au/about-usq/about-us/plans-reports

University of Tasmania (2014), *Curriculum Principles for the University of Tasmania*, http://www.utas.edu.au/__data/assets/pdf_file/0006/567744/7825_A3_Curriculum-Principles1.pdf

Wenk, B. (2010), *Open Educational Resources Inspire Teaching and Learning*, Paper presented at the IEEE EDUCON Education Engineering 2010 — the Future of Global Learning Engineering Education, 14-16 April, Madrid.

Willems, J. and Bossu C. (2012), Equity Considerations for Open Educational Resources in the Glocalization of Education, *Distance Education*, 33(2), pp. 185-199, http://dx.doi.org/10.1080/01587919.2012.692051

Index

This book need not end here…

At Open Book Publishers, we are changing the nature of the traditional academic book. The title you have just read will not be left on a library shelf, but will be accessed online by hundreds of readers each month across the globe. OBP publishes only the best academic work: each title passes through a rigorous peer-review process. We make all our books free to read online so that students, researchers and members of the public who can't afford a printed edition will have access to the same ideas.

This book and additional content is available at:
http://www.openbookpublishers.com/isbn/9781783742783

Customize

Personalize your copy of this book or design new books using OBP and third-party material. Take chapters or whole books from our published list and make a special edition, a new anthology or an illuminating coursepack. Each customized edition will be produced as a paperback and a downloadable PDF. Find out more at:

http://www.openbookpublishers.com/section/59/1

Donate

If you enjoyed this book, and feel that research like this should be available to all readers, regardless of their income, please think about donating to us. We do not operate for profit and all donations, as with all other revenue we generate, will be used to finance new Open Access publications.

http://www.openbookpublishers.com/section/13/1/support-us

Like Open Book Publishers

Follow @OpenBookPublish

Read more at the Open Book Publishers BLOG

You may also be interested in…

Digital Humanities Pedagogy
Practices, Principles and Politics
Edited by Brett D. Hirsch

http://dx.doi.org/10.11647/OBP.0024
http://www.openbookpublishers.com/product/161

The Universal Declaration of Human Rights
in the 21st Century
Edited by Gordon Brown

http://dx.doi.org/10.11647/OBP.0091
http://www.openbookpublishers.com/product/467

 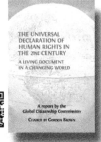

Oral Literature in the Digital Age
Archiving Orality and Connecting with Communities
Edited by Mark Turin, Claire Wheeler
and Eleanor Wilkinson

http://dx.doi.org/10.11647/OBP.0032
http://www.openbookpublishers.com/product/186

Lightning Source UK Ltd.
Milton Keynes UK
UKOW07f2354071216
289453UK00001B/1/P